John Keay is the author of three acclaimed histories: *The Honourable Company*, about the East India Company; *Last Post*, about imperial disengagement in the Far East; and the two-volume *Explorers of the Western Himalayas*. His books on India include *Into India* and *The Great Arc: The Dramatic Tale of How India was Mapped and Everest was Named*. John Keay is married with four children, lives in Scotland and is co-editor with Julia Keay of the *Collins Encyclopaedia of Scotland*.

INDIA
DISCOVERED

*The Recovery of a Lost
Civilization*

JOHN KEAY

HarperCollins*Publishers*

HarperCollins*Publishers*
77–85 Fulham Palace Road,
Hammersmith, London W6 8JB

www.fireandwater.com

This paperback edition 2001
1 3 5 7 9 8 6 4 2

First published in Great Britain in 1981
First published in paperback by William Collins 1988

ISBN 0 00 712300 0

Set in Linotron Sabon by Ace Filmsetting Ltd, Frome

Printed and bound in Great Britain by
Omnia Books Limited, Glasgow

Contents

Author's Note To Third Edition

When I was writing this book, the 'orientalist' scholarship with which it is concerned came in for a savaging at the hands of Professor Edward Said (see his book *Orientalism*, published in 1978). Reviewing Western portrayals of, and investigations into, the Islamic Middle East, Said discerned an ignorant and disparaging commentary prompted by acquisitive and self-serving motives. This pejorative aspect of 'orientalism' has since been enforced by his numerous disciples and critics. *India Discovered* is, however, quite innocent of it. Most of the text was written before Said's great work appeared, and I doubt whether I would have written it differently had it been otherwise.

India is not like the Middle East and its colonial exposure was of a different order. For every act of vandalism there were several of conservation, and for every paragraph of orientalist disparagement there was a page of wide-eyed wonder. Both are frankly represented in the text which follows. On balance, though, I believe that to the scholars of the Raj, India's heritage came to represent not some antithetical 'other' to be denigrated and marginalized but a spectacular survival with which they were anxious and proud to be associated, a jewel, indeed, in the crown. Of course such studies gratified the imperialist mind-set. No scholarship is entirely disinterested, be it orientalist or a critique of the same.

Just as the intellectual climate has changed, so has my own perspective. Since this book was written I have learned much more about Indian history. The jaunty assertion in the Introduction that India's early history is devoid of the personalities and anecdotes which make the past palatable cannot go unchallenged. As the author of a recent work replete with just such detail (*India: A History*), I stand severely self-corrected. There are other generalizations which, were I writing this book today, I would avoid, although they scarcely detract from what is essentially an account of eighteenth–nineteenth century enquiry. And there are instances, particularly in respect of Harappan studies (Chapter 12), where the pace of current research means that anything in print is already out of date.

The book originally appeared under the same title but in a large format with many colour illustrations. This smaller format makes for more manageable reading and the new illustrations convey a greater sense of period. They were collected by Joy Law, to whom I am most grateful.

Argyll, January 2001

Chronology 1765–1927

1765 East India Company granted *diwan* of Bengal

1774 Warren Hastings first Governor-General

1783 Mackenzie arrives in Madras. Jones arrives in Calcutta

1784 Asiatic Society of Bengal founded

1786 Calcutta Botanical Garden founded

1790 Third Mysore War. Twining's travels

1793 Roxburgh arrives in Calcutta

1794 Jones dies

1797 Wellesley Governor-General

1798 Fourth Mysore War

1800 Mysore Survey – Buchanan, Mackenzie and Lambton take the field

1803 Maratha War; acquisition of Delhi and Agra

1806 Tod's first visit to Udaipur. Salt and Valentia visit Salsette caves

1807 Buchanan begins survey of Bengal and Bihar

1810 Lambton completes trig survey of south. Buchanan at Boddh Gaya

1813 Wallich superintendent of Calcutta Botanical Garden

1816 Colebrooke declares Himalayas the highest in world

1817 Tod returns to Rajasthan

1819 Prinsep arrives in India. Fell visits Sanchi. Dangerfield discovers Bagh. Franklin discovers Khajuraho

1820 Hodgson posted to Kathmandhu

1822 De Koros in Himalayas. Tod visits Abu and Girnar

1823 Everest succeeds Lambton as Superintendent of GTS

1824 Alexander visits Ajanta

1825 Bishop Heber begins tour of India

1830 Ventura opens Manikyala *stupa*

1833 Masson discovers coins in Begram. Hodgson's report on Ashoka pillars published

1834 Fergusson tours north India

1835 Macaulay's Minute. Cunningham opens Dhamekh *stupa*

1836 Publication of Fa Hsien. Gandhara sculpture found at Mathura. Ralph/Gresley report on Ajanta. Kittoe finds Orissa rock inscription

1837 Prinsep deciphers pillar inscriptions

1838 Burt visits Khajuraho. Postans visits Girnar. Prinsep deciphers Kharosthi and is invalided home

1841 Blyth appointed curator of Asiatic Society's museum

1842 Ellenborough proposes restoration of Somnath gates. Fergusson tours south India

1844 Gill begins copying Ajanta frescoes

1845 Everest starts North-East Himalaya series

1848 Hooker visits India. Cunningham finds Gandhara sculpture in Punjab

1851 Cunningham at Sanchi

1853 Cunningham first visits Mathura

1857 Indian Mutiny or National Uprising

1858 Demise of East India Company, exile of Moghul emperor

1861 Cunningham appointed Archaeological Surveyor

1862 Cunningham at Boddh Gaya

1865 Cunningham at Khajuraho

1867 Publication of Jerdon's *Mammals of India*

1872 Griffiths starts copying Ajanta frescoes

1873 Cunningham discovers Bharhut

1881 Cole restores Sanchi. Keith restores Gwalior

1897 Publication of Ajanta frescoes

1899 Curzon arrives as Viceroy

1902 Marshall arrives as Director of Archaeology

1908 Havell's *Indian Sculpture and Painting* published

1910 Controversy over Indian art at Royal Society of Arts

1913 Marshall begins excavations at Taxila

1920 Ajanta restorations begin

1921 Banerji discovers Mohenjo-daro

1924 Excavation of Mohenjo-daro begins

1927 Coomaraswamy's *Indian and Indonesian Art* published

List of Illustrations

32. Mohenjo-daro Girl.
33. Seals from the Indus Valley civilization.

The author and publisher are grateful to the following for their kind permission to reproduce the above illustrations: the India Office Library, British Museum for nos. 1–5, 7, 11, 13–16, 19, 22, 25–30; the Victoria & Albert Museum for nos. 6, 9, 17, 18, 23 and 24; the British Museum for nos. 10 and 33; the Werner Forman Archive, London for no. 12; the British Architectural Library, RIBA for no. 20; the National Portrait Gallery no. 31; and the National Museum, New Delhi for no. 32. Illustration no. 8 is reproduced from *Archaeological Survey of India, Report of a Tour in the Central Provinces Lower Gangetic Doab 1880–81* by Alexander Cunningham, Vol. XVII, Plate xxi.

Introduction

*Some day the whole story of British Indology will
be told and that will assuredly make a glorious,
fascinating and inspiring narrative.*

A. J. Arberry, *British Orientalists* (1943)

Two hundred years ago India was the land of the fabulous and
fantastic, the 'Exotic East'. Travellers returned with tales of marble
palaces with gilded domes, of kings who weighed themselves in gold,
and of dusky maidens dripping with pearls and rubies. Before this
sumptuous backdrop passed elephants, tigers and unicorns, snake
charmers and sword swallowers, pedlars of reincarnation and magic,
long-haired ascetics on beds of nails, widows leaping into the pyre. It
was like some glorious and glittering circus – spectacular, exciting, but
a little unreal.

Now, in place of the circus, we have the museum. India is a supreme
cultural experience. Instead of the rough and tumble of the big top, we
have meditation and the subtle notes of the sitar. It is temples and
tombs, erotic sculpture, forlorn palaces and miniature masterpieces.
Hinduism is studied in deadly earnest; the ascetic no longer needs a
bed of nails to ensure an audience. Even the elephants and tigers have
become too important to be fun; they too must be carefully studied
and preserved.

This dramatic change in attitude was principally brought about by a
painstaking investigation of all things Indian. No subject people, no
conquered land, was ever as exhaustively studied as was India during
the period of British rule. It is this aspect of the British affair in India
which forms the subject of this book.

The nineteenth century was the age of enquiry. It was perhaps
inevitable that India should have its Darwin, its Livingstone and its
Schliemann. There was also something in the paternalistic nature of
British imperialism that attracted the scholar and the scientist. The
men who discovered India came as amateurs; by profession they were

soldiers and administrators. But they returned home as giants of scholarship.

And then, above all, there was India itself, exercising its own irresistible fascination. The more it was probed the greater became its antiquity, the more inexhaustible its variety, and the more inconceivable its subtleties. The pioneers of Indian studies, described in this book, rose to the challenge. 'Man and Nature; whatever is performed by the one or produced by the other' would be the field of their enquiries.

The results, even in an age of discoveries, were as sensational as the country and the scope of the undertaking. For a start, Indian history was pushed back two thousand years, roughly from the age of William the Conqueror to a millennium or so before that of Tutankhamun. In the process two great classical civilizations were discovered, and one of the richest literary traditions was revealed to the outside world. So were the origins of two of the world's major religions. What Lord Curzon called 'the greatest galaxy of monuments in the world' was rescued from decay, classified and conserved. Ancient scripts were deciphered, dated and used to disentangle the history of kings and emperors. Coins and paintings by the hundred were discovered, and their significance charted. Western sensibilities struggled to come to terms with the discovery of erotic sculptures in places of worship. In the natural sciences one of the most exciting flora and fauna was studied and catalogued; so too was the incredibly rich human miscellany of racial, linguistic and religious groups. The entire sub-continent was surveyed and mapped; in the process the world's highest mountains were measured. And so on. In short the modern image of India was pieced together.

In tracing this process, I have tried to convey something of the wonder of each new discovery and the excitement of each new deduction. The men who stumbled upon sites like the temple complex of Khajuraho or the painted caves of Ajanta, felt as if they had suddenly come upon the Uffizi swathed in creepers, swarming with bats and unvisited for a thousand years. It is not hard to understand their astonishment. Parts of India are still littered with monuments and ruins that have never attracted the attention of conservationists. Herdsmen bivouac in royal palaces, mirror-work mosaics crunch underfoot, and bees' nests hang from painted ceilings. It is one of India's perhaps ironic glories that, in addition to the more popular and spectacular sites, she still has real ruins, untended, still crumbling, still succumbing to the rains and the vegetation.

The discovery of these varied and magnificent monuments stimulated curiosity about India's past. It is hard to appreciate now that as late as the end of the eighteenth century nothing whatsoever was known of Indian history prior to the Mohammedan invasions. 'It is at this epoch [AD 1000]', wrote Thomas Twining in 1790, 'that we come to a line of shade beyond which no object is distinctly discernible. What treasures might not be discovered if the light of science should ever penetrate this darkness.' To Twining, Indian history was like some deep Aladdin's cave. The outer chambers were well lit thanks to recent Mohammedan chroniclers, but beyond them the cave was in darkness. How far back it went no one could tell. There was just one uncertain clue – the invasion of Alexander the Great in 326 BC. By exploring every possible source, and by combining guesswork with some brilliant deduction, the orientalists successfully penetrated this darkness. The excitement when, deep in the gloom, some new light was shed, was tremendous. But much remained in the gloom; whole centuries defied illumination.

For all the excitement and the very considerable achievements, Indian history is still far from complete. There are almost no ancient historical works to provide a framework, no chronologies to provide the dates and, above all, no contemporary chronicles to provide the detail. It is devoid of almost everything that traditionally makes history palatable for the general reader. There are no anecdotes, no scandals, no well-documented campaigns and no personalities. A chronological approach soon becomes an incredibly confusing list of dynasties and kings, reigning in obscurity, to whom neither reliable dates nor defined kingdoms can be attributed.

To some extent the same goes for Indian art and architecture. The artists, builders and sculptors are mostly anonymous and so, in many cases, are their patrons. We know little about how they worked and nothing of the problems they encountered. In Indian painting, for example, there is a near hiatus of some 1000 years which makes any discussion of the subject highly conjectural.

In this book I have concentrated more on the historians than the history, more on the Indologists than India. The careers of men like Sir William Jones, James Prinsep, Sir Alexander Cunningham, James Fergusson – and many more – reveal almost as much about British

India as about the centuries that preceded it. Moreover, the problems and prejudices they had to surmount in coming to terms with a very alien art and culture are the same as those that any non-Indian unfamiliar with the subject has still to face. The story of the pioneers makes an excellent guidebook to an understanding of India.

To appreciate this story it is not necessary to be in sympathy with the British raj. The government's role in it was the usual one of too little too late. It was a constant source of shame that, whereas other European governments generously supported research on Indian subjects, the British authorities displayed little interest. The field was left to individual initiative. The men who took up the challenge were no more enlightened or liberal in their attitudes than other British officials of the day. Some were deeply respectful of all things Indian. They criticized government policy and were themselves pilloried as 'Brahminized'. Others, perhaps the majority, regarded contemporary Indians as quite unworthy of their glorious heritage. Either they attributed all that was finest in Indian culture to outside influences, or they portrayed Indian history as one of steady decline towards cultural bankruptcy and moral degeneracy.

This story would not be complete without also including those servants of empire who, acting often out of the worthiest of motives, were nothing short of iconoclasts and vandals. The damage wrought on India's fortresses by British cannon was surpassed by that caused by British officers in their search for suitable barracks. And there were engineers whose appetite for in-fill for their dams and railway embankments resulted in some of the most tragic archaeological depredations. Even the zoologists were sometimes sportsmen who could see no contradiction in studying India's wildlife and contributing towards its gradual extinction.

But none of this need detract from the achievement. (The vandals were eventually stopped; even the government was brought to some awareness of its responsibilities.) The products of British scholarship deserve to stand alongside those more commonly cited legacies of the raj – the railways, the judiciary and civil service, democracy. In any large library, India requires a quite disproportionate length of shelf space (in the London Library nearly five times that of China). To work, or just to walk, along those groaning shelves is a stimulating experience. Take away the travelogues and memoirs, the political commentaries and the official papers, and the shelves are still crammed – 200-odd volumes on archaeology, a similar number on the work of the surveyors, nearly fifty concerned purely with ancient inscriptions. Here surely is an aspect of the raj of which an Englishman can be proud without reservation, a unique salute by a conquering power to an older, nobler and more enduring civilization.

CHAPTER ONE
This Wonderful Country

On 1 September 1783 the *Crocodile*, five months out of Portsmouth, struck sail and anchored off Madras. On board Sir William and Lady Jones eyed with concern the wall of spray where the rollers of the Indian Ocean crashed onto the offshore reefs. With the other passengers – the ladies in voluminous, rustling gowns and the men all cocked hats and swords, silk stockings and buckled shoes – they trooped into wooden cages and were lowered over the side. Below, an armada of canoes and catamarans manoeuvred for custom; duckings were commonplace, drownings not unusual.

The first glimpse of India, in the shape of the boatmen, was also less than reassuring. They 'wear no sort of covering but a small piece of rag, not entirely hiding their members', wrote William Hickey, 'a very awkward exhibition this for modest girls on their first arrival.' The brown bodies glistened with the spray and rippled with each stroke of the paddle. And – an early lesson in the nature of British rule in India – these stalwarts had the fine ladies and gentlemen entirely in their power: safely through the foaming breakers, each passenger had to embrace one of those hard brown torsoes for a piggyback through the shallows.

Arriving in Madras was not a dignified business. But on the beach, a parade of well-dressed gentlemen and handsome carriages awaited the new arrivals. Behind, the city shone in the sunshine, white and neoclassical amidst the waving palms, 'rather resembling the images that float in the imagination after reading *The Arabian Nights*'. This at last was India, home for months or years to come, a place where a gentleman could live like a lord and simultaneously amass a fortune.

Sir William Jones was no exception. His first priority was to attain financial independence, or to be precise, a clear £30,000. On the strength of his appointment to the post of Supreme Court judge in Calcutta, he had been knighted and had married. His salary, he calculated, would enable him and Anna Maria to save the £30,000 within six years. Then back to England, to his books and his friends.

But he was already more predisposed towards the East than most new arrivals. His professional qualifications as a jurist were unique. Edward Gibbon, then writing *The Decline and Fall of the Roman Empire*, described Jones as 'the only lawyer equally conversant with the year-books of Westminster, the commentaries of Ulpian, the Attic pleadings of Isaeus, and the sentences of Arabian and Persian *cadhis* [judges]'. On board the *Crocodile*, Jones had continued his studies in Persian law. He needed to make a small fortune, but he also expected to administer justice to the people of Bengal according to their own laws, and indeed, to study and clarify these.

Elsewhere Gibbon described Jones as more than a lawyer; he was 'a genius'. And it was for his other attainments, considerable by any standards, spectacular by those of British India, that he was already best known. The son of an eminent mathematician, he was a keen student of mathematics, astronomy and the sciences – and yet first achieved distinction as a classical scholar. Greek and Latin literature were his passions; he modelled his letters on Cicero, his speeches on Demosthenes, and spattered both with classical allusions. At Oxford he turned to modern languages and then Persian and Arabic. His first published works were typical: a Persian grammar and a translation from Persian into French. He was also a much acclaimed poet, was intensely interested in music, and had the bottomless memory so vital to any polymath; aged eleven, it is said, he amazed his schoolfellows by supplying them with the entire text of *The Tempest* out of his head.

But oriental literature was now his leading interest. Whilst in India he intended to collect manuscripts; he was even prepared to invest some of the £30,000 in them. As the *Crocodile* had sped across the Arabian Sea, with India ahead and Persia to port, he had been overcome with a flush of intense excitement. Culturally speaking, what a vast and unexplored field lay about him; what untold riches were hidden there; and what a glorious achievement if he could lead men in their systematic discovery.

After a couple of days in Madras, the Joneses were back on board 'the sweet little *Crocodile*' and heading for Calcutta. Madras, once the pride of the British settlements in India, had already been eclipsed. Calcutta, founded less than 100 years before, was now the great attraction. Through Clive's treaty with the Moghul emperor in 1765, the whole of Bengal, stretching from Benares to Burma, had been ceded to the East India Company. Commercial priorities were giving way to administrative and fiscal necessities. Casually, precariously, but inexorably, British dominion in India was being created. Jones himself described Bengal as 'this wonderful country which fortune has thrown into Britain's lap while she was asleep'. Administrative responsibility meant collecting revenue, developing communications, regulating trade and administering justice; hence the judiciary and the Supreme Court, not to mention the network of civil and military officials. From being a trading settlement for seventy years, Calcutta had suddenly become a colonial metropolis.

It is hard now to imagine the city as the gay and elegant capital of the East. Few places can have gained quite such an opposite reputation in the space of a couple of centuries – like Regency Bath turning into the Bronx. Contemporary paintings by the likes of Thomas Daniell show spacious Palladian mansions, wide thoroughfares and stately gardens bordered by the blue waters of the Hughli river – no crowds, no dust; it even looks cooler. As the *Crocodile* sailed upriver the Joneses passed their future home on Garden Reach – a nine-mile stretch of 'elegant mansions'. 'They are all white, their roofs invariably flat and surrounded by colonnades, and their fronts relieved by lofty columns supporting deep verandahs.' Each, according to a gossipy contemporary, 'surrounded by groves and lawns, which descend to the water's edge, and present a constant succession of whatever can delight the eye or bespeak wealth and elegance in the owners'. Then came the fort, also on the eastern bank and 'so well kept and everything in such excellent order that it is quite a curiosity to see it – all the slopes, banks and ramparts are covered with the richest verdure, which completes the enchantment of the scene'. Finally, the city itself, flanking the fort with government offices and the homes of the military. 'As you come up past Fort William and the Esplanade, it has a beautiful appearance. Esplanade Row, as it is called, seems to be composed of palaces.' Indeed, Calcutta was known as 'the City of Palaces'.

It was also, in Clive's view, 'one of the most wicked places in the Universe ... Rapacious and Luxurious beyond concepcion [sic]'. Fortunes, so easily made, were as easily lost at the whist table. The day was dominated by dinner at about 2 p.m. – 'a soup, roast fowl, curry and rice, a mutton pie, a forequarter of lamb, a rice pudding, tarts, very good cheese, fresh churned butter, fine bread and excellent Madeira', and that was assuming there were no guests. After dinner the gentleman of the house downed his three bottles of claret and retired to bed until it was time for the evening promenade, supper and a ball, or another round of drinking. Pert little Emma Wrangham and the ravishing Madame Grand provided the scandals; for those too sozzled or syphilitic to stand their pace, there were also legions of 'sooty *bibis*' (prostitutes). Factional quarrels were a way of life at every level. It was only three years since Warren Hastings, the Governor-General, had fought his famous duel with Sir Philip Francis, a senior member of the Governing Council. Yet it was all intensely exciting, like a combination of Paris in the naughty nineties and the Klondike.

The other surprising thing about this city that was to be Jones's home for the next eleven years was its insularity. Although it was the headquarters of a sizeable chunk of India, Calcutta was less Indian even than Madras or the struggling little colony at Bombay. Clive had foreseen the possibilities of an Indian empire and Warren Hastings was aware that with government there came profound responsibilities for the Indian people. Yet there was no general awareness of such things. More typical was the attitude of Sir Philip Francis who never stirred more than a mile or two outside the city. The only British empire known to most was the one in North America that had just been lost. In India the settlement mentality prevailed. What went on in the *Mofussil* outside Calcutta was a mystery; what went on amongst the country powers beyond was an irrelevance. Strictly speaking, the East India Company's administration of Bengal was just another favour granted by the Moghul emperor in Delhi and not so very different from the commercial concessions won in the previous century. 'Up-country disturbances' were deplorable if they upset the flow of trade; but not for another twenty years would the British feel constrained to do anything about them.

William Hodges, the artist, who was touring India when Jones arrived, thought it 'a matter of surprise that of a country so closely allied to us so little should be known. Of the face of the country, of its arts and crafts, little has yet been said.' After several unsuccessful attempts, Hodges managed to get as far inland as Agra and Gwalior, reminding his contemporaries of the glories of the Taj Majal and of Gwalior's massive hill fortress, 'the Gibraltar of the East'. They made little impression on the socialites of Calcutta. The price of indigo, Miss Wrangham's engagement, and the shocking case of William Hunter and the three mutilated maidens were more to their taste.

In this philistine and grasping society Sir William Jones could hardly be other than a conspicuous exception. In London he had been accused of showing an ill-tempered reticence in company, and though he quite reasonably objected, it was to the ill-temper rather than the reticence. As befitted a man of letters, he was reserved in the company of others unless they were his intellectual equals – and there would be precious few of these in Calcutta. Nor had he any time for factions and politics. An unhappy experience as prospective MP for Oxford, plus the drudgery of having had to promote his career by seeking favours, had embittered him. Finally, he was now married and very happily so. Anna Maria, beautiful, accomplished and devoted, was his great delight. Her health would be his only real anxiety in India, and her companionship was one of the major factors in the confidence with which he set about his work. In a society so rife with scandal, it was no small achievement to remain forever untouched by it. Only one other relationship in India could rival theirs – that between another Anna Maria and her husband, Warren Hastings.

Whatever had been achieved in the way of Indian studies before Jones was due to Hastings. The first Governor-General of India (Clive had been Governor of Bengal only), he was also the greatest. Faced with the challenge of governing several million Indians, he conceived the novel and momentous idea of trying to do so with their approbation. Little was yet understood of their customs, whether Muslim or Hindu, and few thought much of their character. 'As degenerate, crafty, wicked and superstitious a people as any race in the known world,' thought a contemporary, adding 'if not more so.' Hastings differed. He spoke Urdu, Bengali and some Persian; he could understand them and in turn respected them. If British rule in India was to prosper and to last, British administrators must themselves become partly Indianized. They must learn the languages, study the customs. The government must work within existing institutions, not try to impose a whole new set of Western ones. There must be an intellectual exchange, not a walkover; and if there were flagrant abuses in Indian society they must be reformed from within, not proscribed from without. Hastings, according to an eminent historian, 'loved the people of India and respected them to a degree no other British ruler has ever equalled'.

If this ambitious scheme was to be realized, the first essential was that all would-be administrators should be able to speak the language. Persian was the language of diplomacy and was already widely used in government circles. Bengali, the local vernacular, was less known; but by the time Jones arrived, the first Bengali grammar, written by

Nathaniel Halhed, an old Oxford friend of Jones, and printed by Charles Wilkins, was already in circulation. Bengali was thus the first of the Indian languages to be made available to scholars; and Wilkins, who cast the type with his own hand, was the first to print in the vernacular in India. The repercussions of this achievement would be enormous, not only for the British for whom the work was intended, but for Indian letters.

One other work of importance had been completed and another was already in manuscript. To enable lawyers to conduct their cases in the native courts, Halhed had followed his grammar with a *Code of Gentoo* [i.e. Hindu] *Laws*. This was a digest assembled by Brahmins working under his supervision. Jones would find it inadequate as a legal code, but it was a step in the direction Hastings wanted the whole administration to take. The other work was potentially much more exciting. Wilkins, having established his Bengali press, won the confidence of the local Brahmins and, with their help, started to learn Sanskrit.

Sanskrit is the sacred language of the Hindus. Its origins were then unknown and, as a spoken language, it was as dead as ancient Greek. But it was the medium in which the earliest religious compositions of the Aryan settlers in India had been expressed; and in the jealous possession of the priestly Brahmin caste, it had been preserved and augmented for centuries. It thus seemed to be the key to the discovery of ancient India: whatever there might be of literary, historical and scientific merit in the pre-Islamic culture of India was composed in Sanskrit or one of its later derivations.

The first Europeans to gain any knowledge of the language were probably Portuguese priests in the sixteenth century. To strengthen their hand in religious disputations with the Brahmins, at least two of the fathers had penetrated its secrets, though without showing any appreciation of its literary wealth. The first Englishmen to show any interest in such matters were equally blind. 'There is little learning among them [the Hindus],' wrote a eighteenth-century traveller, 'a reason whereof may be their penury of books which are but few and they manuscripts.' He was right about the books. There were only manuscripts and they too were carefully guarded. But he overlooked the oral tradition. As every Sanskrit scholar would discover, finding the right *pandit* (teacher) to interpret them was every bit as important as possessing the manuscripts.

All we know about Wilkins's pioneering efforts in Sanskrit is that by the time Jones arrived on the scene he had almost completed the first translation of a Sanskrit work into English. He had chosen the *Bhagavad Gita*, a long extract from that longest of epics, the *Mahabharata*. The *Gita* was the best loved devotional work in India and its publication was to cause a sensation. But first Wilkins sent the work to his patron, Warren Hastings. Would the Governor-General recommend that the East India Company finance its publication?

> I hesitate not to pronounce the *Gita* a performance of great originality [wrote Hastings], of a sublimity of conception, reasoning and diction almost unequalled; and a single exception, amongst all the known religions of mankind, of a theology accurately corresponding with that of the Christian disposition, and most powerfully illustrating its fundamental doctrines. ... I should not fear to place, in opposition to the best French versions of the most admired passages of the Iliad or Odyssey, or of the first and sixth books of our own Milton ... the English translation of the *Mahabharata*.

Hastings was overwhelmed. 'Not very long since, the inhabitants of India were considered by many as creatures scarce elevated above the degree of savage life.' Now their civilization was being revealed in this masterpiece from an age 'preceding even the first efforts of civilization in our own quarter of the globe'. For the benefit of the Company's hard-headed directors, he pointed out that the publication could produce only gratitude from their Indian subjects and greater understanding from their officers. And he ended with a prophetic and resounding pronouncement on the whole body of Indian writings. 'These will survive when the British dominion in India shall have long ceased to exist, and when the sources which it once yielded of wealth and power are lost to remembrance.'

It was as if he was already aware that, however great and lasting the British raj, the discoveries of the orientalists would transcend it. Buried in antiquity there lay the structure of a remarkable civilization; unearthed and reconstructed, it could become the noblest of all monuments to the British period in India.

For this task no man was better qualified than the new Supreme Court judge. Jones combined the broad, bold vision of Hastings with the incisive intellect of Wilkins. In addition, his personality and his enthusiasm for the task had a magnetic quality. Coming straight from England, he was above the pettiness and hedonism of Anglo-Indian life. His stature lent a new respectability to those who took Indian culture seriously. Hastings could encourage others, but Jones had the rare gift of inspiring them.

Before he had even found a Calcutta home, he got in touch with Hastings's protégés. Wilkins and the rest had been working each in his own vacuum. They were flattered. On 15 January 1784, less than sixteen weeks after his arrival, Jones invited thirty kindred and influential spirits to the High Court jury room.

> The proceedings were opened by Sir William Jones who delivered a learned and very suggestive discourse on the Institution of a Society for enquiring into the History, Civil and Natural, the Antiquities, Arts, Sciences and Literature of Asia. The address was enthusiastically received, and a resolution was come to establishing the Society under the name of the Asiatic Society.

Supposedly modelled on the Royal Society, the Asiatic Society owed everything to Jones and was really closer to Dr Johnson's celebrated club, of which Jones had been a member. It was highly informal; there were no rules and the only qualification for membership was a voluntarily-expressed 'love of knowledge'. After Jones, much of this informality would be changed; but his other stipulation remained. The field of enquiry was to be all-embracing. 'You will investigate whatever is rare in the stupendous fabric of nature, will correct the geography of Asia, ... will trace the annals and traditions of those nations who have peopled or desolated it; you will examine their methods in arithmetic and geometry, in trigonometry, mensuration, mechanics, optics, astronomy, and general physics; ... in morality, grammar, rhetoric, and dialectic; in medicine ... anatomy and chemistry. To this you will add researches into their agriculture, manufacture and trade ... music, architecture and poetry ... If now it be asked what are the intended objects of our enquiries within these spacious limits, we answer Man and Nature; whatever is performed by the one or produced by the other.'

To draw up such a comprehensive scheme was an achievement in itself. But Jones was also the only man of his generation who could himself make a distinguished contribution in all these fields. During his ten years as president he stamped the Society with his own unique brand of universality. His contributions included papers on Indian music, on a cure for elephantiasis, on Chinese literature, on the scaly anteater, on the course of the Nile, on Indian chronology, on the Indian zodiac, on the Indian origin of chess, on a new species of haw-finch, on Indian botany, on spikenard, on mystical poetry and on the slow-paced lemur – and all this in addition to his more seminal studies of Hinduism, Indian history and the language and literature of Sanskrit which were embodied in his annual discourses to the Society.

To the far-flung official with a cherished interest in crustaceans, meteorology or Arabic, it came as a revelation that here was a Society anxious to hear from him, and a man who knew enough about the subject to guide his studies and publish his findings. From Benares to Chittagong, and in far away Madras and Bombay, men sat up and took notice of their surroundings. Reports of manuscripts, monuments, inscriptions, old coins, strange customs, forgotten tribes and rare birds began to pour in. Through the Society, Jones was able not only to collate and pass on all this material but to publicize it. The first volume of *Asiatick Researches*, the Society's journal, appeared in 1789. Four more followed during Jones's decade as president and each caused a successively greater sensation in Europe.

Previously the great bar to Indian studies among those who acknowledged that there might be something to study was the idea that they were somehow disreputable. What could one expect to learn from idolators who worshipped cows and monkeys, and who yet presumed to claim a history that out-distanced that of classical Greece, and a religious tradition that discredited the accepted chronology of Genesis? Why should one bother with sculpture that was invariably suggestive and often obscene, or with a religion that enjoined widows to burn themselves? The Hindus apparently condoned infanticide and, according to a seventeenth-century writer, considered the most disgusting eccentricities as evidence of sanctity.

> Some yogis go stark naked, several of which I have seen in India, and 'tis reported that the Hindu women will go to them and kiss the yogi's yard. Others lie something upon it when it stands, which the yogis take to buy victuals with; and several come to stroke it, thinking that there is a good deal of virtue in it, none having gone out of it, as they say, for they lie not with women nor use any other way to vent their seed.
>
> They can hold their breath and lie as if dead for some years, all of which time their bodies are kept warm with oils etc. They can fly and change souls, each with the other or into any beast. They can transform their bodies into what shape they

please and make them so pliable that they can draw them
through a little hole, and wind and turn them like soft wax.
They are mighty temperate in diet, eating nothing but milk
and a sort of grain they have.

By the late eighteenth century it was not usual to be quite as candid
as John Marshall had been. But reports like this were common knowledge. How could such people, 'scarce elevated above the degree of
savage life', be worthy of serious study except by anthropologists?

On the other hand, Hastings's eulogy on the *Gita* suggested that, for
all its modern absurdities, Hinduism was based on the loftiest of
religious sentiments. It was also being said that the Hindus really only
worshipped one god, though in many guises. This immediately made
the subject more respectable. Jones, though, was more intrigued by the
many guises. 'I am in love with the *gopis*,' he wrote to Wilkins in 1784,
'charmed with Krishna, an enthusiastic admirer of Rama and a devout
adorer of Brahma. Yudhisthir, Arjun, Bhima and other warriors of the
Mahabharata appear greater in my eyes than Agamemnon, Ajax and
Achilles appeared when I first read the Iliad.' As if to make the whole
pantheon of Hindu gods more acceptable to Western tastes, one of his
first papers was on *The Gods of Greece, Italy and India*. Deploying his
immense classical learning, he identified many of the Indian gods with
their classical counterparts and even suggested that the Greeks might
have imported many of their deities from India. Zeus and company
might not be entirely respectable, but their exploits had never been
considered reason for ignoring classical studies. Likewise with the
Hindu pantheon. Siva's wife, Parbati, corresponded well with Venus;
Jones could not resist reminding his audience that Venus was occa-
sionally portrayed in the form of a 'conical marble' for which 'the
reason appears too clearly in the temples and paintings of India'. The
lingam or phallus was indeed a formidable hurdle for any good
Christian Englishman who might be mildly intrigued by Hinduism or
Indian sculpture. But, as Jones observed, in Hinduism 'it never seems
to have entered the heads of the legislators or peoples that anything
natural could be offensively obscene, a singularity that pervades all
their writings and conversations, but is no proof of depravity in their
morals'.

This is an argument that the British were never able to swallow.
Jones is almost unique in his acceptance of the erotic in Indian art and
of its place in the Hindu religion. Having disposed of the obvious
stumbling blocks, he was ready to launch into a sympathetic discovery
of India's past.

CHAPTER TWO

An Inquisitive Englishman

In the winter of 1784–5 the Joneses made a tour up the Ganges to Benares and back by way of the ancient cities of Gaya and Gaur. Sir William was getting a feel for 'this wonderful country', meeting the men who corresponded with him, and stalking the precious manuscripts. A copy of the legal code of Manu, the ancient law-giver whom he had previously compared with Moses, was his most prized acquisition. He planned to use it as the basis for a new compendium of Hindu law which would replace Halhed's. He also considered how to outmanoeuvre the Brahmins on whom the courts had to rely for the interpretation – not always impartial – of Sanskrit laws. But he finally resolved to learn Sanskrit himself only when Wilkins announced his intention to leave India. Wilkins was still the only Englishman who had mastered the language. Jones would therefore be the second.

In autumn 1785 the Joneses moved to Krishnagar, sixty miles upriver from Calcutta. There, beside the ancient seat of Bengali scholarship at Nadia, they rented a bungalow, built 'entirely of vegetable materials', and Jones approached the local Brahmins for instruction in Sanskrit. In spite of considerable cash inducements, they refused and eventually decamped for a religious festival. In their absence Jones found Ramlochand, a doctor who, though not a Brahmin, knew and had taught Sanskrit. With reservations he accepted the new pupil.

For the next six years the Joneses returned to Krishnagar and Ramlochand every autumn. Nadia became Jones's 'third university'. He adopted the Indian dress of loose white cotton; their thatched bungalow became the scene of a pastoral idyll that was the antithesis of Calcutta life. Even Anna Maria, who though 'not always ill, is never well', seemed to revive there. The days passed in a routine of simple pleasures and hard study.

Sanskrit proved an extremely difficult language even for a polyglot. But 'I am learning it more grammatically and accurately than the indolence of childhood and the impatience of youth allowed me to learn any other.' Perhaps it was this highly systematic approach which enabled him to make his first major discovery. For, within six months, he was experiencing a sense of *déjà vu*; the grammar, the vocabulary even, seemed to bear some resemblance to Greek and Latin. The Sanskrit for mother was *matr*, mouse *mus* and so on. For someone with no Sanskrit–English dictionary, groping to catch the phrases and inflections of a glib *pandit*, it was not as obvious as it seems now. Nor were the implications clear. It could just be that there were a few borrowed words, either from Sanskrit to Greek or vice versa. Jones, though, guessed that he was on to something more important and in February 1786 he presented his theory to the Asiatic Society.

> The Sanskrit language, whatever be its antiquity, is of a wonderful structure; more perfect than the Greek, more copious than the Latin, and more exquisitely refined than either; yet bearing to both of them a stronger affinity, both in the roots of verbs and the forms of grammar, than can possibly have been produced by accident; so strong, indeed, that no philologer could examine them all without believing them to have sprung from *some common source*, which perhaps no longer exists. There is similar reason though not quite so forcible, for supposing that both the Gothick [i.e. Germanic] and Celtick, though blended with a different idiom, had the same origin with Sanskrit; and the old Persian might be added to the same family.

It was the genius of Sir William Jones that in the chance discovery of what would look to most like a minor coincidence, he could recognize and interpret a cardinal concept. He had not only discovered what later became known as the Indo-European family of languages and indicated that they had a common lost origin; he had in fact laid down the principles of comparative philology. If the study of languages could reveal something as shattering as the common Aryan origin of the ancient peoples of Europe and north India it could clearly be used as a method of historical research. Languages evidently evolved in much the same way as, say, architectural styles. The state of a language at any given period could be used as an indicator of the degree of civilization reached by those who used it. Equally, it could be a way of giving an approximate date to literary compositions of unknown antiquity. Philological studies have since helped to prise open the secrets of many ancient civilizations. India, with its wealth of ancient literature and inscriptions, has benefited more than most, and the dates now ascribed to its earliest literary compositions depend entirely on the evidence of philology.

More immediately, Jones's discovery clearly showed that the people of northern India, far from being savages, were actually of the same ethnic origin as their British rulers. Also, if Sanskrit was 'more perfect' etc. than Greek or Latin, then the record of civilization in India might be longer than in Europe. However sobering for the *sahibs*, it was a tremendous boost for oriental studies. The translation of Sanskrit literature suddenly became a matter of much wider interest. What might it not tell of the civilization of this ancient people, and perhaps of the common origins of all the Aryan peoples? And what about the chronology? Just how old were the various Sanskrit writings?

In what leisure was left after a strenuous life in the courts, Jones forged ahead with his studies. 'I hold every day lost in which I acquire no new knowledge of man or nature,' he wrote in 1787. 'It is my ambition to know India better than any other European ever knew it. I rise an hour before the sun and walk from my garden to the fort, about three miles; ... by seven I am ready for my *pandit* with whom I read Sanskrit; at eight come a Persian or Arab alternately with whom I read till nine; at nine come the attorneys with affidavits; I am then robed and ready for court.' Dinner was at 3 p.m. 'When the sun is sunk in the Ganges we drive back to the Gardens either in our post-chaise or Anna's phaeton drawn by a pair of beautiful Nepal horses. After tea time we read; and never sit up, if we can avoid it, after ten.' He was teaching Anna Maria algebra, and together they were reading Dante, Ariosto and Tasso in the original. Life in Garden Reach had become as idyllic as at their bungalow in Krishnagar. Together they studied botany: Anna Maria drew and painted the plants; Sir William classified them according to the system of Linnaeus and wrote a Latin description of each.

He drew the line at actually picking the flowers. Much as he loved the natural sciences, he had a very Buddhist aversion to destroying life in any form. His studies encouraged botany in India but temporarily stalled zoology. 'I cannot reconcile to my notions of humanity the idea

of making innocent beasts miserable and mangling harmless birds.'
The livestock that thronged their garden responded to this humane
outlook. From the Joneses' dairy came 'the best butter in India'. Their
sheep and goats, safe from the butcher's knife, would feed from Anna
Maria's hand. It was all 'like what the poets tell us of the golden ages;
... you might see a kid and a tiger playing at Anna's feet. The tiger is
not as large as a full grown cat, though he will be as large as an ox: he is
suckled by a she-goat and has all the gentleness of his foster-mother.'
Jones always insisted that even in England he had never been
unhappy; 'but I was never happy till I settled in India'.

He was also in a state of intense excitement. 'Sanskrit literature is
indeed a new world; the language (which I begin to speak with ease) is
the Latin of India and a sister of Latin and Greek. In Sanskrit are
written half a million of stanzas on sacred history and literature, epic
and lyric poems innumerable, and (what is wonderful) tragedies and
comedies not to be counted, about 2000 years old, besides works on
law (my great object), on medicine, on theology, on arithmetic, on
ethics and so on to infinity.' He felt like a man who had stumbled
unawares on the whole corpus of classical literature. How could he
convey this excitement?

> Suppose Greek literature to be known in modern Greece
> only, and there to be in the hands of priests and philosophers;
> and suppose them to be still worshippers of Jupiter and
> Apollo; suppose Greece to have been conquered successively
> by Goths, Huns, Vandals and Tartars, and lastly by the
> British; then suppose a court of judicature to be established
> by the British parliament, at Athens, and an inquisitive
> Englishman to be one of the judges; suppose him to learn
> Greek there, which none of his countrymen knew, and to read
> Homer, Pindar, Plato, which no other European had ever
> heard of. Such am I in this country; substituting Sanskrit for
> Greek, the Brahmins for the priests of Jupiter, and Valmiki,
> Vyasa and Kalidasa for Homer, Plato and Pindar.

Jones had no doubts that Sanskrit literature, like the language itself,
was in every way the equal of Greek or Latin literature. He was now,
in 1787, translating a drama by Kalidasa, 'the Indian Shakespeare'.
Completed in 1788 and published the following year, *Sakuntala* fully
justified his expectations. It was the first Sanskrit work to be translated
purely for its literary merit. Despite the omission of some passages too

bold for contemporary tastes – like the one detailing the heroine's swelling breasts – the comparison of Kalidasa with Shakespeare was not excessively partisan. *Sakuntala* was strongly reminiscent of *The Tempest* or *A Midsummer Night's Dream* and was an instant success. The Calcutta edition was followed by two London editions within the space of three years.

Jones was, however, wrong about one thing. Kalidasa was known to have lived in the age of a king called Vikramaditya, but Jones's dating of 'above 2000 years old' was a few centuries out. Vikramaditya was the title of several Indian sovereigns, and Kalidasa's patron reigned about AD 400. He was thus a contemporary of St Augustine, not Homer.

As the literary evidence of a great classical age in Indian history accumulated, the question of dates became more and more vexed. Sanskrit literature included some long lists of kings, but no chronicles – and nothing that could be regarded as historical writing. This was a bitter disappointment. Where was the Indian Tacitus? And, without him, how could this civilization be fitted into any kind of historical context? Jones heard tell of the *Rajatarangini*, a Kashmiri work of the twelfth century which we now know to be the only historical work relating to pre-Islamic India. But in time and place it is far removed from the classical age, and anyway, Jones was not able to get a copy.

Failing that, there was just one date in the whole of ancient Indian history – 326 BC which, as every schoolboy was expected to know, was the year that Alexander the Great had invaded the Punjab. Strangely, this event, so significant to western historians, seemed to have entirely escaped the attention of Sanskrit authors. Nowhere did Jones find any mention of Greeks or any sign of Greek influence.

Through the early 1790s he continued to broaden the scope of his Sanskrit reading. He had already discovered that chess and algebra were of Indian origin; to these, after studying a Sanskrit treatise on music, he added the heptatonic scale. He was also making progress with his legal code and creating something of a reputation in the courts. 'I can now read both Sanskrit and Arabic with so much ease that the native lawyers can never impose upon the courts in which I sit.' To the acclaim of scholars all over the world (Dr Johnson called him 'one of the most enlightened of the sons of men') was added the sincere regard and affection of Bengalis, whether petitioners or *pandits*.

India was exercising its spell on him. His planned stay of six years was up; but he no longer yearned to return to England. He might make a visit to Europe, but he planned to be still in India at the turn of the century. Hinduism he found increasingly attractive and the doctrine of reincarnation seemed 'incomparably more rational, more pious and more likely to deter men from vice than the horrid opinions inculcated by Christians of punishment without end'. But he was not tempted to forsake Christianity. Indeed there was no need; the *Thirty-nine Articles*, if written in Sanskrit, would pass for the work of a Brahmin and be quite acceptable to Hindus.

By now the Joneses had become something of an institution. Young Thomas Twining, only seventeen and just arrived in India, was so honoured by an invitation to dine with them that he filled a whole page of his journal with an account of the visit.

> The party consisted of Sir William and Lady Jones, another gentleman and myself. Sir William was very cheerful and agreeable. He made some observations on the mysterious word *om* of the Hindoos, and other Indian subjects. While sitting after dinner he suddenly called out with a loud voice 'Othello, Othello'. Waiting for a minute or two and Othello not coming, he repeated his summons, 'Othello, Othello'. His particularly fine voice, his white Indian dress, surmounted by a small black wig, his cheerfulness and great celebrity, rendered this scene extremely interesting. I was surprised that no one, Muslim or Hindoo, answered his summons. At last I saw a black turtle of very large size, crawling slowly towards us from an adjoining room. It made its way to the side of Sir William's chair, where it remained, he giving it something it seemed to like. Sir William observed that he was fond of birds, but had little pleasure seeing them or hearing them unless they were at liberty; and he no doubt would have liberated Othello if he had not considered that he was safer by the side of his table than he would be in the Ganges.
>
> I passed a most pleasant day in the company of this distinguished and able man. He was so good as to express some approbation of my Persian studies, and repeated to me two lines of a Persian couplet, and also his translations of them —
>
> > Kill not that ant that steals a little grain;
> > It lives with pleasure, and it dies with pain.

Sitting in the shade on the banks of the Hughli, surrounded by venerable *pandits* and tame livestock, with Anna Maria sketching quietly in the background, he seemed the archetype of the Indian teacher – scholar and law-giver, patron to man and beast. It was the same at the Asiatic Society. He presided at almost every meeting, and at the beginning of each year delivered a challenging discourse on some different aspect of oriental studies. Right from the start there had been something Socratic in his manner – You will investigate this, enquire into that, etc., etc. – and in his last discourse he referred to the Society as a 'symposiack assembly'. Revered and loved (though rarely seen) by Calcutta society, he was indeed the Indian Socrates.

In 1793 he delivered his tenth discourse and celebrated the occasion by casually coming out with the long-awaited breakthrough on Indian chronology. 'The jurisprudence of the Hindus and Arabs being the field I have chosen for my regular toil, you cannot expect that I should greatly enlarge your collection of historical knowledge; but I may be able to offer you some occasional tribute, and I cannot help mentioning a discovery which accident threw my way.' He had already laid down the basis of literary and linguistic studies; now, at last, he had unearthed a foundation from which a start could be made with the reconstruction of India's ancient history. The discovery may have been accidental, but it was his greatest; no one without his immense learning and his genius for spotting a relevant fact could have made it.

First there was the Greek background. Following the invasion by Alexander the Great, Seleucus Nicator, his successor in Asia, had sent an ambassador named Megasthenes to India. This man's report had subsequently been raided by numerous classical writers for their descriptions of India and so, though the original was lost, it could be largely reconstructed. It appeared that Megasthenes had found the Indian court at a place named Palibothra, at the junction of the Ganges and the Erranaboas. He had given a long and interesting account of the court and its ruler, Sandracottus; but where Palibothra was, which river the Erranaboas was supposed to be, and who Sandracottus was, all remained mysterious. One geographer had maintained that the Erranaboas must be the Jumna and that therefore Palibothra must be the modern Allahabad at the junction of the Ganges and the Jumna. There were several other claimants including Kanauj and Rajmahal, but the most promising was Patna, the ancient name for which was known to have been Pataliputra. This sounded very close to the Greek; but there was a problem. No river joins the Ganges at Patna. In the 1770s the great geographer James Rennell revealed that once upon a time the Son river might have joined the Ganges at Patna, though it had since taken up a course much further east. But how could the Son river be the Erranaboas, especially when Megasthenes had mentioned the Son as a quite separate river?

This conundrum must have been on Jones's mind as he waded through the Sanskrit literature. The first connection came when he stumbled upon a reference to the Son as the *Hiranyabahu*, or golden-armed. Immediately he realized that Erranaboas could be a Greek attempt at *Hiranyabahu*; in which case Erranaboas was the Son after all and Megasthenes was wrong when he thought them two separate rivers. And if the Erranaboas was the Son then Palibothra must indeed be Pataliputra, the modern Patna. That left just Sandracottus, the Indian ruler whom Megasthenes had so much admired. He was evidently an adventurer and usurper but a man of considerable ability and the creator of a vast empire. Yet no such name appeared in any of the Sanskrit king lists.

Jones went on reading. In an obscure political tragedy he found what purported to be the story of Chandragupta; he was described as a usurper who chose Pataliputra as his capital and received foreign ambassadors there. This proved the point; Chandragupta must be Sandracottus. The later discovery of an alternative spelling for Sandracottus as Sandraguptos clinched it. Going back to classical sources, it was also known that, before sending Megasthenes, Seleucus Nicator had himself visited, or rather invaded, India. He had been beaten back but his adversary, even then, had been Sandracottus, whose dominion was already established right across northern India. Seleucus returned west and was known to have reached Babylon in 312 BC. So Sandracottus must have ascended the throne before this date, but after Alexander's visit – somewhere between, say, 325 BC and 313 BC.

Thus, to within a decade, one event in India's ancient history had been given a date. It is impossible to exaggerate the importance of this discovery. Fortuitously Alexander, Seleucus and Megasthenes had blundered into Indian history at a crucial moment. Chandragupta would soon be revealed as a sort of Indian Julius Caesar, the creator of an empire and the founder of a dynasty unique in Indian history. The date of his ascent to the throne was thus a crucial one. Working backwards from it to the birth of Buddha, and forwards using the Sanskrit king lists, the whole chronology of Indian history could be, and was, based upon it.

Six months after announcing his discovery, Jones wrote to a close friend in England. 'This day ten years ago ... we landed at Calcutta; and if it had not been for the incessant ill-health of my beloved Anna, they would have been the happiest years of a life always happy ...' But now Anna Maria must go home; to stay longer would endanger her life. Jones himself would follow 'as soon as I can, consistent with my own plans ... but having nothing to fear from India, and much to enjoy in it, I shall make a great sacrifice whenever I leave it'.

> In fact I shall leave a country where we have no Royal Court, no House of Lords, no clergy with wealth or power, no taxes, no fear of robbers or fire, no snow and hard frosts followed by comfortless thaws, and no ice except what is made by art to supply our deserts; add to this, that I have twice as much money as I want, and am conscious of doing very great and extensive good to many millions of native Indians, who look to me, not as their judge, but as their legislator. Nevertheless a man who has nearly closed the forty-seventh year of his age, and who sees younger men dying around him constantly, has a right to think of retirement in this life, and ought to think chiefly of preparing himself for another ...

Already his eyesight was deteriorating, and in November he collapsed with a fever. He recovered, but rheumatism and a tumour continued to give him great pain. Anna Maria sailed for home. Jones immersed himself ever deeper in his studies. Seven volumes of the digest of Hindu law were now complete. A year more of intensive study, and the remaining two volumes should be ready. He officially requested permission to resign his judgeship and return to England in 1795. A month after making the request he collapsed. Doctors linked the tumour to an inflammation of the liver. Again he seemed to recover. On 26 April 1794, the doctors thought him well enough to face an immediate voyage to England. The next day, as if shattered by the thought of such an abrupt departure, 'the father of oriental studies' died.

Jones's discoveries – of the Indo-European family of languages, of the riches of Sanskrit literature, and of the first date in ancient Indian history – were all milestones. But in retrospect, his most important achievement was the founding of the Asiatic Society. Had he left no such institution, his death might well have created an unbridgeable void in the ranks of the orientalists; the reconstruction of India's ancient history might have been delayed by decades. As it was, there was no hiatus. Henry Thomas Colebrooke, another brilliant scholar, who had read his first paper to the society just before Jones's death, completed the digest of Hindu laws. He also assumed the mantle of Jones as the champion of Hindu civilization and the exponent of Sanskrit literature; indeed, Professor Max Muller, the great German orientalist, considered Colebrooke the finer scholar.

Many other notable figures assisted in the exploration of Sanskrit and in the study of how India's vernacular languages had developed from it. Indirectly, they also contributed to the reconstruction of Indian history and the appreciation of Indian art and architecture. But the more sensational discoveries would be made elsewhere. Sanskrit literature proved too unreliable on facts and dates, too hard to authenticate and too diffuse to assimilate; sometimes it was positively misleading.

But if Jones had concentrated on literature, he had also provided for and encouraged the widest possible use of research: 'Man and Nature – whatever is performed by the one or produced by the other.' Every branch of Indian studies owed something to his inspiration and, without this, no true picture of India would ever have emerged.

He had also succeeded in making Indian studies respectable. In England, Calcutta was now compared to Florence; there was talk of an Indian-based renaissance; and Jones and his successors were compared to the great Italian humanists. The 'Exotic East' had taken on a new meaning. It was no longer possible to view India as an extravagant and titillating circus. For scholars it was a challenge, for administrators a responsibility. Various reforms were making India less attractive to the adventurer and speculator. Jones's fame ensured that their place would be taken by the soldier-scholars and collector-scientists who became the true glory of the raj.

CHAPTER THREE
Thus Spake Ashoka

The trappings of government set up in Calcutta to cope with the sudden acquisition of Bengal included not only a judiciary but also a mint. It was as Assistant Assay-Master at this mint that James Prinsep arrived in India in 1819. The post was an undistinguished one; Prinsep, far from being a celebrity like Jones, could expect nothing better. He was barely twenty and, according to his obituarist, 'wanting, perhaps, in the finish of classical scholarship which is conferred at the public schools and universities of England'. As a child, the last in a family of seven sons, his passion had been constructing highly intricate working models; 'habits of exactness and minute attention to detail' would remain his outstanding traits. He studied architecture under Pugin, transferred to the Royal Mint when his eyesight became strained, and thence to Calcutta. 'Well grounded in chemistry, mechanics and the useful sciences', he was not an obvious candidate for the mantle of Jones and the distinction of being India's most successful scholar.

In the quarter century between Jones's death and Prinsep's arrival the British position in India had changed radically. The defeats of Tipu Sultan, ruler of Mysore, of the Marathas, and of the Gurkhas had left the British undisputed masters of as much of India as they cared to digest. Indeed the British raj had begun. The sovereignty of the East India Company was almost as much a political fiction as that of their nominal but now helpless overlord, the Moghul emperor. Both, though they lingered on for another thirty years, had become anachronisms.

From Calcutta a long arm of British territory now reached up the Ganges and the Jumna to Agra, Delhi and beyond. A thumb prodded the Himalayas between Nepal and Kashmir, while several stubby fingers probed into Punjab, Rajasthan and central India. In the west, Bombay had been expanding into the Maratha homeland; Broach and Baroda were under British control, and Poona, a centre of Hindu orthodoxy and the Maratha capital, was being transformed into the legendary watering place for Anglo-Indian bores. In the south, all that was not British territory was held by friendly feudatories; the French had been obliterated, Mysore settled, and the limits of territorial expansion already reached.

Visitors in search of the real India no longer had to hop around the coastline; they could now march boldly, and safely, across the middle. Bishop Heber of Calcutta (the appointment itself was a sign of the times; in Jones's day there had not been even a church in Calcutta) toured his diocese in the 1820s. The diocese was a big one – the whole of India – and 'Reginald Calcutta', as he signed himself, travelled the length of the Ganges to Dehra Dun in the Himalayas, then down through Delhi and Agra into Rajasthan, still largely independent, and came out at Poona and thence down to Bombay.

The acquisition of all this new territory brought the British into contact with the country's architectural heritage. Two centuries earlier Elizabethan envoys had marvelled at the cities of Moghul India 'of which the like is not to be found in all Christendom'. The famous buildings of Agra, Fatehpur Sikri and Delhi, 'either of them much greater than London and more populous', they had described in detail. When, therefore, the first generation of British administrators arrived in upper India they showed genuine reverence for the architectural relics of Moghul power. Instead of the landscapes of Hodges and the Daniells, their souvenirs of India would be detailed drawings of the Taj Mahal and the Red Fort. Their curiosity also extended to buildings sacred to the non-Mohammedan population; Khajuraho, Abu and many other sites were discovered between 1810 and 1830. The raw materials for a new investigation of India's past were accumulating. But it was another class of monuments, predating the Mohammedan invasions and with unmistakable signs of extreme antiquity, which would become Prinsep's speciality.

The first of these monuments – one could scarcely call them buildings – to attract European attention were the cave temples in the vicinity of Bombay. The island of Elephanta in Bombay harbour had been known to the Portuguese and became the subject of one of the earliest archaeological reports received by Jones's new Asiatic Society.

The cave is about three-quarters of a mile from the beach; the path leading to it lies through a valley; the hills on either side beautifully clothed and, except when interrupted by the dove calling to her absent mate, a solemn stillness prevails; the mind is fitted for contemplating the approaching scene.

The approaching scene was not of some natural cave with a few prehistoric scratchings, but of a spacious pillared hall, with delicate sculptural details and colossal stone figures – an architectural creation in all but name; for the whole thing was hacked, hewn, carved and sculpted out of solid rock.

North of Bombay, the island of Salsette boasted more groups of such caves. In 1806 Lord Valentia, a young Englishman whose greatest claim to fame must be the sheer weight of his travelogue (four quarto volumes of just on half a hundredweight), set out to explore them. He took with him Henry Salt, his companion and artist, to help clear a path through the jungle that surrounded the caves. Outside the Jogeshwar caves they hesitated before the fresh pug marks of a tiger; according to the villagers, tigers actually lived in the caves for part of the year.

Salt found that the other Salsette caves at Kanheri and Montpezir had also been recently occupied. To the Portuguese, the pillared nave and the transepts had spelt basilica; there was even a hole in the façade for a rose window. They had just smothered the fine, but pagan, carving in stucco and consecrated the place. Salt chipped away at the stucco and observed how well it had preserved the sculpture.

Though these figures are by no means well proportioned, yet their air, size and general management give an expression of grandeur that the best sculptors have often failed in attaining; the laziness of attitude, the simplicity of drapery, the suitableness of their situation and the plainness of style in which they are executed ... all contribute towards producing this effect.

He was getting quite a feeling for ancient art treasures. In Lord Valentia's train he would move on to Egypt, stay on there as British consul, and become so successful at appropriating and selling the art treasures of the Pharaohs that he rivalled the great tomb-robber Belzoni.

Meanwhile in India more rock-cut temples had come to light. The free-standing Kailasa temple at Ellora, cut into the rock from above like a gigantic intaglio, was discovered in the late eighteenth century. It was followed by the famous caves at Ajanta and Bagh. 'Few remains of antiquity,' wrote William Erskine in 1813, 'have excited greater curiosity. History does not record any fact that can guide us in fixing the period of their execution, and many opposite opinions have been formed regarding the religion of the people by whom they were made.' From the statuary at Elephanta and Ellora, particularly the figures with several heads and many arms, it was clear that these at least were Hindu. But why were they in such remote locations and why had they been so long neglected? What, too, of the plainer caves like Kanheri and the largest of all, Karli in the Western Ghats? Lord Valentia was pretty sure that the sitting figure, surrounded by devotees, at Karli was 'the Boddh'; he had just come from Ceylon where Buddhism was still a living religion, though it appeared to be almost unknown in India.

Other critics who looked to the west for an explanation of anything they found admirable in Indian art, insisted that the excellence of the sculpture indicated the presence of a Greek, Phoenician or even Jewish colony in western India. Yet others looked to Africa: who but the builders of the pyramids could have achieved such monolithic wonders? These theories were based on the idea that such monuments were exclusive to western India, which had a long history of maritime contacts with the West. They became less credible with the discovery of the so-called Seven Pagodas at Mahabalipuram near Madras. Here, a thousand miles away and on the other side of the Indian peninsula, were a group of temples cut not out of solid rock, but sculpted out of boulders. At first glance they looked like true buildings, a little rounded like old stone cottages, but well proportioned — up to fifty-five feet long and thirty-five feet high — with porches, pillars and statuary. It was only on closer inspection that one realized that each was a single gigantic stone sculpted into architecture. 'Stupendous,' declared William Chambers who twice visited the place in the 1770s (though his report had to wait for the Asiatic Society's first publication in 1789), 'of a style no longer in use, indeed closer to that of Egypt.'

Five years later, a further account of the boulder temples, or *raths*, was submitted by a man who had also seen Elephanta. To his mind there was no question that in style and technique the two were closely related. Had he also seen the intaglio temple of Ellora he might have been tempted to postulate some theory of architectural development; first the cave temple, then the free-standing excavation, and finally the boulder style, freed at last from solid rock. It was as if India's architecture had somehow evolved out of the earth's crust. Elsewhere, stone buildings have always evolved from wooden ones; but in India it was as if architecture was a development of sculpture. The distinctive characteristic of all truly Indian buildings is their sculptural quality. The great Hindu temples look like mountainous accumulations of figures and friezes; even the Taj Mahal, for all its purity of line, stays in the mind as a masterpiece of sculpture rather than of construction.

There was yet one other type of ancient monument which had intrigued early visitors. Thomas Coryat, an English eccentric who turned up in Delhi in 1616, was probably the first to take notice of it. South of the Moghul city of Delhi (now Old Delhi) lay the abandoned tombs and forts of half a dozen earlier Delhis (now, confusingly, the site of New Delhi). The ruins stretched for ten miles, overgrown, inhabited by bats and monkeys. But in the middle of this jungle of crumbling masonry Coryat saw something that made him stop; it did not belong. A plain circular pillar, forty feet high, stuck up through the remains of some dying palace and, in the evening light so proper to ruins, it shone. At a distance he took it for brass, closer up for marble; it is in fact polished sandstone. Of a weight later estimated at twenty-seven tons, it is a single, finely tapered stone, another example of highly developed monolithic craftsmanship. But what intrigued Coryat was the discovery that it was inscribed. Of the two principal inscriptions one was in a script consisting of simple erect letters, a bit like pin-men, which Coryat was sure were Greek. The pillar must then, he thought, have been erected by Alexander the Great, probably 'in token of his victorie' over the Indian king Porus in 326 BC.

Fifty years later another such pillar was discovered by John Marshall, an East India Company factor who has been called 'the first Englishman who really studied Indian antiquities'. He was certainly less inclined to jump to wild conclusions. His pillar was 'nine yards nine inches high' and boasted a remarkable capital: 'at the top of this pillar ... is placed a tyger engraven, the neatliest that I have seene in India'. It was actually a lion. But perhaps the most interesting thing about this pillar was that it was in Bihar, a thousand miles from Delhi and many more from the rock-cut monuments around Bombay and Madras.

Writing similar to that found on the Delhi pillar was also found on some of the cave temples; and at Karli there was actually a small pillar outside the cave. Clearly all these monuments were somehow connected. But it was doubtful whether Alexander had ever reached Delhi, let alone Bihar. The existence of a similar pillar there put paid to Coryat's idea of their commemorating Alexander's victories, although the possibility that the letters were some corrupt form of Greek would linger on for many years.

With the foundation of the Asiatic Society there was at last a forum in which a concerted investigation into all these monuments could take place. Reports of more pillars and caves were soon trickling in. Jones himself was rightly convinced that the mystery of who created them, when and why, could be solved only if the inscriptions could be translated. Some ancient civilization, some foreign conqueror perhaps, or some master craftsman, seemed to be crying out for recognition. Another breakthrough seemed imminent; and with it another chunk of India's lost history might be restored.

Thanks to Charles Wilkins, the man who preceded Jones as a Sanskritist, progress was at first encouraging. At one of the earliest meetings of the Society he reported on a new pillar, also in Bihar.

> Sometime in the month of November in the year 1780 I discovered in the vicinity of the Town of Buddal, near which the Company has a factory, and which at that time was under my charge, a decapitated monumental pillar which at a little distance had very much the appearance of the trunk of a coconut tree broken off in the middle. It stands in a swamp overgrown with weeds near a small temple. . . . Upon my getting close enough to the monument to examine it, I took its dimensions and made a drawing of it. . . . At a few feet above the ground is an inscription, engrained in the stone, from which I took two reversed impressions with printer's ink. I have lately been so fortunate as to decipher the character.

Though very different from Devanagari, the modern script used for Sanskrit, it was clearly related to it and Wilkins was not surprised to discover that the language was in fact Sanskrit. To historians the translation was a disappointment; the Buddal pillar told them nothing of interest. But the deciphering was an important development. Nowadays it is recognized that the modern Devanagari script has passed through three distinct stages; first the pin-men script that Coryat thought was Greek (Ashoka Brahmi); second a more ornate, chunky script (Gupta Brahmi); and third, a more curved and rounded script (Kutila) from which springs the washing-on-the-line script of

Devanagari. The Buddal pillar was Kutila, and once Wilkins had established that it had some connection with Devanagari, the possibility of working backwards to the earlier scripts was dimly perceived.

As if to illustrate this, Wilkins next surprised his colleagues by teasing some sense out of an inscription written in Gupta Brahmi. It came from a cave near Gaya which had been known for some time though never visited; a Mr Hodgekis, who tried, 'was assassinated on his way to it'. Encouraged by Warren Hastings, John Harrington, the secretary of the Asiatic Society, was more successful and found the cave hidden behind a tree near the top of a hill. The character of the inscription, according to Wilkins, was 'undoubtedly the most ancient of any that have hitherto come under my inspection. But though the writing is not modern, the language is pure Sanskrit'. Wilkins, tantalizing as ever about how he made his breakthrough, apparently divined that the inscription was in verse. It was the discovery of the metre that somehow helped him to the successful decipherment. But again, there was little in this new translation to satisfy the historian's thirst for facts.

A far more promising approach to the problem, indeed a short cut, seemed to be heralded in a letter to Jones from Lieutenant Francis Wilford, a surveyor and an enthusiastic student of all things oriental, who was based at Benares. Jones had been sent copies of inscriptions found at Ellora and written in Ashoka Brahmi, the still undeciphered pin-men. He had probably sent them to Wilford because Benares, the holy city of the Hindus, was the most likely place to find a Brahmin who might be able to read them. In 1793 Wilford announced that he had found just such a man.

> I have the honour to return to you the facsimile of several inscriptions with an explanation of them. I despaired at first of ever being able to decipher them. ... However, after many fruitless attempts on our part, we were so fortunate as to find at last an ancient sage, who gave us the key, and produced a book in Sanskrit, containing a great many ancient alphabets formerly in use in different parts of India. This was really a fortunate discovery, which hereafter may be of great service to us.

According to the ancient sage, most of Wilford's inscriptions related to the wanderings of the five heroic Pandava brothers from the *Mahabharata*. At the unspecified time in question they were under an obligation not to converse with the rest of mankind; so their friends devised a method of communicating with them by 'writing short and obscure sentences on rocks and stones in the wilderness and in characters previously agreed upon betwixt them'. The sage happened to have the key to these characters in his code book; obligingly he transcribed them into Devanagari Sanskrit and then translated them.

To be fair to Wilford, he was a bit suspicious about this ingenious explanation of how the inscriptions got there. But he had no doubts that the deciphering and translation were genuine. 'Our having been able to decipher them is a great point in my opinion, as it may hereafter lead to further discoveries, that may ultimately crown our labours with success.' Above all, he had now located the code book, 'a most fortunate circumstance'.

Poor Wilford was the laughing stock of the Benares Brahmins for a whole decade. They had already fobbed him off with Sanskrit texts, later proved spurious, on the source of the Nile and the origin of Mecca. After the code book there was a geographical treatise on *The Sacred Isles of the West*, which included early Hindu reference to the British Isles. The Brahmins, to whom Sanskrit had so long remained a sacred prerogative, were getting their own back. One wonders how much Wilford paid his 'ancient sage'.

Jones was already a little suspicious of Wilford's sources, but on the code book, which was as much a fabrication as the translations supposedly based on it, he reserved judgement until he might see it. He never did. In fact it was never heard of again. But in spite of these disappointments Jones continued to believe that in time this oldest script would be deciphered. He had been sent a copy of the writings on the Delhi pillar and told a correspondent that they 'drive me to despair; you are right, I doubt not, in thinking them foreign; I believe them to be Ethiopian and to have been imported a thousand years before Christ'. It was not one of his more inspired guesses and at the time of his death the mystery of the inscriptions and of the monoliths was as dark as ever.

And so it remained until the labours of James Prinsep. Jones had given oriental studies a strongly literary bias and his successors continued to concentrate on Sanskrit manuscripts. Archaeological studies were ignored in consequence, and so were inscriptions. Wilkins's few translations had led nowhere and the most intriguing of the scripts remained undeciphered. Indeed even the translation of the Gupta Brahmi script from the cave at Gaya was forgotten in the general waning of interest; it would have to be deciphered all over again.

During his first twelve years in India Prinsep confined his attention to scientific matters. He was sent to Benares to set up a second mint and while there redesigned the city's sewers. He also contributed a few articles to the Asiatic Society's journal ('Descriptions of a Pluviometer and Evaporameter', 'Note on the Magic Mirrors of Japan', etc.).

But in 1830 he was recalled to Calcutta as assistant to the Assay-Master, Horace Hayman Wilson, who was also secretary of the Asiatic Society and an eminent Sanskrit scholar. At the time Wilson was puzzling over the significance of various ancient coins that had recently been found in Rajasthan and the Punjab. Prinsep helped to catalogue and describe them, and it was in attempting to decipher their legends that his interest in the whole question of ancient inscriptions was aroused. Although his ignorance of Sanskrit was undoubtedly a handicap, here, in the deciphering of scripts, was a field in which his quite exceptional talent for minute and methodical study could be deployed to brilliant advantage.

Since Jones's day another pillar like that at Delhi had been found at Allahabad; in addition to a Persian inscription of the Moghul period, it displayed a long inscription in each of the two older scripts (Ashoka Brahmi and Gupta Brahmi). A report had also been received of a rock in Orissa covered with the same two scripts. In 1833 Prinsep prevailed on a Lieutenant Burt, one of several enthusiastic engineers and surveyors, to take an exact impression of the Allahabad pillar inscription.

The facsimiles reached Prinsep in early 1834. With an eminent Sanskritist, the Rev. W. H. Mill, he soon resolved the problem of the Gupta Brahmi. This was the script that Wilkins had deciphered nearly fifty years before, though his achievement had since been forgotten. The same thing was not likely to happen again; for this time the inscription had something to tell. Evidently it had been engraved on the instructions of a king called Samudragupta. It recorded his extensive conquests and it mentioned that he was the son of Chandragupta. The temptation to assume that this Chandragupta was the same as Jones's Chandragupta, the Sandracottus of the Greeks, was almost irresistible. But not quite. For one thing Jones's Chandragupta had not, according to the Sanskrit king lists, been succeeded by a Samudragupta; they did, however, mention several other Chandraguptas. But if Prinsep and Mill were disappointed at having to deny themselves the simplest and most satisfying of identifications, there would be compensation. They had raised the veil on a dynasty now known as the Imperial Guptas. According to the Allahabad inscriptions Samudragupta had 'violently uprooted' nine kings and annexed their kingdoms. His rule stretched right across northern India and deep into the Deccan. Politically, here was an empire to rival that of Jones's Chandragupta. But, more important, the Gupta period, about AD 320–460, would soon come to be recognized as the golden age of classical Indian culture. To this period belong many of the frescoes of Ajanta, the finest of the Sarnath and Mathura sculptures, and the plays and poems of Kalidasa, 'the Indian Shakespeare'.

But at the time Prinsep and Mill knew no more about these Guptas than what the pillar told them – and much of that they were inclined to regard as royal hyperbole and therefore unreliable. Prinsep, anyway, was more interested in the scripts than in their historical interpretation. Unlike Jones, he did not indulge in grand theories. He was not a classical scholar, not even a Sanskritist, but a pragmatic, dedicated scientist.

In between experimenting with rust-proof treatments for the new steamboats to be employed on the Ganges, he wrestled next with the Ashoka Brahmi pin-men on the Allahabad column. Coryat's idea that it was some kind of Greek was back in fashion. One scholar claimed to have identified no less than seven letters of the Greek alphabet and another had actually read a Greek name written in this script on an ancient coin. Prinsep was sceptical. The Greek name was only Greek if read upside down. Turn it round and the pin-men letters were just like those on the pillars.

But as yet he had no solution of his own. 'It would require an accurate acquaintance with many of the languages of the East, as well as perfect leisure and abstraction from other pursuits to engage upon the recovery of this lost language.' He guessed that it must be Sanskrit and thought the script looked simpler than the Egyptian hieroglyphs. It was still beyond him, though, and he could only hope that someone else in India would take up the challenge 'before the indefatigable students of Bonn and Berlin'.

No one reacted directly to this appeal, but in far away Kathmandu the solitary British resident at the court of Nepal, Brian Houghton Hodgson, read his copy of the Society's journal and immediately dashed off a pained note. No man made more contributions to the discovery of India than Hodgson, or researched in so many different fields. From his outpost in the Himalayas he deluged the Asiatic Society with so many reports that it is hardly surprising some were mislaid. This was a case in point. 'Eight or ten years ago' (so some time in the mid 1820s), he had sent in details of two more inscribed pillars. Prinsep could not find them. But Hodgson also disclosed that he had now found yet a third. It was at Bettiah (Lauriya Nandangarh) in northern Bihar and, like the others, very close to the Nepalese frontier. Could they then have been erected as boundary markers?

More intriguing was the facsimile of the inscription on this pillar which Hodgson thoughtfully enclosed. It was Ashoka Brahmi and Prinsep placed it alongside his copies of the Delhi and Allahabad inscriptions. Again he started to look for clues, concentrating this time on separating the shapes of the individual consonants from the vowels which were in the form of little marks festooning them. Darting from one facsimile to the other to verify these, he suddenly experienced that shiver down the spine that comes with the unexpected revelation. 'Upon carefully comparing them [the three inscriptions] with a view to finding any other words that might be common to them ... I was led to a most important discovery; namely that all three inscriptions were identically the same.'

Any surprise that he had not noticed this before must be tempered by the fact that the inscriptions, all of 2000 years old, were far from perfect. Many letters had been worn away and in one case much of the original inscription had been obliterated by a later one written on top of it. The copies from which Prinsep worked also left much to be desired. Apart from the errors inevitable when someone tried to copy a considerable chunk of writing in totally unfamiliar characters, one copyist working his way round the pillar had managed to transpose the first and second halves of every line.

By correlating all three versions it was now possible to obtain a near perfect fair copy. At the same time even the cautious Prinsep could not resist offering a few conjectures 'on the origin and nature of these singular columns, erected at places so distant from each other and all bearing the same inscription'.

> Whether they mark the conquests of some victorious raja; – whether they are, as it were, the boundary pillars of his dominions; – or whether they are of a religious nature ... can only be satisfactorily solved by the discovery of the language.

Clearly this people, this kingdom, this religion, was of significance to the whole of north India. It was altogether too big a subject to be left to chance. Prinsep, well placed now as secretary of the Asiatic Society to assess the various materials (Wilson had retired to England), re-solved to undertake the translation himself. In 1834 he tried the obvious line of relating this script to that of the Gupta Brahmi which he had just deciphered. For each, he drew up a table showing the frequency with which individual letters occurred, the idea being that those which occurred approximately the same number of times in each script might be the same letters. It was worth a try, but obviously would work only if both were in the same language and dealt with the same sort of subject. They did not, in fact they were not even in the same language, and Prinsep soon gave up this approach.

Next he tried relating the individual letters from each of the two scripts which had a similar conformation. This was more encouraging. He tentatively identified a handful of consonants and heard from a correspondent in Bombay, who was working on the cave temple inscriptions, that he too had identified these and five others. Armed with these few identifications, he attempted a translation, hoping that the sense might reveal the rest. But some of his letters were wrongly identified, and anyway he was still barking up the wrong tree in imagining that the language was pure Sanskrit. The attempt was a dismal failure. Discouraged, but far from defeated, Prinsep returned to the drawing board.

For the next four years he pushed himself physically and mentally towards the brink. Outside his office Calcutta was changing. The Governor-General had a new residence modelled on Kedleston Hall, but considerably grander: the dining-room could seat 200 and over 500 sometimes attended the Government House balls. Society was less boorish than in Jones's day. The hookah had gone out and so had most of the 'sooty bibis'; the *memsahibs* were taking over. But the only innovation Prinsep would have been aware of was the flapping *punkah*, or fan, above his desk. Now the Assay-Master, he spent all day at the mint and all evening with his coins and inscriptions or conferring with his *pandits*. By seven in the morning he was back at his desk. There is no record, as with Jones, of an early morning walk or ride, no mention of leisure. Instead he lived vicariously, through the endeavours and successes of his correspondents.

Jones, as president and founder of the Asiatic Society, and the most respected scholar of his age, had both inspired and dominated his fellows. Prinsep was just the opposite. He was the secretary of the Society, not the president, a plain Mr with few pretentions other than his total dedication. But this in itself was enough. His enthusiasm communicated itself to others and was irresistible. When he asked for coins and inscriptions they came flooding in from every corner of India. Painstakingly, he acknowledged, translated and commented upon them. By 1837 he had an army of enthusiasts – officers, engineers, explorers, political agents and administrators – informally collecting for him. Colonel Stacy at Chitor, Udaipur and Delhi, Lieutenant A. Connolly at Jaipur, Captain Wade at Ludhiana, Captain Cautley at Saharanpur, Lieutenant Cunningham at Benares, Colonel Smith at Patna, Mr Tregear at Jaunpur, Dr Swiney in Upper India ... the list was long.

It was from one of these correspondents, Captain Edward Smith, an engineer at Allahabad, that in 1837 there came the vital clue to the mysterious script. On Prinsep's suggestion, Smith had made the long journey into central India to visit an archaeological site of exceptional interest at Sanchi near Bhopal. Prinsep wanted accurate drawings of its sculptural wonders and facsimiles of an inscription in Gupta Brahmi which had not yet been translated. Smith obliged with both of these and, noticing some further very short inscriptions on the stone railings round the main shrine, took copies of them just for good measure.

> These apparently trivial fragments of rude writing [wrote Prinsep] have led to even more important results than the other inscriptions. They have instructed us in the alphabet and language of these ancient pillars and rock inscriptions which have been the wonder of the learned since the days of Sir William Jones, and I am already nearly prepared to render the Society an account of the writing on the *lat* [pillar] at Delhi, with no little satisfaction that, as I was the first to analyse these unknown symbols ... so I should now be rewarded with the completion of a discovery I then despaired of accomplishing for want of a competent knowledge of the Sanskrit language.

Typically, Prinsep then launched into a long discussion of the sculpture and other inscriptions, keeping his audience and readers on tenterhooks for another ten pages. But to Lieutenant Alexander Cunningham, his protégé in Benares, he had already announced the discovery in a letter.

23 May 1837.
My dear Cunningham, *Hors de département de mes études!* [a reference to a Mohammedan coin that Cunningham had sent him]. No, but I can read the Delhi No. 1 which is of more importance; the Sanchi inscriptions have enlightened me. Each line is engraved on a separate pillar or railing. Then, thought I, they must be the gifts of private individuals where names will be recorded. All end in *danam* [in the original characters] – that must mean 'gift' or 'given'. Let's see ...

He proved his point by immediately translating four such lines, and then turned to the first line of the famous pillar inscriptions: *Devam piya piyadasi raja hevam aha*, 'the most-particularly-loved-of-the-gods raja declareth thus'. He was not quite right; the r should have been l, *laja* not *raja*. But he was near enough. *Danam* giving him the d, the n and the m, all very common and hitherto unidentified, had been just enough to tip the balance.

With the help of a distinguished *pandit* he immediately set about the long pillar inscriptions. It was June, the most unbearable month of the Calcutta year; to concentrate the mind even for a minute is a major achievement. By now the Governor-General and the rest of Calcutta society were in the habit of taking themselves off to the cool heights of Simla at such a time. Prinsep stayed at his desk. The deciphering was going well but he had at last acknowledged the unexpected difficulty of the language not being Sanskrit. As Hodgson had suggested, it was closer to Pali, the sacred language of Tibet, or in other words it was one of the Prakrit languages, vernacular derivations of the classical Sanskrit. This made it difficult to pin down the precise meaning of many phrases. Prinsep also had, himself, to engrave all the plates for the script that would illustrate his account.

Nevertheless, in the incredibly short space of six weeks, his translation was ready and he announced it to the Society. As usual he treated them to a long preamble on the discoveries that had led up to it and on the difficulties it still presented. But, unlike other inscriptions, these had one remarkable feature in their favour. There was an almost un-Indian frankness about the language, no exaggeration, no hyperbole, no long lists of royal qualities. Instead there was a bold and disarming directness:

Thus spake King Devanampiya Piyadasi. In the twenty-seventh year of my anointment I have caused this religious edict to be published in writing. I acknowledge and confess the faults that have been cherished in my heart ...

The king had obviously undergone a religious conversion and, from the nature of the sentiments expressed, it was clearly Buddhism that he had adopted. The purpose of his edicts was to promote this new religion, to encourage right thinking and right behaviour, to discourage killing, to protect animals and birds, and to ordain certain days as holy days and certain men as religious administrators. The inscriptions ended in the same style as they had begun.

In the twenty-seventh year of my reign I have caused this edict to be written; so sayeth Devanampiya; 'Let stone pillars be prepared and let this edict of religion be engraven thereon, that it may endure into the remotest ages.'

Something about both the language and the contents was immediately familiar: it was Old Testament. Even Prinsep could not resist the obvious analogy – 'we might easily cite a more ancient and venerable example of thus fixing the law on tablets of stone'. Perhaps it was just out of reverence that he called them edicts rather than commandments. But the message was clear enough. Here was an Indian king uncannily imitating Moses, indeed going one better; as well as using tablets of stone, he had created these magnificent pillars to bear his message through the ages.

But who was this king? 'Devanampiya Piyadasi' could be a proper name but it was not one that appeared in any of the Sanskrit king lists. Equally it could be a royal epithet, 'Beloved of the Gods and of gracious mien'. At first Prinsep thought the former. In Ceylon a Mr George Turnour had been working on the Buddhist histories preserved there and had just sent in a translation that mentioned a king Piyadasi who was the first Ceylon king to adopt Buddhism. This fitted well; but what was a king of Ceylon doing scattering inscriptions all over northern India? One of the edicts actually claimed that the king had planted trees along the highways, dug wells, erected travellers' rest houses etc. How could a Sinhalese king be planting trees along the Ganges?

A few weeks later Turnour himself came up with the answer. Studying another Buddhist work he discovered that Piyadasi was also the normal epithet of a great Indian sovereign, a contemporary of the Ceylon Piyadasi, and that this king was otherwise known as Ashoka. It was further stated that Ashoka was the grandson of Chandragupta and that he was consecrated 218 years after the Buddha's enlightenment.

Suddenly it all began to make sense. Ashoka was already known from the Sanskrit king lists as a descendant of Chandragupta Maurya (Sandracottus) and, from Himalayan Buddhist sources, as a legendary patron of early Buddhism. Now his historicity was dramatically established. Thanks to the inscriptions, from being just a doubtful name, more was suddenly known about Ashoka than about any other Indian sovereign before AD 1100. As heir to Chandragupta it was not surprising that his pillars and inscriptions were so widely scattered. The Mauryan empire was clearly one of the greatest ever known in India, and here was its noblest scion speaking of his life and work through the mists of 2000 years. It was one of the most exciting moments in the whole story of archaeological discovery.

CHAPTER FOUR

Black and Time-Stained Rocks

Having broken the Ashoka Brahmi code, Prinsep was now in full cry. If mind and body could stand it, he would round onto the cave temple inscriptions, try the coins again, and finally double back to the long rock inscriptions. Only then would it be possible to assess the full importance of his discovery and to set Ashoka in perspective. But even as he worked, more monolithic finds were accumulating.

Thanks largely to Hodgson's discoveries along the Nepalese frontier, Prinsep knew of five Ashoka columns. As he deciphered their messages a sixth came to light in Delhi (the second to be found there). Broken into three pieces and buried in the ground, it was thought to have been the casualty of an explosion in a nearby gunpowder factory sometime in the seventeenth century. The inscription was badly worn, though evidently the same as that on the other pillars. In due course the whole pillar was offered to the Asiatic Society for their new museum. They accepted it but found the difficulties and cost of transporting it to Calcutta to be prohibitive; eventually they settled for just the bit with the inscription on it.

The question of how these pillars had originally been moved round India, and whether they were still in their ordained positions, was an intriguing subject in itself. It was now appreciated that they were all of the same stone, all polished by the same unexplained process, and therefore all from the same quarry. Prinsep thought this was somewhere in the Outer Himalayas, although we now know their source to have been Chunar on the Ganges near Benares. Either way, they had somehow been moved as much as 500 miles, no mean feat considering that the heaviest weighed over forty tons.

Presumably river transport was the answer. An interesting sidelight on this had just been shed by the study of the Mohammedan histories of India. These revealed that neither of the Delhi pillars had originally been erected in Delhi; they had evidently been moved there to adorn the capital of the early Mohammedan kings or Sultans. The first pillar was in the ruins of the palace of Feroz Shah, a Sultan of the fourteenth century. According to contemporary chronicles he had ordered the pillar to be brought there from a site up the Jumna river near Khizrabad.

> When the Sultan visited that district and saw the column in the village of Tobra, he resolved to move it to Delhi, and there erect it as a memorial to future generations. After thinking over the best means of lowering the column, orders were issued commanding the attendance of all the people dwelling in the neighbourhood ... and all soldiers, both horse and foot. They were ordered to bring all materials and implements suitable for the work. Directions were issued for bringing parcels of the cotton of the silk-cotton tree. Quantities of this silk cotton were placed round the column, and when the earth at its base was removed, it fell gently over on the bed prepared for it. The cotton was then removed by degrees, and after some days the pillar lay safe upon the ground. The pillar was then encased from top to bottom in reeds and ram skins so that no damage might accrue to it. A carriage with forty-two wheels was constructed, and ropes were attached to each wheel. Thousands of men hauled at every rope, and after great labour and difficulty the pillar was raised onto the carriage. A strong rope was fastened to each wheel and 200 men pulled at each of these ropes. By the simultaneous exertions of so many thousands of men, the carriage was moved and was brought to the banks of the Jumna. Here the Sultan came to meet it. A number of large boats had been collected, some of which could carry 5000 and 7000 maunds [ten tons] of grain. The column was very ingeniously transferred to these boats and was then conducted to Firozabad [Delhi] where it was landed and conveyed into the palace with infinite labour and skill.

Re-erection of the column was also a ticklish business, especially since Feroz Shah had ordained that it should stand on the roof, nine storeys up. After much more shunting about on beds of cotton, and an ingenious system of windlasses, 'it was secured in an upright position, straight as an arrow, without the smallest deviation from the perpendicular'. Feroz Shah then proudly showed off his new acquisition and asked for an explanation of the strange inscriptions. 'Many Brahmins and Hindu devotees were invited to translate them, but no one was able.' Prinsep could feel justly proud.

The Feroz Shah column still stands in Delhi, and Hodgson's at Lauriya Nandangarh, though not the most elegant, is the only one that still retains its original capital. Others have fared less well. Of the Bihar columns two appear to have been used for cannon target practice during the Moghul period. And in the 1840s the remains of at least two more pillars were dug up at Sanchi. Local tradition had it that they had been broken up by an Indian industrialist for use as rollers in a gigantic sugar cane press. Of one only the base remained; the other was found in three pieces with the chisel marks still visible where it had been intentionally broken.

For British antiquarians a potentially more embarrassing case of vandalism was the persistent rumour that the road roller being used by a zealous engineer at Allahabad was actually an Ashoka pillar. If there was any substance in this, it is to be hoped that it was just a broken fragment. The only pillar that was quite definitely thrown down by the British was the other, much studied one at Allahabad. It had evidently been in the way of a new embankment which was part of an eighteenth-century refortification programme. Filled with remorse, the Asiatic Society, and even the government, arranged for its re-erection. Captain Edward Smith, the man who had procured for Prinsep the vital facsimiles from Sanchi, designed a new pedestal for it, which came in for much praise. Unfortunately, he went further and also designed a new capital. It was meant to be a lion in the style of that of Lauriya Nandangarh; but it was not exactly the 'neatliest engraven'. According to Alexander Cunningham 'it resembles nothing so much as a stuffed poodle on top of an inverted flower pot'.

We now know of at least nine inscribed Ashoka columns, but these are considerably outnumbered by the Ashoka inscriptions carved on convenient rocks. The pillars naturally claimed attention first, but in fact the rock inscriptions proved more interesting both in content and location. The pillars were found only in the north of India (Sanchi was the most southerly), widely scattered round the Ganges basin. The rock inscriptions were found much further afield, from Mysore in the south to near Peshawar in the extreme north-west; and from near the coast of Orissa in the east to the coast of Saurashtra in the west. These last two, the first at Dhauli in Orissa, the second at Girnar in Gujerat, were the only ones known to Prinsep. Luckily they were two of the most informative.

The Orissa inscription had been discovered in early 1837. Lieutenant Markham Kittoe had been sent into the wilderness of Orissa to search for coalfields. Left much to his own devices he also searched for antiquities and soon stumbled on a whole network of ancient caves and sculptures. He described his find to the Asiatic Society:

> I have further great pleasure in announcing the discovery of the most voluminous inscription in the column character that I have ever heard of. ... There is neither road nor path to this extraordinary piece of antiquity. After climbing the rock through thorns and thickets, I came of a sudden on a small terrace open on three sides with a perpendicular scarp on the fourth or west from the face of which projects the front half of an elephant of elegant workmanship, four feet high; the whole is cut out of the solid rock. On the northern face beneath the terrace, the rock is chiselled smooth for a space of near fourteen feet by ten feet and the inscription, neatly cut, covers the whole space.

He spent a day taking a facsimile and returned to the spot again in November of the same year to complete the job. In places the rock was badly worn but he found that the shadow thrown by the evening sun enabled him to pick out letters that were not otherwise apparent. In spite of several gaps, Prinsep immediately attempted a translation and made out a number of intriguing phrases. But he gave up the task in early 1838 when a copy of the much better preserved Girnar inscription came to hand.

This had first been noticed by Colonel James Tod, another legendary figure in this story, who had been on a tour of Gujerat in 1822.

> The memorial in question, evidently of some great conqueror, is a huge hemispherical mass of dark granite, which, like a wart upon the body, has protruded through the crust of mother earth, without fissure or inequality, and which, by the aid of the 'iron pen', has been converted into a book. The measurement of the arc is nearly ninety feet; its surface is divided into compartments or parallelograms, within which are inscriptions in the usual character.

In Tod's time the script was still, of course, a mystery. The Colonel was one of those who thought it might be Greek. But he was nearer the mark when he confidently predicted that, sooner rather than later, someone at the Asiatic Society would solve the problem. Meantime he had taken copies of only two short sections.

Fifteen years later, a Bombay antiquarian, hearing of Prinsep's translation of the pillar inscriptions, quickly headed for Girnar. He wanted to see if the new code would work on Tod's inscription. 'To my great joy, and that of the Brahmins with me, I found myself able to make out several words.' The engraving was still amazingly sharp; it was possible to make an impression, filling the letters with ink and pressing a cloth over them. From this he made a reduced copy – on the original each letter was nearly two feet high – and sent it off to Calcutta.

Prinsep, turning from the Orissa inscription to this new one, again experienced that shiver down the spine. Bar two extra paragraphs on the Orissa inscription, the two were identical. Ashoka was proclaiming his edicts from one corner of India to the other, across an empire far greater than that of British India and comparable only to that of the Moghuls. But still more surprising was a claim made in one of the edicts. If Prinsep's reading was right, Ashoka had set up hospitals for men and animals throughout his kingdom, including the extreme south of the peninsula 'and moreover within the dominions of Antiochus the Greek'. He also claimed that the gospel of non-violence and respect for all living creatures was being acknowledged even 'by the kings of Egypt, Ptolemy and Antigonus and Magas'.

This said a great deal for Ashoka's international standing. But, more important, here at last was another point of contact – the first since Jones's identification of Sandracottus – between India's ancient history and that of the West. As Prinsep leafed through the classics to discover which Ptolemy and which Antiochus these might be, he sent an urgent message to Kittoe who was still in Orissa. Would the coal prospector quickly go to Dhauli and recheck the edicts in which these names appeared? Kittoe reacted at once.

> On my arrival at Cuttack I received a letter from my friend the Secretary of the Asiatic Society, informing me of his discovery of the name of Antiochus in the Girnar and Dhauli inscriptions, and requesting me to recompare my transcript and correct any errors. I instantly laid my *dak* [organized transport] and left at 6 p.m. for Dhauli, which curious place I reached before daybreak and had to wait till it was light; for

the two bear cubs which escaped me there last year, when I killed the old bear, were now full grown and disputing the ground. At daybreak I climbed to the Aswastuma [the rock] and cutting two large forked boughs of a tree near the spot, placed them against the rock; on these I stood to effect my object. I had taken the precaution to make a bearer hold the wood steady, but being intent on my interesting task I forgot my ticklish footing; the bearer had also fallen asleep and let go his hold, so that having overbalanced myself the wood slipped and I was pitched head foremost down the rock, but fortunately fell on my hands and received no injury beyond a few bruises and a severe shock; I took a little rest and then completed the job.

Simultaneously Prinsep tried to get the Girnar inscription rechecked. The vital edict containing the mention of Ptolemy was badly damaged with many of the letters missing altogether. Tentatively he approached the government, an unthinkable idea only a few months previously. But by now the excitement caused by his revelations was considerable. The government agreed to help and, within a couple of weeks, a Lieutenant Postans was on his way to Girnar.

Mrs Postans went too, anxious like everyone else to be in on the elucidation of what she called 'this black and time-stained rock'. Funded by the government, the operation was conducted with unheard-of thoroughness. The great rock was swathed in sturdy ladders and scaffolding; an awning was erected overhead to shade the workers from the sun; the whole inscription was then divided into numbered sections, and for three weeks Postans and his men crawled about on its vast surface taking impression after impression.

As my first plan, the letters were carefully filled with a red pigment (vermilion and oil), every attention being paid to the inflexions and other minute though important points. A thin and perfectly transparent cloth was then tightly glued over the whole of one division, and the letters as seen plainly through the cloth, traced upon it in black; in this way all the edicts were transcribed and the cloth being removed, the copy was carefully revised letter by letter with the original. The very smooth and convex surface of the rock on this side was highly favourable to this method, but it is tedious and occupied ten days of incessant labour.

I need not observe that it became a matter of primary interest to find some clue to the discovery of the missing portion of the rock on the eastern side, as the highly important eighteenth edict, containing the names of Ptolemy etc., had principally suffered from the mutilation. All our enquiries led to the conclusion that the rock had been blasted to furnish materials for the neighbouring causeway; to remove ... this would have been attended with an expense which I did not feel myself authorized in incurring but the whole soil at the base of the rock was dug up to a considerable distance and as deep as could be gone.

In this way two or three inscribed fragments were found. But it was impossible to decide where they came from. Postans had to rest content with his vastly improved facsimiles of the rock itself and these were duly sent off to Calcutta. They arrived in early November 1838, just a day after a ship called the *Hertfordshire* had sailed away down the Hughli. On board was James Prinsep, demented and dying.

While wrestling with the first transcriptions from Dhauli and Girnar, he had fought off headaches and sickness. Rapidly the illness developed into 'an affectation of the brain'. By the time he was bundled aboard the *Hertfordshire*, 'his mind was addled'. He reached England but never recovered his sanity, dying a year later at the age of forty.

'That he was a great man, it would not perhaps be strictly correct to assert,' wrote a friend and obituarist (he was probably thinking of Jones with whom Prinsep was so often compared). 'But he was one of the most useful and talented men that England has yet given to India.' His genius lay not so much in his scholarship as in his tenacity, 'his burning, irrepressible enthusiasm'. Ultimately it proved his undoing, for his obsessive dedication to the Indian scripts had both unhinged his mind and wrecked his physique. But it had also gained for him, and for the study of India's past, a new band of determined scholars. 'We felt as if he observed and watched over us,' wrote one. And, of course, it led him, perhaps drove him, to the solution of India's greatest historical enigma.

One of his last achievements had been two carefully engraved plates showing the development of each letter of the modern Devanagari script from its origin in the Ashoka Brahmi. He illustrated nine distinct stages and gave a date to each. This was of immense value to philologists and constituted a worthy and succinct summary of his life's work. Though since added to and qualified, it remains the basis for a study of India's scripts. But, as Prinsep fully appreciated, it had a still more important aspect. 'The table furnishes a curious species of palaeographic chronometer by which any ancient inscription may be consigned with considerable accuracy to the period at which it was written, even though it possesses no actual date.' It was, in effect, a ready reckoner not only for inscriptions but also for the monuments on which they were found. And since almost every building in India contains some inscription he had thus casually opened the way to a new and even more dramatic branch of Indology, the systematic study of Indian architecture.

But of more immediate significance was his unveiling of Ashoka. Hitherto all contact with ancient India had seemed impossibly vague. The great classical civilization hinted at by the glories of Sanskrit literature could be viewed only at about three removes – in translations of minor classical authors relaying information gleaned many centuries before by Megasthenes on his, probably brief, visit to north India. It was rather like trying to make out the history of the Plantagenets with nothing more to go on than a modern historical romance. Now, suddenly, it was like coming into possession of the text of the Magna Carta. In Ashoka here at last was a genuine historical figure, an emperor – apparently one of the most influential and powerful – whose very words expressing the rationale of his rule had been miraculously preserved.

From the mention of contemporary rulers like Ptolemy and Antiochus, his dates – about 269 to 232 BC – are more certain than those of any other Indian king before AD 1000. We know that his capital was Pataliputra (Patna) and that his empire stretched from Orissa to the Khyber Pass and from the Himalayas to at least as far south as Madras. Within this vast area there were independent tribes in the forests and hills as indeed remained the case until British times. They must have represented a real threat, since Ashoka seems to have adopted a firm if not repressive policy towards them. In other respects, his edicts favour tolerance and passivism. In the early years of his reign he had waged war in Orissa. The bloodshed and horrors of this campaign caused him to forswear further aggression. Whether he was actually a Buddhist monk or whether he even understood Buddhist theology is doubtful. But there is no question that the result of his conversion was an unwavering commitment to the ethics of that most humane and endearing religion.

'The greatest and noblest ruler India has known', according to Professor Basham, he was 'indeed one of the great kings of the world. ... Ashoka towers above the other kings of ancient India, if for no other reason than that he is the only one among them whose personality can be constructed with any degree of certainty.' It is this personal dimension that makes Ashoka so intriguing. His disapproval of any non-religious jollifications, and the austerity and directness of his language, suggest a Cromwellian puritanism – and yet he seems so typically Indian; vegetarianism, non-violence, reverence for life in all forms, tolerance to men of other religions were as important to Ashoka as to Mahatma Gandhi. The building of rest houses and the planting of trees along the highways were measures which recommended themselves to many of India's great rulers, including the Moghuls and the British. And then there was what, by western standards, can only be called the naivety of Ashoka. To Christians the idea of moral reform on a world scale is irrevocably tied up with the ideas of sacrifice, suffering and persecution. But for Ashoka, as for most Indian reformers, regeneration springs from within and can be spread by conviction, precept and example. Like the Buddha, Ashoka's conversion stemmed from a renunciation; like the Mahatma, he directed his appeal at something deep within the Indian soul.

CHAPTER FIVE

The Legacy of Pout

The hill of Sanchi, source of the short inscriptions which gave Prinsep the key to breaking the Ashoka script, is one of the loveliest archaeological sites. Miles from anywhere, in the dead centre of the Indian subcontinent, the hill rises gently from a sea of scrubby jungle, the haunt of tigers and aboriginal tribesmen. On its flat summit the architectural shapes are weird and unfamiliar; the very silence suggests extreme antiquity. Yet it prompts no quavering of the spirit like the austere dawn-of-creation ruggedness of Stonehenge, nor that flutter of the emotions evoked by the chaste lines of the Parthenon or the scented splendour of the Taj. Instead there is a soothing sense of peace, and, despite the wilderness setting, an overwhelming impression of civilization. For more than a thousand years Sanchi was a cherished centre of worship, learning, art and trade. The panels of sculptural relief that cover the gateways portray the Buddha's life and Buddhist history in crowded, bustling scenes. All creation seems to be represented, all human moods portrayed. No written work of history could possibly convey so vividly the reality of civilized society two millennia ago.

Yet, if the atmosphere is almost tangible, the setting and the buildings defy description. The first man to attempt an account of what he called 'the Ancient and Remarkable Building near Bhilsa' was Captain E. Fell. He had made the sixty-mile trek out from Bhopal in 1819 on the recommendation of a friend. Doubtless he had some idea of what to expect; and he was far from disappointed. But how to convey to the readers of the *Calcutta Journal* some idea of even the main *stupa*, or *tower*?

On a tableland of a detached hill ... is an ancient fabric of a
hemispherical form, built of thin layers of free-stone, in the
nature of steps, without any cement and, to all appearances,
solid; the outside of which has been faced throughout with a
coat of *chunam* mortar ... The monument (for such I will call
it) is strengthened by a buttress of stone masonry, twelve feet
high and seven broad, all around the base, the measured
circumference of which is 554 feet.

It was really a sort of circular pyramid, and Fell thought that it
might not in fact be solid. If there were any hidden chambers they
might prove 'highly interesting and worthy of being examined'.

The monument is surrounded by a colonnade of granite
pillars, ten feet high, distant from each other a foot and a half,
connected by parallels also granite, of an elliptical form,
united by tenons ... At the East, West and North points are
gateways [the south gateway had already collapsed], plain
parallelograms, the extreme height of each of which is forty
feet and the breadth within the perpendiculars nine feet.

It was as if Buddhist architects had been determined to do everything the hard way. Where several small stones would do the job of
one big one they chose the one big one. They whittled temples out of
rock, erected pillars that looked as if they had been turned on a lathe,
and here they were again treating sandstone as if it were wood. The
rails of the colonnade were jointed to the uprights by mortice and
tenon, and the lintels of the great gateways were shaped as if to
anticipate bowing.
But Fell, like every subsequent visitor, was soon absorbed by the
carving.

The perpendiculars of the gateways are divided into four
almost equal compartments. In the lower are statues of
door-keepers ... In another compartment is a representation
of the monument [the *stupa*] surrounded by figures in groups,
some standing, others sitting cross-legged, others bowing, all
with joined hands, and in the act of worship ... In another is a
small convex body in a boat, the prow of which is a lion's
head and the stern the expanded tail of a fish, over which is
suspended a long cable. In the boat are three male figures, two
of whom are rowing and the third holding an umbrella over

the convex. The vessel is in an open sea, in the midst of a tempest; near it are figures swimming and endeavouring by seizing piles to save themselves from drowning. One, on the point of drowning, is making an expiring effort to ascend the side; the features of all fully portray their melancholy situation. In another compartment is the sacred tree and altar, surrounded by groups of figures, both male and female, some beating tympans, others playing cymbals, others dancing; ... in short it is hardly possible to conceive sculpture more expressive of feeling than this.

Fell did his best; but how could someone 'inexperienced in the power of description,' give even a very faint idea of the magnificence of such stupendous structures and exquisitely finished sculpture? He was not even sure to what religion the site belonged. The hill-top was strewn with statues. He thought he had recognized Brahma of the Hindus and Parasnath of the Jains, but the predominant figure was certainly the Buddha. If Sanchi was Buddhist though, where were the Buddha's followers today?

The answer was almost everywhere – Ladakh, Nepal, Tibet, China, Burma, Thailand and Ceylon – except India. Buddhism encircled the subcontinent, but in India it was unknown. To Jones and his colleagues, immersed in their Sanskrit studies, it had looked as if Hinduism must have pre-empted the country. *Stupas* were thought to have been dedicated to the Hindu god, Siva, and to have been inspired by the Egyptians. 'Whether Buddha was a sage or a hero,' wrote Francis Wilford, 'the founder of a colony or a whole colony personified, whether ... black or fair', he was assuredly 'either an Egyptian or an Ethiopian'. Jones agreed. He identified Sakyasinha, one of the Buddha's epithets, with the Egyptian god Sesostris. But he also subscribed to the widely held belief that Buddha was just another name for the Norse god Woden, who in turn was Mercury of the Romans. Buddha was the son of Maya and Mercury the son of Maia. And there was an even simpler equation; Wednesday, or *Wodenstag*, of Germanic languages was *Buddhwar*, or Buddha's day, of Sanskrit languages and also *Mercredi*, or *Mercurii dies* of Latin languages.

This sort of speculation went on well into the nineteenth century. It was only from non-Indian sources that gradually a true and wholly unexpected picture of the origins of Buddhism emerged. William Chambers, the man who had first reported on the boulder temples of

Mahabalipuram, read a French account of Thailand and made the important identification of the Thai god, known as Pout or Codom, with the Ceylonese deity known as Buddha or Gautam. He also suggested that this Pout or Codom had once been worshipped in parts of India. This was borne out by Francis Buchanan, a naturalist and surveyor, who visited Burma in the late 1790s. He made a useful study of Buddhist ritual there as well as reporting that the Buddha had been an Indian from Bihar.

Ten years later Buchanan's surveying actually took him to Bihar: it was not long before he found further evidence. At Boddh Gaya, the name of which was a clue in itself, he declared that the extensive ruins, including the pyramidal temple, were clearly Buddhist in origin. Statues of the Buddha were scattered through the neighbourhood to a radius of fifteen miles and were now objects of worship to the Hindus. Indeed the temple itself was now in the charge of Brahmins. But they admitted to being puzzled by its origins. Every now and then strange visitors from far-off lands would descend on them and reverently tour the overgrown ruins with ancient books in their hands. Only the previous year, 1811, one such, 'a man of some rank with several attendants [who] came from a country called Tamsa-dwip-maha-amarapura-paigu' had arrived out of the blue. He claimed that the place had once been the residence of Gautama and that the temple was built by 'Dharma Ashoka, king of Pandaripuk'. Buchanan knew that Gautama was the Buddha and correctly identified the strangers as from Burma; but Ashoka and Pandaripuk (Pataliputra) meant nothing to him. Neither did he realize that Boddh Gaya was venerated, not as the residence of the Buddha, but as the place of his enlightenment.

It was not till the 1820s that Buddhist studies really got off the ground. Brian Hodgson had visited Sanchi soon after Captain Fell. His curiosity was aroused and, as the lone British representative in Kathmandu, he resolved to take advantage of his unique position in a still partly Buddhist country. 'Although the regular investigation of such a subject was foreign to my pursuits, [I commenced] a full and accurate investigation of this almost unknown subject.' The Nepalese monks were far from co-operative, but Hodgson soon accumulated a horde of Buddhist scriptures and then found 'an old Buddha residing in the city of Patan' who was willing to divulge some of the sect's secrets. Hodgson drew up a detailed questionnaire and, on the basis of the old man's answers, prepared a sketch of Buddhist beliefs. But when he proceeded to compare the results of the questionnaire with the textual evidence, he almost gave up. 'I began to feel my want of languages, and (to confess the truth) of patience.'

His collection of manuscripts was getting out of hand. It was already the largest hoard in existence and included two copies of the Tibetan encyclopaedia of sacred learning, which runs to 367 volumes, each of more than 100,000 leaves and each leaf about two feet long. Donated by the trunkload to the libraries of London, Paris and Calcutta, this collection was destined to provide the foundation for all future Buddhist studies. But Hodgson's immediate problem was that there seemed to be considerable divergence between Buddhism as now practised and traditional Buddhism as revealed in the texts. Even on the subject of the Buddha's birthplace there was no agreement; 'but all the places named are Indian'. Clearly both doctrine and practice had undergone a long process of change. On the other hand it was interesting that Buddhism, like Hinduism, was still a living religion and a thriving culture. To scholars used to the idea that all classical civilizations were dead civilizations, it came as a revelation that in Asia they tended to be still going strong. One really could study the past through the present. Jones himself had been struck by the idea that it was like discovering an enclave of Greeks who still spoke ancient Greek, read their Homer and consulted the Delphic oracle. Hodgson, with his questionnaire, was exploiting this situation. He was, for instance, able to provide a guide to the stylistic conventions used in sculptures of the Buddha. And he furnished an engraving of a modern Nepalese *stupa* which was clearly a descendant of Sanchi's.

Meanwhile, far away in the western extremity of the Himalayas, another scholar, in rather different circumstances, was poring over the sacred texts of the Tibetans. Alexander Czoma de Koros had originally armed himself with a stout stick and set off to walk from his native Hungary to China. In 1822, two years and several thousand miles later, he ran into William Moorcroft, the legendary explorer of the Western Himalayas. Moorcroft had travelled in Tibet and was deeply attracted to Buddhism. He urged de Koros to take up the study of the Tibetan texts and provided him with the limited funds he needed (de Koros lived off Tibetan tea, and his only possessions were a single change of clothes). Moorcroft then headed for Afghanistan and promptly disappeared; but, thanks to the intervention of the Asiatic Society, de Koros continued to receive a frugal stipend. In the cliff-top monasteries of Ladakh and Kinnaur he sat cross-legged through the cruel Himalayan winters, oblivious of all but the text before him. He compiled the first-ever Tibetan dictionary and grammar and began to make important contributions to the elucidation of the Buddhist mysteries.

With Hodgson and de Koros able to provide textual interpretations, archaeological discoveries came into their own. In the early 1820s the British representative at Bhopal, Henry Maddock, inspired by Fell's hint that there might be hidden chambers in the Sanchi *stupas*, attempted to open the Great Stupa. If it was indeed a pyramid of some sort it might contain treasure, or at least some clue to its origin and purpose. But Maddock was disappointed. The *stupa* did not consist of sealed chambers, but was indeed a solid mass of masonry. He retired with nothing to show for his labours but a gaping hole in one side of the monument, a mound of rubble, another collapsed gateway, and a lasting reputation as one of the raj's vandals.

Inspired by no nobler motives, a further attempt was made to explore a *stupa* in 1830. This time the would-be tomb-robber was one of a band of ex-Napoleonic officers now serving under the independent rajah of the Punjab, Ranjit Singh. The *stupa* in question was a lofty domed edifice at Manikyala, near Rawalpindi, in what is now Pakistan. Encamped in the vicinity with no obvious employment for his soldiery, General Ventura directed them to dig into the ruin. A British mission twenty years earlier had thought it might be Greek; it was worth investigating. Like Maddock, Ventura first tried to excavate a hole in the side and succeeded only in collapsing vast quantities of rubble. But, with time and unlimited labour, he adopted a different approach and started burrowing down from the top of the dome. Only three feet down, he found his first coins. More followed at intervals, and then came small compartments containing cylindrical boxes and canisters of gold and copper in which were scraps of material, jewellery and more coins.

The coins, many of which were gold, had important consequences for the reconstruction of Indian history. Ventura's initiative was accounted a considerable success and brought him, besides some saleable treasure, renown as an archaeologist. Other European officers in Ranjit Singh's service joined the fray and, in the Punjab and neighbouring Afghanistan, there followed a period of intense *stupa* raiding. As yet there was little conclusive evidence, but it was beginning to look as if the *stupas* and their relics were Buddhist. Moreover the success of these new archaeological ventures provided a powerful stimulus to would-be archaeologists across the frontier in British India.

In 1834, Lieutenant Alexander Cunningham, only twenty years old and just arrived in India, began to take an interest in the well-known *stupa* at Sarnath just outside the city of Benares. Forty years earlier, in the days of Sir William Jones, an Indian contractor had used the site as a hardcore quarry for a new market place in Benares. He had dug up a stone urn 'of the size and shape of the Barberini vase', and a statue. The urn contained another of marble which, with its contents of a few bones, some gold leaf and pearls, was presented to the Asiatic Society as a curiosity. The statue was a seated Buddha. Here was incentive enough to explore further, and Cunningham, himself an engineer, enlisted the financial support of James Prinsep for his dig.

Of several ruinous mounds at Sarnath, the Dhamek *stupa*, with its superb bands of sculptural ornament, was much the best preserved and most inviting. Learning from Ventura's experience, Cunningham decided to start from the top and drive a shaft right down the middle. But the first problem was to get up there; the *stupa* was 143 feet high.

> On the 18th January 1835 my scaffolding was completed and I stood on the top of the great tower. On cutting the long grass [there were also several trees on the top] I found two iron spikes each eight inches long and shaped like the head of a lance. On the following day I removed the ruined brick pinnacle and began sinking a shaft or well, about five feet in diameter; at three feet from the top I found a rough stone; and on the 25th January, at a depth of ten and a half feet, I found an inscribed slab.

After Ventura's discoveries, these were nothing to get excited about; Cunningham pressed on. At first he made good progress, but seventy feet down he struck solid stone. Was this the casing of some chamber? In spite of the cost it looked too promising to give up now.

> The labour of sinking the shaft through the solid stone-work was very great as the stones, which were large (from two to three feet in length, eighteen inches broad and twelve inches thick), were all secured to each other with iron cramps. Each stone had usually eight cramps, four above and as many below, all of which had to be cut through before it could be moved. I therefore sent for regular quarrymen to quarry out the stones, and the work occupied them for several months.

And still there was no find. Only a man who was gradually discovering his true vocation in life could have kept at it.

> At length, at a depth of 110 feet from the top of the monument, the stone gave way to brickwork made of very large bricks. Through this the shaft was continued for a further depth of twenty-eight feet, when I reached the plain soil beneath the foundation. Lastly a gallery was run right through the brickwork of the foundation ... but without yielding any result. Thus ended my opening of the great tower, after fourteen months labour and at a cost of more than five hundred rupees.

Cunningham was bitterly disappointed. All he had to show was a stone with an unknown inscription on it. But this was better than nothing and he sent a copy of the inscription to Prinsep. The letters were of the Gupta Brahmi script and the whole was identical to one recently found on a broken pedestal in northern Bihar. Prinsep thought he could read it; but it did not make much sense, some sort of invocation apparently. By chance, Alexander Czoma de Koros happened to be down from the mountains at the time, and, in view of a possible Buddhist connection, was asked for his opinion. Instantly he recognized it as the standard Buddhist formula or confession of faith. There was therefore no question that the Dhamek *stupa* was a Buddhist monument of the Gupta period and that the key to understanding the purpose and sculptures of all the *stupas* lay in Buddhism. Not only had the Buddha been an Indian, but his religion had evidently been widespread in India and had flourished there for several centuries.

Further dramatic evidence of this would soon be provided by the translation of the Ashoka edicts, and by 1838 it was even being asked whether perhaps Buddhism antedated Hinduism or, as Prinsep put it, 'whether the Buddhists or the Brahmins may claim precedence in the history of Indian civilization'. The Sanskrit of the ancient Hindus appeared to be much earlier than the Prakrit used for Buddhist texts. Yet in terms of architecture – rock-cut temples, pillars, or structural *stupas* – and inscriptions, the evidence seemed to favour Buddhism.

The same also seemed to be true of sculpture. Whilst excavating the Dhamek *stupa*, Cunningham met an old man who had taken part in that quarrying operation, forty years earlier, in an adjacent mound. He not only remembered where the stone urn had been discovered, but also directed Cunningham to a spot where he recalled seeing a whole subterranean room full of statues.

> I at once commenced an excavation on the spot pointed out by Sangkar ... At a depth of two feet below the surface I found about sixty statues and bas-reliefs in an upright position, all packed closely together within a small space of less than ten feet square.

Superstition had evidently prevented the previous diggers from disturbing this collection and Cunningham was thus able to exploit the first major discovery of Sarnath scupture. He singled out those figures that bore inscriptions or that were best preserved, including a magnificent Buddha, and sent them off to the Asiatic Society.

> The remaining statues, upwards of forty in number, together with most of the other carved stones that I had collected, and which I left lying on the ground, were afterwards carted away by the late Mr Davidson and thrown into the Barna river under the bridge to check the cutting away of the bed between the arches.

Though himself an engineer, Cunningham could not condone such behaviour. It was his first brush with the iconoclasts – but by no means his last.

Fortunately it was not the end of Sarnath's riches either. Scarcely any site in India has yielded so much in the way of archaeological data and sculpture. Cunningham himself made further finds, and excavations continued to be richly rewarded well into the twentieth century. In 1904 the remains of yet another Ashoka pillar were found, together with its miraculously preserved capital, the lion capital of Sarnath – the most celebrated piece of Indian sculpture and now the symbol of the Republic of India.

But what was so special about Sarnath? Why had the Buddha's followers lavished so much skill and money on the adornment of this particular spot just outside the Hindus' most sacred city? Since the *stupa* contained neither relics nor ashes it was clearly not the burial place of some Buddhist saint. What then was it? Cunningham was at first mystified. But in 1836, the year he ended operations at Sarnath, two eye-witness accounts of Buddhist India were published. All was made clear.

Until this time the only first-hand account of ancient India was that of Megasthenes by way of later Greek and Latin authors. Unfortunately for students of Buddhist history, Megasthenes had stumbled onto the Indian scene in the reign of Chandragupta Maurya, Ashoka's grandfather; he was thus just two generations too soon to witness the rise of Buddhism under royal patronage. Now, by an equally circuitous route, a Buddhist account of India at the beginning of the fifth century AD was brought to light; and it was soon followed by another from the mid-seventh century. These were the travelogues of Fa Hsien and Hsuan Tsang, Chinese Buddhists who journeyed through India in search of sacred manuscripts and to visit the scenes of the Buddha's life. The travelogues were acquired by French orientalists, translated in Paris and expounded by Prinsep's old boss, Horace Hayman Wilson, who was now the first professor of Sanskrit at Oxford.

As befitted monks on pilgrimage, the two Chinese were reticent about temporal affairs. But it was significant that Fa Hsien's visit had coincided with the Gupta period to which so much in the way of sculpture and architecture (including Cunningham's Dhamek *stupa*) was being ascribed. Evidently Buddhism was still very much in the ascendant under the Guptas, 700 years after Ashoka, although Hindu beliefs were also widespread. Most impressive, too, was the fact that the whole of north India was then at peace. Crime and repression were equally unknown, and Fa Hsien could travel from one end of the country to the other without let or hindrance. Compared with the state of the Roman Empire at that time, it looked as if India under the Guptas was the most congenial place in the world.

By the time of Hsuan Tsang's visit things had changed. In the seventh century Buddhism appeared to be on the retreat; many of the shrines were in ruins and Buddhists were actually being persecuted in Kashmir and Bengal. The roads were no longer safe and though Hsuan Tsang had great respect for King Harsha, who was trying to restore some of the lost glory of the Guptas, there had clearly been a social and cultural decline.

All this was of the utmost interest to historians; but to Alexander Cunningham the main point was that Buddhist India had been brought to life. 'It is almost impossible to exaggerate the importance of these travels'; he wrote, 'before, all attempts to fathom the mysteries of Buddhist antiquities were but mere conjecture.' The purpose of the *stupas* was unknown, as was their significance, and even the names of the shrines and cities they had adorned. Now all was made clear. These eye-witness accounts explained the nature of the sites and described their locations and lay-outs so clearly that they amounted to a map of Buddhist India and site plans of all the main shrines.

Sarnath, for instance, was indeed a notable spot. It was none other than the deer park where the Buddha had preached his first sermon. Fa Hsien found four *stupas* there and two monasteries. By Hsuan Tsang's time it had grown considerably. There was a vast monastery, 1500 monks, lakes and gardens and, amongst the *stupas*, one 300 feet high. Hsuan Tsang also noted the sculptures and recorded that the oldest *stupa* and the pillar had been set up by Ashoka.

Cunningham could only fantasize, but what might he have achieved if he had had all this information a couple of years earlier? More important, what of all the other Buddhist sites mentioned by the Chinese travellers? 'With what joy would not one trace Fa Hsien's route from Mathura to his embarkation for Ceylon?' There was now the possibility of identifying so many of the mounds and ruins that littered India. Indian archaeology had a chance to begin at the beginning, and the idea filled Cunningham with exhilaration.

CHAPTER SIX

The Old Campaigner

Sir Mortimer Wheeler, the last British director of India's Archaeological Department, singled out three men as pioneers in the study of India's history and civilization – Jones, Prinsep and Cunningham. Of the three, Cunningham alone really knew India. Sir William Jones was the founding genius and figure-head, Mr Secretary Prinsep the organizer and scientist, and Alexander Cunningham the explorer and field-worker. During more than fifty years in India he travelled from the steaming jungles of Burma to the arid hills bordering Afghanistan, and from the remotest tracts of Central India to the Tibetan lands beyond the Great Himalaya. He probably marched more miles on Indian soil than any of his contemporaries. Not only was he 'the father of Indian archaeology' but, for a quarter of a century, he *was* Indian archaeology. And all this at a time when the British seemed to have turned their backs on Indian civilization.

Cunningham had arrived, as a Lieutenant in the Royal Engineers, in 1833. His father, the Scots poet Allan Cunningham, had enlisted the help of his old friend Sir Walter Scott in procuring commissions in India for both his boys. For a man who wrote 'It's hame, and it's hame, hame fain wad I be', India was an odd choice for his sons. But the Cunninghams were not wealthy, and a career in India, if no longer a short cut to fortune and fame, offered many possibilities and had now become highly respectable.

After three years in Benares, and the excavation at Sarnath, Cunningham was called to Calcutta to serve as an ADC to Lord Auckland. In the Governor-General's party he made the annual pilgrimage up to Simla and paid his first visit to Ranjit Singh's Punjab. Emily Eden, Auckland's caustic sister, found the young 'AC' attentive and agreeable. With an eye for the picturesque, she sketched such antiquities as fell along their route; the studious ADC, meanwhile, ferreted about for coins and inscriptions and offered quaint explanations of their history.

To Emily Eden this was just a mild eccentricity, although to others such behaviour now appeared distinctly unsound. A cold wind of intolerance and distaste for India and its civilization was sweeping through the British ranks. That deep sense of wonder experienced by Jones, shared by the men like Fell who first discovered India's monuments, and still cherished by the likes of Prinsep and Cunningham, was no longer in fashion. All that remained was the passing fancy for the picturesque shown by Emily Eden; and this was too insubstantial to conceal deeper feelings of outrage and disgust. The Orientalists, who not long before had been hailed as equals of the Renaissance humanists, were in disgrace. Warren Hastings's ideal of a partially Indianized civil service had been rejected and the Indian raj was slowly making way for the British Empire.

Three new influences were at work. On the one hand there were the Evangelicals, horrified by the idea that Christians could take the idolatry and improprieties of a pagan culture seriously, seeing in India an unlimited field for missionary activity, and insisting that it was part of a Christian government's duty to promote this. Then there were the Utilitarians, pouncing on India as prime territory for putting into effect their cherished reforms aimed at 'the greatest good for the greatest number'. This was what civilization was all about and, since progress and utility did not appear to feature in India's so-called civilizations, they were hardly worthy of serious attention. James Mill, father of John Stuart, had published his history of India in 1818. Though Mill spoke no Indian languages, indeed had never been to India, his damning indictment of Indian society and religion had become the standard work – required reading for all who would serve in India.

Finally, unifying these two opposing themes, there was the rising crescendo of national superiority. No longer did the British feel any sneaking sense of surprise at their success in India. Clearly it was ordained, either by the Almighty as the Evangelicals would have it, or by history as the Utilitarians preferred. Even the Moghul emperor need no longer be treated with respect. He was a joke, and so too was Ranjit Singh. Fifty years before, Tipu Sultan had been accorded a certain respect, but Ranjit Singh, the only native prince who could still deal the British a serious blow, was the subject of drawing room titters.

Hadn't he urinated in the presence of the Governor-General? The word nigger was slowly coming into fashion; 'no — ten thousand pardons, not niggers, I mean natives — sons of the soil — Orientals — Asiatics', wrote Atkinson in the 1850s. He was caricaturing an up-country judge whose interest in such people amounted to a weird and old-fashioned eccentricity. British society was growing more exclusive; the *memsahibs* had arrived in force, the club was about to make its appearance. 'Brahminized' old-timers were just an embarrassment to the service.

The inevitable collision between the Orientalists and their new opponents was signalled in 1835. Thomas Babington Macaulay, during his brief spell in India, won the support of Auckland's predecessor for withholding government finance from all institutions that used languages other than English. In support of a move that amounted to outlawing all Sanskrit and vernacular studies, as well as imposing English as the only language of education, Macaulay delivered his celebrated Minute.

> It is, I believe, no exaggeration to say that all the historical information that has been collected to form all the books written in the Sanskrit language is less valuable than what may be found in the most paltry abridgements used at preparatory schools in England. In every branch of physical or moral philosophy the relative position of the two nations is nearly the same ...
>
> The question before us is simply whether ... we shall teach languages [Sanskrit and Arabic] in which, by universal confession, there are no books on any subject which deserve to be compared to our own; whether, when we can teach European science, we shall teach systems which, by universal confession, whenever they differ from those of Europe, differ for the worse; and whether, when we can patronize true philosophy and sound history, we shall countenance, at the public expense, medical doctrines which would disgrace an English farrier — astronomy, which would move laughter in girls at an English public school — history, abounding with kings thirty feet high, and reigns thirty thousand years long — and geography, made up of seas of treacle and butter.

Later, in the House of Commons, he directed his attack towards Hinduism.

In no part of the world has a religion ever existed more unfavourable to the moral and intellectual health of our race. The Brahminical mythology is so absurd that it necessarily debases every mind which receives it as truth; and with this absurd mythology is bound up an absurd system of physics, an absurd geography, an absurd astronomy ... All is hideous and grotesque and ignoble. As this superstition is of all superstitions the most irrational, and of all superstitions the most inelegant, so it is of all superstitions the most immoral.

Macaulay chose his ground carefully. Moreover there can be no question that he had India's best interests at heart. Indeed, many, even Indians, argue that he was right about insisting that the country's development was only possible through the adoption of English. But, however noble his motives and sound his judgement, there can be no forgiving the viciousness and insensitivity of his rhetoric. One flinches to read it, even now. The impression it must have made on Orientalists, let alone Indians, is horrifying. And, combined with the vaunting of British superiority in everything from morality to medicine, the airing of such views can have done the *Sahibs* themselves nothing but harm.

This was the background against which Prinsep and Cunningham worked during the 1830s. No wonder that their discoveries made so little impact outside the world of scholarship; or that Prinsep was so apprehensive about asking Lord Auckland for help in getting a copy of the Girnar inscription.

No wonder, too, that Cunningham had to wait so long before pursuing Indian archaeology. In response to repeated representations from the Asiatic Society, Markham Kittoe, the coal prospector, was given some limited archaeological responsibilities in the late 1840s. But the funds provided were inadequate. Kittoe could spare little time from other duties, and anyway he soon died. In the words of a later Governor-General, 'the scheme appears to have been lost sight of within two or three years of its adoption'.

Meanwhile, Cunningham continued to correspond with the Asiatic Society. In 1839 he was sent to survey the sources of the Ravi and Chenab rivers on the frontier of Kashmir; while there, he took the opportunity to collect inscriptions. In 1842 he was in central India but was recalled to the Punjab to serve in the First Sikh War. In 1847, now a Captain, he was sent to Ladakh, or Indian Tibet, to head a boundary commission. He thus had a chance, like Hodgson and de Koros, to study Buddhism in operation. He also toured the antiquities of the Kashmir valley and returned with no boundary – the Tibetans had failed to appear – but with a camel-load of Buddhist statuary, three unknown Sanskrit dramas and 'the oldest dated inscription hitherto found in India'. He was just in time to take part in the Second Sikh War, and then served at Gwalior and at Multan.

At about this time his brother, Joseph Cunningham, was appointed political agent at Bhopal in central India – the state that held Sanchi; the chance was too good to miss. In January 1851 Alexander Cunningham was back amongst the *stupas*. He was much taken by the famous gateways: their bas-reliefs 'are more original in design and more varied in subject matter than any other examples of eastern sculpture that I have seen'. As at Sarnath, he drove a shaft down the Great Stupa and again found no relics. But the main purpose of his visit was to explore the other two *stupas* on the Sanchi hill and the many other *stupas* and cave temples in the vicinity. In a *stupa* just a few yards to the north of the main one, Cunningham was at last rewarded. Under a vast slab of stone five feet square his shaft found two stone boxes. Inside each box was a small steatite relic casket, covered with a thin saucer of black pottery. Inside each casket were fragments of bone and beads. But the most dramatic discovery was that the boxes were engraved. One bore the name of Sariputasa, the other, Maha-Mogalanasa. These were two of the Buddha's foremost disciples; it was like finding the graves of Saints Peter and Paul. At last Cunningham experienced the thrill of handling secrets undisturbed for two millennia. And, on the strength of this identification, Sanchi, which centuries before had slipped from Buddhist memory, again became a place of Buddhist pilgrimage.

Cunningham published his findings in a book, *The Bhilsa Topes*, and took the opportunity to plead, ever so gently, the cause of Indian archaeology. The money saved by no longer financing the publication of Sanskrit works could well be spent on exploring other *stupas*. If the British public needed some convincing about the worthwhile character of India's Buddhist legacy, why not have the two fallen gateways at Sanchi removed to England and re-erected in the British Museum, 'where they would form the most striking objects in the Hall of Indian Antiquities'? The weight of anti-Orientalist prejudice had fallen on Hindu literature, so Cunningham tried to make it clear that archaeology was worthy of separate consideration and that Buddhism was altogether less objectionable than Hinduism. Buddhist sculpture was never obscene and, since Buddhism was dead in India, there was no question of offering encouragement to pagans.

But still the time was not ripe; Cunningham would have to wait another ten years. In 1856, now a Lieutenant-Colonel, he was posted to Burma to set up a public works department. While he was there British India reaped the rewards of Macaulay's rhetoric and thirty years of insensitivity. The Mutiny, or the National Uprising, may not have changed much; if anything it hardened attitudes. But it did show that the British must needs be a bit more conciliatory, a bit less outspoken. An interest in native culture could now be forgiven, even applauded, on the grounds of its political expediency. More obvious effects of the Mutiny were the demise of the East India Company and of the Moghul emperor. India was now the direct responsibility of the British government and Queen Victoria was its sovereign. Under these circumstances it was reasonable to expect a more responsible attitude towards the national heritage. More often than not the government would try to dodge this responsibility, but the preservation of national monuments could no longer be totally ignored. If places like the Taj Mahal were allowed to fall into ruin, 'the brightest jewel in the imperial crown' would begin to look distinctly tawdry.

In 1861 Cunningham, now aged forty-seven, retired from the army with the rank of Major-General. He had never ceased to press for an archaeological appointment and now, in the evening of his career, he had at last received a favourable reaction. Officially, he outlined his scheme to Lord Canning, the first Viceroy.

> During 100 years of British dominion in India, the government has done little or nothing towards the preservation of its ancient monuments which, in the almost total absence of any written history, form the only reliable source of information as to the early condition of the country. Some of these monuments have already endured for ages, and are likely to last for ages to come; but there are many others which are daily suffering from the effects of time, and which must soon disappear altogether unless preserved by the accurate drawings and faithful descriptions of the archaeologists. ... In the present proposed investigation I would follow the footsteps of the Chinese pilgrim Hsuan Tsang who, in the seventh century of our era, traversed India from west to east and back again.

The Chinese pilgrims had noted Hindu temples as well as the Buddhist sites. Cunningham proposed to do the same. But the Buddhist bias of his researches was something for which he would be much criticized. Indian studies, having started with a strong literary and Hindu bias under Jones, were now swinging too far towards Buddhism and archaeology. But given the Evangelical legacy, it is hard to see the government willingly financing a specific study of, say, Hindu sculpture. It is to Cunningham's credit that he managed to embrace such subjects at all. In the short list of sites to be immediately investigated, which he enclosed with his letter to Canning, was Khajuraho.

The other significant point about his recommendation was that it had little to do with archaeology as we now know it. Cunningham was not proposing to dig, not even to conserve, but simply to survey and to draw. Lord Canning, in accepting the recommendation, expressed his anxiety over the neglect of architectural remains.

> By neglect I do not mean only the omission to restore them or arrest their decay; for this would be a task which, in many cases, would require an expenditure of labour and money far greater than any government of India could reasonably bestow upon it. But ... there has been neglect of a much cheaper duty, that of investigating and placing on record, for the instruction of future generations, many particulars that might still be rescued from oblivion and throw light upon the early history of England's great dependency.

Clearly a more ambitious scheme would never have been approved. In Canning's view the beauty of a survey was that it cost very little, should take only a couple of years and would commit the government to nothing. Cunningham managed to make it last for a quarter of a century. He did do some conservation and exploration, and he made sure that the responsibility for serious conservation could never again be so complacently shrugged away. The criticism that he left India's monuments in much the same state as he found them should be directed at the government rather than at the new Archaeological Survey.

With a modest caravan Cunningham took to the field in December 1861. Bihar was his first destination. At Boddh Gaya he confirmed its Buddhist associations. It was in fact the site of the Buddha's enlightenment. He found the pillars and railings, similar to those at Sanchi, which were later re-erected at Lord Curzon's instigation, and after much controversy he dated the temple itself to about AD 200. North of the Ganges he visited Hodgson's three Ashoka pillars and beside one of them found burial mounds in which were huge lead coffers, nine feet long, containing 'unusually long human skeletons'. Dated to about 1000 BC, these were the oldest finds yet made on Indian soil.

The next year he worked his way up the Ganges and Jumna to Mathura and Delhi; then the Punjab, where he discovered the ancient city of Taxila; then central India; then back to Bihar, Benares and Allahabad. And so it went on. With a short break in the late 1860s, the old General stomped back and forth across northern India for twenty-five years. There was so much to record, so many new sites; a week here, a week there, he could never afford more. It was boom-time in the building of roads and especially railways. In the plains, rock was scarce and the contractors were grabbing every bit of stone and masonry they could lay their hands on. If Cunningham could never concentrate his energies on a major dig nor undertake any sustained conservation work, he could at least try to block the contractors. Every site recorded might be a site saved. He was too late at Sultanganj, where the ruins 'furnished brick ballast for many miles of the line'; the only good to come of the depredations was the discovery of a famous bronze Buddha. Too late at Rajaona, Masar and Tiwar. Too late, too, at Tigowa where at least thirty-six temples 'had been utterly destroyed by a railway contractor using 200 carts; his name, which is still well remembered, was Walker'. But Cunningham was amazingly thorough and the wealth of archaeological remains that survive is largely due to him.

In the process he came to know northern India better perhaps than any contemporary. A little crusty as he approached his seventies, very possessive about his own discoveries and jealous of his unquestioned pre-eminence, Cunningham and his Archaeological Survey became an institution. One can imagine the little caravan descending on some forgotten group of temples. The tents are up as the old General emerges, stooping, from a sculpture-encrusted *mandapam*. His tweeds reek with the sickly smell of bat dung; but a quick 'tub' and he is back to work, recording the day's discoveries on a shaky camp table. As the sun dips behind the trees and the parakeets go screeching home to roost, the lamp is lit, and the General, issuing instructions for an early start in the morning, retires to bed with a dog-eared copy of Hsuan Tsang.

For a man whose career seems to have revolved around the great Buddhist shrines of Sarnath in 1835, Sanchi in 1851, Boddh Gaya in 1862, it was wholly appropriate that his last major discovery should be another *stupa*. Marching cross-country for Nagpur on a November's day in 1873, he paused to investigate a rumoured site at the remote village of Bharhut. The site proved to be a flat-topped mound of rubble, but sticking up out of it was a section of collapsed railing almost identical to the mortice and tenon colonnade of Sanchi. Beside it stood a column which Cunningham immediately recognized as the upright of a gateway. Three months later he was back at Bharhut and spent ten days, a long time for the restless Archaeological Survey, digging into the mound and unearthing the heavily sculpted stones.

> The curious sculptures were a source of much wonder to the people who visited the place by hundreds every day. But the inscriptions excited even greater curiosity when it was known that I was able to read them. At every fresh discovery I was importuned to say what was the subject of the writing, and great was the disappointment when I made known the simple words of gifts to the stupa or of the names of the guardian *yakshas, devatas* and *nagas*. Few natives of India have any belief in disinterested excavations for the discovery of ancient buildings. ... Their only idea of such excavations is that they are really intended as a search for hidden treasure, and from the incredulous look of many of the people, I have no doubt that I was regarded as an arch-deceiver who was studiously concealing the revelations made by the inscriptions as to the position of the buried treasures.

The *stupa* itself had gone, removed brick by brick to furnish building materials; the village of Bharhut boasted 200 houses, every one of them built out of purloined bricks. Many of the railing's pillars had also been dispersed: they made excellent roof beams and lintels. A cross piece of one of the gateways was found embedded in the wall of a local stronghold; another was in use seven miles away as the stone on which the washermen beat their laundry. On his third visit in 1875, Cunningham rounded up these pieces, offering compensation where necessary. He had been known to purchase a field of standing corn if he thought there was was something worth excavating in it; the niceties of rural etiquette were now second nature to him. But he also realized that as soon as the Archaeological Survey turned its back the raiding would begin again.

With this in mind, he recommended that the gateway and the section of railing that he had laboriously pieced together, should be speedily removed to a museum. Judging by the inscriptions, which were in an early form of Ashoka Brahmi, and by the more archaic carving, Bharhut was earlier than the Sanchi gateways (Cunningham thought 250–200 BC though nowadays 150–100 BC is thought more likely). In view of this great antiquity the government agreed, though not without protests from some quarters; 'The scheme carries with it a certain aroma of vandalism', wrote one of Cunningham's correspondents; 'fancy carting away Stonehenge'. But in the event the old General was proved right. When he returned to Bharhut in 1876 after the main items had been removed to the Indian Museum in Calcutta, he found that 'every stone that was removable has since been carted away by the people as building material'.

Indian sculpture is poorly served by artificial light and the museum setting. The carving needs the sharp contrast between light and shade afforded by the Indian sun to bring it to life; the architecture needs the vastness of its rural surroundings, and the wide blue sky to establish its credentials. The beauty of the Sanchi gateways lies in their intricate silhouette and in the way the light glances through their massive superstructures. As sun and shade play upon the voluptuous curves of the famous *yakshi* (nymph and tree spirit) on the east gate she seems to lean still further out into space while the gentle elephants behind her sway ever so gently. But the Bharhut sculptures have no such life. Cunningham had rescued them from oblivion; but he cannot have been entirely happy about consigning them to a museum.

CHAPTER SEVEN
Buddha in a Toga

Bharhut's railing and gateway were particularly vulnerable because, by the time Cunningham discovered them, the vast stones had already been broken into portable pieces. Fortunately this was not true of the two collapsed gateways at Sanchi. Cunningham had proposed that they too be transported to a museum, the British Museum in this case. This was rejected on the grounds that the transport of such enormous chunks of stone would be a costly operation (even for the government), and one fraught with danger to the sculptures. They therefore remained on site. But fifteen years later the Begum of Bhopal, to whom the site nominally belonged, was approached by the French government: how would she feel about one of the fallen gateways being removed to adorn the boulevards of Paris? The Begum's reaction is not recorded, but that of the government of India was prompt enough: nothing was better calculated to dispel official indifference than the appearance of a foreign bidder. Sanchi was declared inviolate and a Major Henry Hardy Cole was sent to scotch any further such bids by procuring plaster casts of one of the gateways. This in itself proved a major operation. With three sappers specially trained in the latest method of 'making elastic moulds with gelatine', twenty-eight tons of materials, and sixty bullock carts, Cole set about the 700 square feet of carving. The final 112 separate castings were duly erected in museums in London, Edinburgh, Dublin and Paris.

Thanks largely to the Asiatic Society – which had a vested interest in seeing that the national heritage remained in India, available to its members – comparatively little in the way of sculpture found its way to Europe. But there were exceptions, and none more celebrated than another masterpiece from the Bhilsa hill – the Sanchi torso. In 1881 the government at last acknowledged that something more positive must be done about conservation. To Major Cole went the job of National Curator, and for three years he did valiant work, not the least of it back at Sanchi. The two fallen gateways were re-erected in their original positions, the breach in the Great Stupa (caused by Maddock's operations) was repaired, and the whole site cleared of vegetation. During these works much broken sculpture was recovered and stored. Not so, however, a particularly fine male torso which found its way to England amongst the effects of the British Agent at Bhopal, General Kincaid. He was Cole's superior during the operations at Sanchi but he claimed that the torso had been legitimately presented to him by the Begum. This may indeed have been the case, but had such presents been commonly accepted, the dissipation of India's treasures would have been considerable. Moreover, it was not government policy to allow its servants to accept gifts.

Kincaid seems to have kept quiet about the torso for five years, and then to have offered it for display at the Victoria and Albert Museum. It went on show in the 1890s and quickly caused a sensation. By 1910 other museums in Europe were rumoured to be negotiating with the owner. 'Rather than risk any rumpus that would ensue if it came out that Germany had bagged the torso', the government authorized its purchase for a not over-generous £80.

The Sanchi torso is now one of the Victoria and Albert's most cherished possessions, and the most revered masterpiece of Indian art outside India. There is something hypnotic about that stylized but supremely graceful pose, something deeply sensuous about the swelling flesh gently submitting to the hard ornamentation of necklace and girdle. Yet, despite its celebrity, its origins confounded the experts until very recently. It was in 1971 that its pair was discovered amongst the broken statuary originally unearthed by Major Cole. From the pair it was possible to deduce its identity – the Boddhisattva Avalokiteswara – as well as its original position and its date – about AD 900. Until then it had usually been hailed as a classic piece of Gupta sculpture (fourth to fifth century AD). Before that, it was considered a typical specimen of what Kincaid called 'Indo-Grecian art' of the first century AD. Perhaps nothing more clearly illustrates the gradual development of European understanding and appreciation of Indian sculpture. And particularly significant is the point that initially its claim to serious attention, indeed its acceptance by the museum, rested on the supposition that its inspiration was Greek. Hellenistic influence provided the first, and in the nineteenth century the only, stimulus to the study of Indian sculpture.

To discover how it was that Greek ideas influenced Indian art and who these Indo-Greeks were, it is necessary to turn again to the 1830s, that most productive period in Oriental studies, and to Prinsep and his colleagues. It is also necessary to introduce yet another source material for the reconstruction of Indian history – ancient coins. Colonel James Tod, the man who discovered the Girnar inscription and most of the other antiquities of western India, is usually credited with launching Indian numismatics. During his long stay among the Rajputs in the 1820s, he casually amassed a collection of some 20,000 coins. Every conceivable size, shape, denomination and metal seemed to be represented and many were clearly very old; some even bore the then undeciphered Ashoka script. If such a collection was representative, then clearly there were enough old coins about to justify serious study. If their legends could be read, their symbols and portraits identified, and their distribution plotted, much might be learnt about India's dynastic history.

Tod made a start, arranging his collection in broad groups and commenting on them as best he could. Well represented were coins of the main dynasties from the time of the Guptas right up till the Mohammedan conquests. Indeed, India's medieval history has since been largely reconstructed on the basis of numismatics. Tod's collection included a few coins which, to judge by the scripts, were earlier than the Guptas. And there were one or two that appeared to be not Indian at all, for they bore dual inscriptions, one indecipherable and the other, quite definitely, Greek.

When General Ventura unearthed a hoard of such coins in the Manikyala *stupa*, interest quickened. From classical sources it was known that after Alexander the Great's invasion in 326 BC his conquests in north-west India had been lost; but it was also known that a Greek kingdom had lingered on, indeed prospered, for many decades in northern Afghanistan, or Bactria. The coins now coming to light looked like the work of these Bactrian Greeks. As well as the series bearing dual inscriptions, there were some particularly fine specimens, perhaps the most magnificent coins ever minted in the ancient world, bearing just a Greek legend. 'King Demetrius', 'the Great King Eucratides', 'King Euthydemus' they declared; and there he was, a fine patrician profile with dramatically classical features and wearing a hat that looked like a centurion's helmet with just a hint of solar topi. On the reverse there was often a naked, muscular Hercules. Moreover, Demetrius, Eucratides etc. were all confirmed as kings of Bactria by the classical authors.

Spurred on by these unexpected discoveries, General Ventura and his fellow officers in Ranjit Singh's service scoured the Punjab for more *stupas* and bombarded Prinsep with their finds. Within a matter of months the Asiatic Society's collection of coins had grown tenfold. And still they kept coming. British travellers to Afghanistan and Central Asia added to the flood and none more so than a mysterious figure who called himself Charles Masson. Masson claimed to be an American citizen – which was not as far-fetched as it sounds: Ranjit Singh employed several Americans. But in Masson's case the nationality, like the name, was assumed. He was in fact one of British India's outcasts – a deserter from the East India Company's ranks, whose real name was James Lewis. Masson's origins, like his later life, are shrouded in obscurity, but for ten perilous years, during most of which he lived and travelled in disguise amongst the fanatical Afghans, he played a role of great importance and considerable daring. In British India he faced a court martial if he returned; in Afghanistan, a knife in the back if he was unmasked. Yet somehow he managed to survive, to reach Kabul, to identify the only strong man in the maelstrom of Afghan politics, to ingratiate himself, and to win a pardon from the British in return for acting as their informant. Almost incidentally, he also revealed to the outside world the archaeological wealth of the Kabul area and in the process discovered one of Asia's most important sites.

In 1832 he had heard 'strange stories of the innumerable coins and other relics' to be found on the plain of Begram, twenty-five miles outside Kabul. Anxious not to arouse suspicion, but 'intensely excited', Masson went to investigate. The people on the spot denied all knowledge of antiquities and spoke only of the danger from bandits. But at last an old, and presumably desperate, Mohammedan produced a small, defaced and utterly worthless coin. Masson paid two paise for it and the floodgates opened.

> [This] induced the appearance of others, until the Hindus ventured to bring forth their bags of old monies from which I selected such as suited my purpose. I had the satisfaction to obtain in this manner some eighty coins of types which led me to anticipate bright results from the future. The fears and

scruples of the owners had been overcome. . . . Before the commencement of winter, when the plain, covered with snow, is closed to research, I had accumulated 1865 copper coins, besides a few silver ones, many rings, signets and other relics. The next year, 1834, the collection which fell into my hands amounted to 1900 copper coins, besides other relics. In 1835 it increased to nearly 2500 copper coins, and in 1836 it augmented to 13,474 copper coins. In 1837, when I had the plain well under control, and was able constantly to locate my people upon it, I obtained 60,000 copper coins, a result with which I was well pleased.

It must rank as one of the greatest numismatic hauls of all time. Masson also located and explored some fifty *stupas* in the same area, and in return for a small grant towards the expenses, gave his collection to the Asiatic Society.

But even this was not the extent of his contribution. For Masson, unlike Ventura, was more than just a field-worker. Though a man of modest education, he was soon studying his coins and it is to him, along with Prinsep and the young Cunningham, that we owe their early identification. Roughly speaking, the coins bearing Greek legends spanned a period of 400 years and charted a gradual waning of Greek influence. The beautifully modelled coins of Alexander's successors gave way to progressively less imposing portrayals and poorer engraving. Hercules was replaced by elephants, lions or bulls. The royal names became less obviously Greek, the noble Greek profiles were replaced by a running wind god with spiky hair and a Mithraic pedigree, with symbols from Buddhist and Hindu mythology, and with a strange war-like figure, bearded and booted with legs wide apart.

In these hybrid coins, which were quite as un-Indian as they were un-Greek, Masson and Prinsep quickly recognized that they had stumbled upon an important and hitherto neglected aspect of India's past. From both classical and Chinese sources it was known that waves of barbarian invaders had swept through Afghanistan and into north-western India during the empty centuries that stretched between the Maurya empire of Chandragupta and Ashoka (third century BC) and the empire of the Guptas (fourth century AD). Identifying these various newcomers and getting them in the right order was a major problem. But it seemed that the Bactrian Greeks were the first culprits. Emulating Alexander, they occupied the Punjab in the second century BC and raided deep into the Ganges basin and down the Indus. Then came Scythians from beyond the Oxus, who overran the Greeks in both Bactria and the Punjab. By about 50 BC the Scythians, or Sakas, controlled the Punjab as far south as Delhi. They in turn were succeeded by the Parthians from Persia in about AD 25 and then by the more important Kushans, a tribe originally from Chinese Central Asia. During the first century AD, the Kushans ruled from Peshawar an empire that stretched as far east as Benares and south to the deserts and jungles of central India.

Matching the various invaders to the different series of coins, and then peopling each dynasty with the kings recorded on the coins, became, for Masson, Prinsep and Cunningham, a highly competitive game. Cunningham in particular was most possessive about his tally of newly-discovered sovereigns, as year by year they pieced together this most confusing period of Indian history. With Masson providing the lead, Prinsep the dedication and Cunningham a few inspired guesses, they also deciphered the unknown script which accompanied the Greek legends. Unlike the Gupta and Ashoka scripts, it read from right to left, like Arabic, and was evidently derived from Aramaic. In 1872 Cunningham discovered a new Ashoka rock inscription which was also written in this script. The rock was at Shahbazgarhi, in the foothills north of Peshawar, and so it was established that this Kharosthi script, borrowed from the Middle East, was as old, if not older, than Ashoka Brahmi.

Whether the art of writing was introduced into India from outside, or whether it was an indigenous development, is still a moot point. But clearly many ideas and influences had penetrated the Indian subcontinent from the north-west. Throughout history the north-west frontier had been more often wide open than not. While the Bactrian, Saka and Kushan empires had actually straddled the Khyber pass, the constant spate of conquests had systematically eroded cultural barriers and washed down onto the Indian plains a rich topsoil of Persian and Mediterranean skills and ideals.

The most obvious example was in the coins themselves. At the time of the Mauryas, Indian coinage was still the unadorned lumps of metal marked with a simple punch that had been in circulation from the earliest times. But the idea of a minted coinage, incorporating a design or portrait and a legend, dates only from the time of these invasions.

The evolution of a specifically Indian coinage is clearly marked in the coins of western India, where markedly Indian profiles start to appear about the second century AD. By the fourth century, the distinctive gold coinage of the Guptas was in circulation throughout north India.

In literature, it has been suggested that Sanskrit drama owed something to Greek influence; Indian playwrights like Kalidasa may have inherited some of the conventions of Greek comedy as performed at the Bactrian court in the Punjab. In architecture there is a more obvious connection. The temple of Jandial at Taxila in Pakistan has Ionic columns and a lay-out not unlike that of the Parthenon on a reduced scale. It could hardly look less Indian and indeed it is not Indian; built by Parthian invaders at the beginning of the first century AD, it was probably used by fire-worshipping devotees of the Persian god Zoroaster. But the significant point is that this temple is the earliest structural, as opposed to rock-cut, temple on Indian soil. So did the ancient peoples of India learn about architecture from the invaders? The answer is certainly no. They had been building on a grand scale in wood and brick for centuries. Megasthenes' description of the gigantic royal palace at Pataliputra is in itself enough to prove the point. But Hellenistic buildings like Jandial did have some impact. In the Himalayan valley of Kashmir the foreign style caught on and produced a distinctive and enduring school of building which employed classical pillars, trefoil arches and triangular pediments.

However, it was in the working of stone and in sculpture that foreign skills really made their mark on India. Craftsmen and masons seem to have moved about the ancient world more freely even than ambassadors. Cunningham was probably the first to remark that the Ashoka pillars with their bell-shaped capitals bore a striking resemblance to the pillars of Persepolis, the ancient Achaemenid capital of Persia. The highly developed modelling shown in the lion capitals found at Sarnath and Sanchi suggested an already well-developed style which must mean that Ashoka borrowed both the idea of the pillars, and the masons to carve them, from Persia.

At Bharhut and Sanchi, Cunningham found yet more evidence of foreign craftsmen. He thought he recognized Kharosthi writing on the best of the carved reliefs at Bharhut, and he explained the disparity in the quality of some of the Sanchi reliefs by assuming the more finished panels were the work of imported craftsmen. As if to prove his point, he discovered at Besnagar, only a couple of miles from Sanchi, a small pillar with an inscription which declared that it had been erected by a

Greek called Heliodorus during the first century BC – the period when the gateways were erected.

Few, however, and certainly not Cunningham, would deny that the inspiration for both the Ashoka columns and the Sanchi reliefs was Indian: they owed as much to earlier indigenous skills in wood and ivory carving as to Greek stone masons. The true Indo-Greek sculptures (called Gandhara, after the name of the region between the Indus and Kabul) were, however, a very different matter.

In 1836 Lieutenant-Colonel Stacy, one of Prinsep's most dogged collectors, was presented with what looked like a massive font carved from a single rectangular block of the local sandstone. It had been found near the city of Mathura, between Agra and Delhi. On the front and back were lively reliefs, and it was the unmistakably classical appearance of these that prompted Stacy to make an immediate report to the Asiatic Society.

> The obverse represents Silenus [Bacchus' alcoholic counsellor] inebriated; he is reclining on a low seat or throne, supported on either side by a young male and female Grecian. Two minor figures support the knees; the attitude of Silenus, the drooping of the head, the lips, and powerless state of the limbs, give an accurate representation of a drunken man. The figure of the youth and the maiden are also in appropriate keeping. The whole is evidently the work of an able artist who could not possibly, in my opinion, have been a native of India.

On the other side there were more Bacchanalian figures. The females showed some concessions to Indian tastes, especially in the lovingly exaggerated bosoms; but they were fully clothed – an unusual circumstance in itself – and their clothing was distinctly Greek, a pleated tunic and flowing drapery that brushed the ground. How on earth had such an improbable piece turned up on the banks of the Jumna?

Prinsep immediately guessed that there might be some connection here with the Indo-Greek coins. But he had serious doubts about it.

> The discovery of a piece of sculpture bearing evident reference to Greek mythology ... might excite less surprise after the elaborate display we have lately had of coins found in upper India and the Punjab with Greek legends and a combination of Greek and Hindu deities. Yet in fact the latter offer no explanation of the former.

Silenus, Bacchus, Dionysos — none of these appeared on the coins and neither was there any Hindu god with whom they might have become identified. Moreover, Bacchic worship did not seem to have featured in Greek Bactria.

Stacy's font therefore remained an unexplained mystery. Only after the British annexation of the Punjab in the late 1840s was anything quite like it found. As usual, Cunningham was in the forefront of the new discoveries. Returning from his abortive boundary commission in Ladakh in 1848, he headed west of Kashmir in search of Fa Hsien's route through the mountains. In the foothills north of Peshawar, he found the ruins of what appeared to be a monastery incorporating Corinthian capitals. The statuary was equally classical and he brought back a whole camel-load. Further excavations were carried out at the same site in the 1850s, and the whole collection was sent to London for the Great Exhibition at the Crystal Palace. Sadly, it perished in the famous fire before it had even been photographed.

Europe had to wait another ten years for a good look at Gandhara sculpture. Dr Gottlieb Leitner, educationist, ethnologist, explorer extraordinary and one of India's most maligned eccentrics, could never resist a sensation. As a schoolmaster in Lahore he spent his vacations wandering in the hills to the north, and in the Swat valley he first encountered Gandhara art. Though neither an archaeologist nor an art historian, he immediately recognized a controversy in the making. He returned to London in 1868 with several crates of statuary.

By now it was established that, despite their classical features, these statues, and the sites from which they came, were for the most part Buddhist. There were exceptions — the odd figure that was straight from classical mythology or Roman history — but even Stacy's Silenus was being identified with the Buddhist *yaksha*, Kuvera. Not that this made the phenomenon any less puzzling. A Buddha in a toga, a Buddha nestling amongst the acanthus leaves of a Corinthian column, a Boddhisattva with moustaches and wearing Athenian sandals? It was all too absurd. Yet for once there was no gainsaying the evidence. As Buddhist scholars had already observed, rigorous iconographic conventions governed any representation of the Buddha. Amongst these were such distinctive features as the protuberance on the crown of the head, the elongated ear lobes, and the suggestion of a third eye in the centre of the forehead. All these were scrupulously incorporated in the Gandhara sculptures; though the figure might look like a good copy of the Apollo Belvedere, there could be no argument that it was in fact the Buddha.

But this raised the most intriguing question of all. The sculptors of Sanchi, Bharhut and Boddh Gaya had carefully avoided any portrayal of the Buddha himself. An empty throne, the sacred Boddhi tree, a footprint or some other symbol was always preferred. There is no known instance of the Buddha being portrayed in human form before the second century AD. Yet the Greeks were now known to have been over-run by 100 BC, at least 200 years earlier. So who carved these Buddhas and, if not the Greeks, who produced these classical forms?

Speculation and controversy simmered throughout the last quarter of the nineteenth century. Broadly speaking, there were two main schools of thought. In India, Cunningham, recalling the very clear Bactrian influence on the Indo-Greek coins, stuck to the idea that the Greeks must somehow be behind all Gandhara art. He suggested that the Bactrians who settled in the Punjab in the second century BC brought their ideals and their artisans with them: the seeds of classicism were thus sown and lingered on long after the eclipse of Greek political power. He further supposed an early date, about 50 BC, for the arrival of the Kushan invaders. The Kushans, and in particular their king Kanishka, were known to have adopted and promoted Buddhism as zealously as Ashoka. *Stupas* and monasteries were suddenly in demand, and what more natural than a revival of the latent skills and ideals of their Greek predecessors? Since the Greeks were accustomed to representing their deities in human form, they automatically attempted to portray the Buddha; the Kushans, converts to Buddhism who knew no better, welcomed the novelty. Gandhara sculptors therefore invented the Buddha image and no doubt it was from them that in due course Indian sculptors borrowed the idea.

Cunningham had the advantage of having discovered many of the sculptures and of having seen most of the others. In India his hypothesis was widely accepted; Major Cole, who himself explored in Swat in 1883 and 1884, was in full agreement. He even revived the idea that the seeds of Hellenism had been sown in the Punjab, not just by the Bactrian Greeks, but by Alexander. In England, though, it was a different matter. On anything to do with Indian art Cunningham now had a formidable rival in James Fergusson, the historian of India's architecture. Fergusson had never visited the Punjab and, anyway, had left India before the main Gandhara finds. He had seen Leitner's collection and studied all available photographs; but understandably, his first complaint was that Cunningham was hogging all the finds and consigning them to Indian museums.

The extraordinary classical character and the beauty of these sculptures ... is of such surpassing interest for the history of Indian art, that it is of the utmost importance their age should be determined, if it is possible to do so. At present, sufficient materials do not exist in this country [Britain] to enable the general public to form even an opinion on any argument that may be brought forward on the subject; nor will they be in a position to do so till the Government can be induced to spend the trifling sum required to bring some of them home. They are quite thrown away where they are now; here they could hardly be surpassed in interest by any recent discoveries of the same class.

This, however, did not stop Fergusson himself from forming an opinion on the subject. Drawing on his considerable knowledge of classical architecture, he made the important observation that Gandhara sculpture owed as much to the Romans as to the Greeks. Indeed, novelties like a figure nestling in the foliage of a Corinthian capital were quite late developments in Roman provincial art (about fourth century AD). Fergusson conceded that in its earliest stages Gandhara art might have owed something to the Greeks, but that it covered a much longer period than Cunningham suggested – right up to the seventh century AD – and was therefore contemporary with the empires of Rome and Byzantium. Just how Roman and Byzantine ideas had reached north-west India without leaving their mark on the intervening lands Fergusson could not say. But he suggested that from time immemorial east–west contacts had been on a much greater scale than was generally appreciated. Stacy had claimed that his Silenus discovery supported Sir William Jones's belief that the gods of India and Greece were somehow interchangeable. Prinsep, and now Fergusson, recalled the tradition that St (Doubting) Thomas had visited the court of Gondophares, one of the Parthian kings of Gandhara. Fergusson also suggested that, if the *Bhagavad Gita* appeared to contain Christian doctrine, this too was no mere coincidence.

In short, if Fergusson's theory was right, just about anything in Indian art and culture which appealed to the Victorians could be explained away as evidence of Greek, Roman, Byzantine or Christian influences. No wonder, then, that in the nineteenth century Gandhara art was the only Indian art that they took seriously. 'Gandhara sculptures', wrote Vincent Smith in 1889, 'would be admitted by most persons qualified to form an opinion to be the best specimens of the plastic art ever known to exist in India.' They were classical and therefore familiar; they were Buddhist and therefore, unlike Hindu art, comparatively innocuous. And they were controversial – an attraction in itself – but this controversy also raised the possibility of an ingenious and consoling explanation for anything that appeared worthy in Indian civilization.

As a result, classical influences in Indian art were, for a time, wildly exaggerated. But fashions change. Where Cunningham had noted 'a boldness of design and a freedom of execution that no eastern artist has ever yet shown', Fergusson 'a beauty of surpassing interest', and Cole much 'delicacy and taste', Ernest Havell in 1890 saw only 'an inferior handicraft ... insincerity and want of spirituality; the Buddhas and Boddhisattvas of this period are senseless puppets, debased types of the Greek and Roman pantheon, posing uncomfortably in the attitudes of Indian asceticism'. Havell, admittedly, was as prejudiced against the Gandhara school as Cunningham or Fergusson for it. The problem for all of them was that no aesthetic valuation was worth much until the chronology of Gandhara art, and therefore the inspiration behind it, had been clarified.

Only with the excavation of Taxila in the 1920s did the necessary evidence come to light. This great site, with its Greek, Parthian and Kushan cities, had been discovered by Cunningham's Archaeological Survey; but as usual the old general had hastened on after doing little more than establish its identity. It was left to Sir John Marshall, Cunningham's successor, albeit after a gap of twenty years, to exploit the find. The wealth of sculptural and architectural remains in each of the old cities provided the data for a thorough classification of all Gandhara art.

Happily, the truth allowed vindication for just about everyone. Cunningham would have been gratified to learn that the beginnings of the school did date back to the first century BC and did represent a revival of Hellenistic art; also that the Kushan period was indeed the most important and that the Gandhara Buddhas were amongst the first representations of the Enlightened One. Fergusson, though, could have consoled himself with the news that he was right about the longevity of the Gandhara school: Marshall identified a quite distinct later school which lasted until the fifth century. He was also right about Roman influence; the classicism of Gandhara seems to have been frequently recharged from the West.

above: In the eighteenth century Aurangzeb's great mosque above Panchganga ghat dominated the Benares waterfront. Built on the site of a vast Hindu temple it helped explain the dearth of pre-Islamic architecture in the sacred city. Yet Benares remained a centre of Hindu scholarship where the first orientalists sought the keys to India's past. (Watercolour by Robt. Smith, 1833.)

below: James Prinsep consulting with Hindu *pandits* in the Sanskrit College in Benares. Founded by one of Warren Hasting's protégés, the institution was the first to attempt the systematic collection and study of India's classical literature. (Lithograph by Sir Chas. D'Oyley.)

above: The rock of Girnar in Gujerat, 'which by the aid of the "iron pen" has been converted into a book', was discovered by Colonel James Tod in 1822. Carrying one of the longest versions of Ashoka's edicts, it was used by Prinsep to help decipher the script and establish Ashoka as the greatest figure in India's ancient history. (Watercolour by Thos. Postans, 1938).

below: Only a few miles from Madras, the temples of Mahabalipuram (here in a painting by Thomas Daniell) puzzled scholars and visitors alike. For they were not in fact architecture but sculpture, each carved and hollowed from a single gigantic boulder.

'Few remains of antiquity have excited greater curiosity.' The engineering skills involved in excavating the cave temples of western India suggested Egyptian involvement while their sculptural elegance was ascribed to Greek influence. Not till the 1830s was it acknowledged that they were in fact Indian – Buddhist in the case of Karli (*above:* lithograph by Henry Salt, 1808), Hindu in the case of Elephanta (*below:* drawing by Bishop Heber).

The ruined temple of Boddh Gaya was being cared for by local Brahmins when Francis Buchanan first identified it as Buddhist. From ancient Chinese texts Cunningham discovered that it was in fact the site of the Buddha's enlightenment. Rehabilitated, it is today a major centre of Buddhist studies and a place of universal pilgrimage. (Watercolour by 'J.C.M.', 1814.)

The *stupas* of Sanchi, and particularly the sculpted reliefs that cover their gateways, proved to be amongst the most enlightening finds. When first discovered in 1819, the Indian origins of Buddhism were still unsuspected. Alexander Cunningham pioneered this field of study and was the first to conduct a systematic examination of Sanchi. But not till the 1880s was the site cleared and partially reconstructed. (Watercolour by William Simpson, 1862.)

A major obstacle to any Victorian appreciation of Indian sculpture was its unabashed sensuality. The *yakshis*, tree and fertility spirits (*left*), once adorned a Buddhist *stupa* railing at Mathura. But exception was made for artefacts of the Gandhara school (first to fifth centuries AD) of the northwest. Here Greek and Roman influence had resulted in the Buddha being decently clothed in a toga (*bottom right*) and in a Boddhisattva (*bottom left*) being endowed with classical features.

Hidden in the jungle, the great temple complex of Khajuraho
(*above*: tenth – eleventh centuries AD) was rediscovered in 1838, but not
greatly publicized. 'The sculptor had at times allowed his subject to grow
a little warmer than there was any absolute necessity for his doing,' wrote
the first visitor with masterly understatement. Many and ingenious are
the explanations which have been advanced for the *mithunas* (love-
making groups) and *apsaras* (dancing girls: *below*), which cover the walls
of almost all the Khajuraho temples.

above: In attempting the monumental task of classifying India's architecture, James Fergusson dubbed as 'Indo-Aryan' those, mainly north Indian, temples with a curvilinear *sikhara* (tower). The *sikhara* took many forms, his favourite being this pineapple shape typical of Orissa. The festival of Jagannath at Puri was reckoned one of India's greatest sights. (Drawing by one of Mackenzie's draughtsmen.)

below: Much of India's architectural heritage was first brought to notice as a result of the travels of surveyors and map-makers. Colin Mackenzie, India's first Surveyor-General, encouraged antiquarian research and expected his surveyors, as here, to measure and sketch all buildings of note. (Drawing, possibly a temple at Vijayanagar, by one of Mackenzie's draughtsmen.)

After spending twenty years over Taxila, Marshall could hardly be expected to embrace Havell's damning aesthetic indictment. In Gandhara, as in every other school of art, there was good and bad; there was development, maturity and decline; there was experimentation and imitation. In the panel reliefs the compositions were often exceptional and the figures charming. Craftsmanship was sometimes of the highest order; the Boddhisattva bust (from Mardan and now in the Peshawar Museum) was superb, 'the beauty of the chiselling as clear-cut and precise as could be found in any school of sculpture, East or West'. But there was also much that was inferior and insipid. The nice clear expressions and the noble features which so appealed to the previous generation smacked too much of a 'smarmy prettiness'. Besides, it was now acknowledged that India had an art of its own that was infinitely more intriguing.

CHAPTER EIGHT

A Little Warmer than Necessary

Included in the list of places Alexander Cunningham submitted to Lord Canning in 1861 as worthy of immediate investigation by the Archaeological Survey, were two sites of outstanding importance for the study of Indian sculpture. The first was Khajuraho, of which notorious place a solitary report had appeared in the Asiatic Society's journal for 1839. It had actually been discovered twenty years earlier. Cornet James Franklin, a military surveyor and the brother of the great Arctic explorer, spotted the temples in what was then dense jungle and duly recorded them as 'ruins'. Unfortunately, Franklin's handwriting was none too clear: the map makers misread his 'ruins' as 'mines' and Khajuraho was thought to contain nothing more exciting than old tin workings. The truth was left for Captain T. S. Burt, one of Prinsep's roving engineers and the man who had procured the first true facsimiles of the Allahabad column inscriptions. While touring in central India in 1838 he heard tell, from one of the men hired to shoulder his palanquin, 'of the wonders of this place – Khajroa near Chatpore he called it'. By double marches, or rather rides (the palanquin bearer must have been regretting his indiscretion), Burt made up the few hours that he thought would suffice for an inspection, and arrived, all unsuspecting, just as the sun was rising above the jungle.

> I was much delighted at the venerable and picturesque appearance these several old temples presented as I got within view of them. They reared their sunburnt tops above the trees with all the pride of superior height and age. . . . My first enquiry, after taking breakfast, was for ancient inscriptions and a temple close by was immediately pointed out as the possessor of one. I went there and sure enough there was an

> inscription in the No. 3 Sanskrit character of the Allahabad
> pillar [Kutila]. ... It was the largest, the finest, the most legible
> inscription of any I had yet met with and it was with absolute
> delight that I set to work to transfer its contents to paper.

A dedicated antiquarian, Burt bent to his task with printer's ink and
wet towels. Like the sportsman who stoops to study a pug mark while,
unseen above him, the leopard looks on, he was still blissfully oblivious of what lay in store. He wanted a date and he found it – 1123 in the
Samvat era, which meant AD 1067.

> Having done this, I took a look round ... and could not help
> expressing a feeling of wonder at these splendid monuments
> of antiquity having been erected by a people who have con-
> tinued to live in such a state of barbarous ignorance. It is a
> proof that some of these men must then have been of a more
> superior caste of human being than the rest.

In a moment he was going to regret these words. Like many of his
contemporaries he subscribed to the idea that for centuries Indian
culture had been steadily degenerating. At first he thought that in
Khajuraho he had found an example of the heights to which it had
once aspired. But as he innocently paused to examine the sculptures,
he had second thoughts: 1067 must have been well into the period of
decline.

> I found ... seven Hindoo temples, most beautifully and
> exquisitely carved as to workmanship, but the sculptor had at
> times allowed his subject to grow a little warmer than there
> was any absolute necessity for his doing; indeed some of the
> sculptures here were extremely indecent and offensive, which
> I was at first much surprised to find in temples that are
> professed to be erected for good purposes, and on account of
> religion. But the religion of the ancient Hindoos can not have
> been very chaste if it induced people under the cloak of
> religion, to design the most disgraceful representations to
> desecrate their ecclesiastical erections. The palki [palanquin]
> bearers, however, appeared to take great delight at those, to
> them, very agreeable novelties, which they took good care to
> point out to all present.

Burt must have been unusually innocent if he was really surprised by
the famous *apsaras* – seductive nymphs – and the *mithunas* – the

love-making couples (and sometimes quadruples) – of the Khajuraho sculptures. Since the seventeenth century the British had been familiar with the so-called Black Temple of Konarak in Orissa, which boasts similar figures – albeit more blurred by erosion. Near the shore of the Bay of Bengal, the Black Temple was commonly a landfall for ships making for the Hughli river and Calcutta. As it hove into sight the old India hands would take the young 'griffins' aside for whispered innuendos about the sexual mores of the Hindu.

Burt, though, seems to have been genuinely scandalized. Turning in acute embarrassment from his sleeve-tugging bearers, he tried to concentrate on the architecture. In the Khandariya Mahadeo temple, the noblest of the 'architectural erections', he determined to get on the roof to inspect the construction of the soaring pinnacles. The only access was from inside, by shinning up the sacred, and not-so-sacred, images.

> From the side wall which was perpendicular I first sent up one of the bearers and then, by laying hold of the leg of one god, and the arm of another, the head of a third and so on, I was luckly enabled, not however without inconvenience, to attain the top of the wall where, on the roof, I found an aperture just large enough for me to creep in at. On entering upon the roof I found that my sole predecessors there for several years before had evidently been the bat and the monkey, and the place for that reason was not the most odoriferous of all places in the world.

Still wary of the *mithunas*, but warming to his subject, Burt toured the whole complex. 'I shall state my opinion that they are most probably the finest aggregate number of temples congregated together in one place to be met with in all India.' He described in detail the great bull, Nandi, outside the Visvanatha temple and the even bigger image of Vishnu in his incarnation as a boar. By his own calculations this statue, a monolith, weighed sixty-eight tons. The female figure representing mankind, and usually borne aloft on the boar's tusks, was missing. Considering that Burt was surrounded by female figures, his distress at this discovery is surprising. 'I would willingly have given a hundred rupees [£10] to have had a good sight of her.'

As he wandered round, penning his thoughts as he went, his style grew increasingly jaunty; he was on the verge of attempting a description of the *mithunas*. But in the end he shied away, contenting himself, before climbing back into his palanquin, with a lively account of another 'ecclesiastical erection'.

> Let us now look at the little Mahadeo, or lingam [the phallus symbol of the god Siva] which is to be seen in another temple. In order to arrive at it, it is necessary to ascend a considerable number of steps, at the top of which is situated the representation of the vital principle. Let us now measure the height of the gentleman. The natives objected to my going inside without taking off my boots, which would have been inconvenient; so standing at the doorway, I saw a bearer measure the height with my walking stick; it amounted to $2\frac{2}{3}$ of its height or eight feet and its diameter to $1\frac{1}{3}$ or four feet. Its weight will be about $7\frac{1}{2}$ tons ... and it is considered by far the biggest lingam in India.

The next account of Khajuraho seems to be Cunningham's. The General finally arrived there in 1865 and, if rather less naïve than Burt, he was certainly not going to be any more explicit; 'all of these [the sculptures] are highly indecent and most of them disgustingly obscene'. He must, though, have paid them a bit more attention. On the Khandariya Mahadeo he counted and measured 872 sculptures, mostly two and a half to three feet high. 'The general effect of this great luxury of embellishment is extremely pleasing although the eye is often distracted by the multiplicity of detail.' He also agreed with Burt about the date. Studying the script of every visible inscription, he came to the conclusion that all the temples dated from the tenth and eleventh centuries, 'a date which I should otherwise be inclined to adopt on account of the gross indelicacy of the principal sculptures'. He also ascribed them to the patronage of the Chandel Rajputs of Chatterpore, who were one of the many rajput clans who so valiantly resisted the Mohammedan invaders.

To Cunningham's mind it was the fact that Khajuraho had been miraculously preserved from the iconoclastic Mohammedans that constituted its real importance. 'The remains are more numerous and in better preservation than those of any other ancient city I have seen.' Hidden away in an extremely remote tract of country, the site had been deserted by the Chandel rajahs before the Mohammedans advanced; then the jungle quickly smothered it as effectively as did the volcanic lava Pompeii. Though never an especially ancient or sacred site, the magnificence and profusion of its temples, their scarcely credible riot of sculpture and relief, and above all the pristine perfection of every detail, gave some idea of the splendour of older and holier cities before the Mohammedan conquest.

In the whole of north India there is scarcely a statue that was not defaced by the Islamic invaders, scarcely a temple that was not ravaged. In Delhi the desecration and destruction were total. And the same was true of Mathura, the other site on Cunningham's list which is of particular relevance to Indian sculpture. Since the discovery of Stacy's 'Silenus', more carvings had come to light there. 'In one of the ancient mounds outside the city the remains of a large monastery have lately been discovered. Numerous statues, sculptured pillars and inscribed bases of columns have been brought to light.' According to Fa Hsien, Mathura had been a thriving Buddhist and Jain centre, and, as the scene of Krishna's youthful exploits, an important place of Hindu pilgrimage. Indeed, the latter it still is. But today not a single building in the Mathura area dates back beyond the seventeenth century. The *stupas*, the monasteries, the temples were all razed to the ground by the invaders.

Fa Hsien reported twenty Buddhist monasteries and 3000 monks, considerably more than Sarnath. In his day the domes of the *stupas* were clad in gold leaf, and the railings and their reliefs brightly painted. The monasteries and temples were covered with frescoes and the stone sculptures could barely compete with the multitude of gold and silver images. (One such, of solid gold, carried away by Mahmud of Ghazni in 1017, weighed half a ton and bore a single sapphire of three and a half pounds; Mahmud's loot also included five more solid gold figures with rubies for eyes and a hundred silver images each of which was heavy enough to constitute a single load for a camel.) To get any idea of what the place must have been like one must also people it with priests and pilgrims, princes and ascetics, moving in procession from shrine to shrine; the maroons and ochres of the monks' robes, a scarlet shawl, a dazzling *dhoti*, mingling amongst the sea of white cottons and glistening brown torsoes. Even the women of ancient India went naked above the waist – naked, that is, except for jewellery. And all the while the air would have been throbbing with the sounds and smells of worship – bells ringing, incense burning, chanting and shouting, the scent of a million marigolds and the murmur of a million prayers.

Turning from that image to the silent halls of today's Mathura Museum, the double tragedy of Indian art strikes one with force. For here, bar a few pieces sent to other museums, is all that is left of Mathura's ancient glory: perhaps a dozen Buddha or Boddhisattva images, all to some extent mutilated, a few bits of railing, an architrave or two, a 'Silenus' like Stacy's, more miscellaneous statuary, and a battery of Hindu deities. And, as if destruction by one set of foreigners were not in itself enough, the reconstruction of this past by another set of foreigners at first totally ignored all aesthetic values. The sculptures in the Mathura Museum are mostly carved out of the none-too-exciting sandstone of Sikri, a lifeless reddish stone marred with white spots. Sun-starved and paraded for inspection rather than effect, they invite the purely antiquarian and archaeological approach to Indian art. This was how Cunningham and his contemporaries saw them, and this is the stigma Indian art still to some extent bears. Sir William Jones would have been horrified. He had always insisted that Indian civilization deserved to be studied for its own sake and that Sanskrit literature, his particular field, could stand comparison with anything that Europe had to offer. But the rhetoric of Macaulay had put paid to all that. The only justification now for studying Indian culture was for the light it might shed on the past. An aesthetic, emotional or spiritual appreciation would have to wait another half century.

Cunningham had first visited Mathura in 1853. He returned with the Archaeological Survey in 1862, 1871 (twice), 1876 and 1882; no other site in the country received so much attention. His own finds and acquisitions were numerous, including the giant *yaksha* (tree spirit) from Parkham, dating from the Mauryan age – the earliest figure sculpture then found in India. He also excavated the first of the famous Mathura railing pillars, each of which is graced with one of those voluptuous, hip-swinging *yakshis* (female tree-spirits), the forerunners of the Khajuraho *apsaras*. But these were almost incidental discoveries. Excavations at the various sites around Mathura went on continuously throughout his long years as the Archaeological Surveyor. The combination of an enlightened District Collector and an ambitious local clearance and rebuilding programme resulted in a steady flow of discoveries. Cunningham's role was essentially interpretative, deciphering the coins and inscriptions and assessing the importance of the finds.

It soon became clear to him that this city had played a crucial role in the development of sculpture. 'Everywhere in the north-west I find that the old Buddhist statues are made of Sikri sandstone, from which it would appear that Mathura must have been the great manufactory for the supply of Buddhist sculptures in northern India.' But it was not only Buddhist sculptures. Hindu, Jain and purely secular pieces were soon coming to light. There were more finds of Gandhara art – another 'Silenus' and a well-draped female figure sometimes identified as Queen Kambojika. There were some classic pieces of Gupta and medieval art including two near-perfect standing Buddhas. And there was a giant warrior, legs apart and feet booted just like the figure first noted on some of the Indo-Greek coins and now identified by an inscription as the great Kushan king, Kanishka. One of the advantages of Mathura art, as opposed to Gandhara, was that most of the pieces bore inscriptions, even dates. Starting with the Parkham colossus of the third century BC, the Mathura finds spanned a period of 1000 years and thus gave a unique panorama of Indian art from its earliest stages to the eve of the Mohammedan invasions.

Moreover, its geographical position between the classically-influenced north-west and the Indian heartland made it an ideal site for studying the inter-action of foreign and indigenous styles. Here the curly haired, clear featured, well draped figures of Gandhara met the soft, bejewelled *yakshas* and the sinuous, flamboyant *yakshis* of the subcontinent. The Gandhara female figure (Queen Kambojika) and a more or less contemporary figure on the recently discovered gateway bracket from Sonkh provide two totally different ideals of femininity. To be fair to Cunningham, there were just no known aesthetic criteria that could be applied to the Indian figure. It was too gross, too primitive. Woman never yet aspired to a shape and a pose quite so blatantly provocative. Indian sculptors seemed to have denied their own experience of human anatomy in order to produce something that was simply and solely erotic. Where was the artistic subtlety in this; where the grace and dignity of womanhood? As much attention had been paid to the lower abdomen as to the face; one could only describe the figure, like the inspiration behind it, as crude. Professor Westmacott's verdict of 1864 may stand for the whole of the nineteenth century.

> There is no temptation to dwell at length on the sculpture of Hindustan [India]. It affords no assistance in tracing the history of art, and its debased quality deprives it of all interest as a phase of fine art.

But happily, if belatedly, a few brave spirits did question it. The aesthetic appreciation of Indian art owes much to Indians themselves and a great deal to Hindu revivalism and the stirrings of Indian nationalism. But it also owes something to Lord Curzon, the first British ruler of India since Warren Hastings to admire Indian civilization, and to his contemporary, the first man to attempt an exposition of Indian art, Dr Ernest Binfield Havell.

Havell's is not a name writ large in the annals of the British raj. He came to India as principal of the Madras College of Art in the 1890s and left as principal of the Calcutta College of Art some twenty years later. But during this period his work and writings exercised considerable influence both in India and in the West. 'Whenever I speak of Indian art,' Sir William Rothenstein of the Royal College of Art told him, 'I say that you were before us all in understanding its qualities.'

Understanding its qualities meant understanding its inspiration, its ideals, its symbolism and its techniques. Havell's then distinctly novel premise was that 'no European can understand or appreciate Indian art who does not divest himself of his western preconceptions, endeavour to understand Indian thought, and place himself at the Indian point of view'. It meant rejecting all comparisons with European art, and all theories of classical or foreign influence, and tackling the whole concept of art from a different direction. A good starting point was the Indian approach to the carving of sacred images. Take, for instance, the two most famous Buddha images from Mathura. The first, a seated figure in red sandstone, dates from the Kushan period and is therefore contemporary with the best Gandhara sculpture. But there is no sign of Gandhara influence. The body is not composed of muscle and bone but simply of flesh, softly swelling. The sculptor has made no attempt to capture reality: the hair and top-knot look more like some kind of hat than real hair; even the smile is not exactly convincing. Much the same goes for the standing Buddha of the Gupta period. In the centuries between, the Mathura artists had adopted a few Gandhara conventions – the curly hair for instance, and the flowing drapery. But there is still no flirting with visual reality; their ideal remains the same. The curls have been reduced to shell-like lumps and the drapery into an abstract pattern of flowing lines which does less to hide the body than to accentuate it. Technique has advanced; there is more refinement in the features, more finished modelling. But still this is not a very convincing figure of a man, or even of a superman.

And there, of course, lay the secret; it was not meant to be a man. European art was still mainly representational: its ideal, according to

Havell, was simply the imitation of nature. But Indian art was conceptual, aiming at the realization of 'something finer and more subtle than
ordinary physical beauty'. The image that the Indian sculptor created
came from inside his head; he had no need of a goose-pimpled model
posing uncomfortably in his studio. His achievement was not that of
capturing real life in art, but of giving birth to an abstract ideal. It was
a bit like the difference between non-fiction and fiction. But life is not
like that, protested the traditionalists. Beauty is, must be, truth; dis-
torting the facts, giving a female figure mountainous breasts or a male
sixteen arms, showed that the artist was either primitive or perversely
depraved. On the contrary, said Havell on the Indian sculptor's
behalf; truth is much more subtle and elusive, and beauty will never be
found in the mere perfecting of reality.

The sculptor of Gandhara, following the classical approach, took
an ideal human figure, added on the necessary top-knot, earlobes etc,
and called him a Buddha. But the Mathura artist started with the
Buddha. First, by study and meditation, he conceived the divine image
in his mind. This needed religious and spiritual development of a high
order. Then, by strictly observing numerous conventions and by constantly consulting his original inspiration, he strove to embody this
image in a shape that fellow believers would recognize. So comprehensive were the various canons about proportions, gestures, features,
etc., that there was certainly very limited scope for individuality and
innovation. But then the Indian sculptor was not in the business of
displaying his own virtuosity or laying claims to immortality. He
usually remained anonymous and, to the extent that his creation
matched up to his original inspiration, it was as much a comment on
his spirituality as his skill.

Havell rightly pounced on this approach to divine beauty as 'the key
to all Indian aesthetic thought'. This did not lead him to a defence of
idolatry, although he did clearly show that the creative process
amounted to one of consecration. Instead, he concentrated on the
purely aesthetic objections to Indian religious art.

> A figure with three heads, and four, six, or eight arms, seems
> to a European a barbaric conception, though it is not less
> physiologically impossible than the wings growing from the
> human scapula in the European representation of angels. ...
> But it is altogether foolish to condemn such artistic allegories
> *a priori* because they do not conform to the canons of the

classic art of Europe. All art is suggestion and convention, and if Indian artists can suggest divine attributes to Indian people with Indian culture, they have fulfilled the purpose of their art.

Just as angels were given wings, or saints halos, or just as the Holy Spirit was portrayed as a dove, so Siva and Vishnu were given extra arms to hold the symbols of their various attributes, or extra heads for their different roles. The fact that invariably the body of a Buddha image was highly generalized and somewhat full was not because the Indian artist could not understand anatomy. It was full because the divine ideal owed much to yoga, the traditional discipline through which man might realize the infinite; a wrapt inward-looking expression conveying transcendental calm and contentment was obviously a manifestation of yogic communion. So too was the holding of the breath, the *prana* or spiritual inflation.

By way of contrast, Havell then showed how consummately the Indian artist could handle movement. Taking as his example one of the famous Nataraj (dancing Siva) bronzes of south India, he first explored its symbolism. No work of Indian art is without a wealth of allegory and symbol, ignorance of which was, and still is, a major stumbling block for most non-Indians. But Havell showed how a formidable collection of mystical and mythical associations need not detract from – and to the Indian, very much enhanced – the beauty of the composition. The Nataraj dealt with the divine ecstasy of creation expressed in dance.

> There is nothing of the mere animal gaiety of the Dancing Faun, nor any suggestion of the dancing frenzy of the Bacchanal. In its technical treatment the figure presents the same broad anatomical generalization and the peculiar type of torso as we have seen in Buddhist sculpture. No one who observes the mastery of the structure of the human figure and the immense technical skill which the Hindu sculptor here shows can believe that it was from want of ability or knowledge that he has left out all indication of the smaller details of the muscular system. The Indian artist as a rule delighted in elaborating detail; but here, as in all his ideals of Deity incarnate, he has deliberately suppressed it.

The same could be said of another favourite subject with Indian artists – animals. Havell chose as his example one of the great war-horses outside the Black Temple of Konarak; but he might just as well have selected an elephant from the Sanchi gateways or from the great mural relief at Mahabalipuram, or a Nandi bull from Khajuraho. None of them was anatomically realistic, yet somehow the Indian artist had gone beyond appearance and captured the peculiar charac-ter of each animal. The playfulness of the monkey, the elegance of the peacock, the timidity of the deer – all are eloquently represented in Indian art. Whereas Leonardo might have dissected a dog before drawing it, the Indian artist was not especially interested in how a dog worked; he wanted to get at the essence of dog.

The Konarak war-horse, prancing into battle with a massively strong warrior striding beside it, appealed to Havell because it also showed that the Indian sculptor was quite capable of handling martial themes. 'Not even the Homeric grandeur of the Elgin marbles sur-passes the magnificent movement and modelling of this Indian Achilles, and the superbly monumental war-horse with its massive strength and vigour is not unworthy of comparison with Verocchio's famous masterpiece at Venice.' None of the then fashionable eques-trian statues in Calcutta and elsewhere could begin to compare with it. Here was an area in which the Indian artist should be encouraged and patronized.

To many, Havell appeared somewhat partisan; he protested too much. But then he was an art teacher, and his concern was not simply to validate Indian art but actively to promote it. He passionately believed that what he called 'the Indo-Aryan master craftsman' was still a vital force. Though suppressed because of Islam's veto on all iconography, and scorned through the ignorance and philistinism of the British, the old skills were still there. A modicum of recognition and patronage could bring about a real renaissance. At Madras and Calcutta, Havell purged his schools of all western influence and encouraged his young painters, sculptors and architects to rediscover their indigenous culture. He inveighed against the sterility of Anglo-Indian art and particularly architecture. It was madness to go on erecting neo-classical – or now, more commonly, neo-Gothic and Scottish baronial – monstrosities when the skills and artistry that had produced the Taj Mahal and the Rajput palaces were still there for the tapping.

Havell totally rejected the idea that Indian culture had declined beyond recognition or redemption. For Burt and Cunningham this theory offered a convenient explanation for the eroticism of places like Khajuraho. Havell could only lamely propose that the sensual *apsaras* were no more than a conventional decorative motif, and that the *mithuna* couples represented 'the extravagance and eccentricity' to which the Indian artist was vulnerable when the lofty ideals of his art deserted him. In other words, for a degree of respectability and perhaps patronage, there was a high price to be paid. All that was sensual in Indian art must be ignored. On no subject had the Indian artist lavished so much skill and affection as the female figure. Yet Havell scarcely mentioned it. Of course, there was nothing wrong with the female nude as such. But the Indian artist was no more content with a naturalistic portrayal of a woman than he was with a true-to-life study of a horse or an elephant. Just as he must present the essence of a horse, so he must celebrate the femininity of a female. And in a society unfettered by the sexual taboos of the West, this meant bringing out her sexual charms.

Hence those gloriously thrusting breasts, the hour-glass waist, and the full and forty hips. No pin-up ever approached the provocative postures, the smouldering looks and the languorous gestures of the Khajuraho nymphs. Serene rather than saucy, intent rather than ecstatic, they go gracefully about their feminine business, adjusting the hair, applying eye shadow, removing a splinter, approaching their lovers; then the kiss, the caress, the passionate love-making of first acquaintance, and the erotic experiments of a mature affection. Here there is love and beauty, passion and joy, instruction even and inspiration; but anything less sordid it is hard to imagine. One can only feel sorry for those generations of Europeans whose own sexual inhibitions prevented them from seeing it that way.

Captain Burt took particular exception to the fact that such sculptures should adorn a place of worship. It made the crime twice as awful. Since his day, many and ingenious have been the explanations for this: advertising the services of the temple courtesans, according to some, allegorizing the soul's longing for communion with the deity, according to others. Or was it to proclaim the vanity of human desires as compared to the inward peace of the temple's interior? Or, again, did it mean that Khajuraho had been a centre for Tantric worship's orgiastic rites? The question is still unsolved and none of these explanations makes much sense when faced with the experience of the sculptures themselves. The Indian artist, though never explicit in a representational sense, was rarely oblique or obscure. It is evidence that his art is still neither fully understood nor appreciated that one must ask, rather than insist, whether he simply wished to proclaim the supreme joy of carnal love. If this still seems out of place in a temple, perhaps the explanation should be sought not in the mind of the artist but of the observer.

CHAPTER NINE

Wild in Human Faith
and Warm in Human Feeling

In 1842 Lord Ellenborough, the most erratic and vainglorious of India's Governors-General, conceived the idea of restoring to the famous temple of Somnath in Gujerat its sandalwood gates. They had been taken to Afghanistan by that arch-vandal, Mahmud of Ghazni. Ellenborough's motives are never easy to determine, but perhaps he thought that such a gesture would help to legitimize the current British occupation of Afghanistan. He was reckoning, though, without Macaulay. It was bad enough that in the past British officers had helped restore the odd temple. 'We decorated the temples of false gods', he told the British parliament, 'we provided the dancing girls, we gilded and painted the images. ...' Now, to 'this most immoral of superstitions in which emblems of vice are objects of worship', Ellenborough was proposing to extend what amounted to official patronage. Worse still, Somnath was a Siva temple. Macaulay hoped there was no need for him to spell out to the House of Commons which 'emblem of vice' was sacred to Siva. 'I am ashamed to name those things to which he [Ellenborough] is not ashamed to pay public reverence.'

In the event the gates proved to be the wrong ones, and the whole idea was lost in the sudden and disastrous rout of the British forces in Afghanistan. But it is interesting that, though prepared to blacken every other aspect of Indian culture, Macaulay stopped short of directly attacking its architecture. Instead he preferred to savage Hinduism and, had the temple been a mosque, would no doubt have given Islam an equally rough ride.

For, as even he would have conceded, India's architecture was in a class apart. Here was one aspect of Indian civilization which the severest critic could not dismiss. Moreover, masterpieces like the Taj Mahal were barely 200 years old, and the lovely palace of Dig had been built within the last century. The theory that Indian culture had been steadily declining for the last millennium – applied so freely to sculpture and literature – obviously did not hold. But why not? The first thing that struck the traveller in India was its extraordinary variety of architectural styles. For example, a south Indian temple of the twelfth century bore no resemblance to a contemporary temple at, say, Khajuraho in central India, or Mount Abu in the west, or Orissa in the east. Likewise, it was extremely difficult to distinguish any chronological development of styles. A prominent feature like the curvilinear tower suddenly appeared from nowhere – no debut as a small protuberance on the roof steadily evolving into the massive superstructure that characterizes the Orissa temples. Instead, it is first found as a fully developed architectural feature.

The bulbous dome too, an equally distinctive feature, this time of Islamic architecture, suddenly appeared from nowhere. Only in this case there was an obvious explanation: the dome might not in fact be Indian. Mohammedan conquerors must have brought the idea with them from Persia or Central Asia. How much more, then, of Islamic architecture, and in particular the celebrated Moghul style, was of alien origin? And could there be some similar explanation for the innovations and variations in pre-Islamic architecture? In short, to what extent were India's monuments testimony to indigenous civilization and products of native craftsmen?

Questions like these much exercised Alexander Cunningham, but by the 1860s a somewhat unlikely amateur had already made the subject peculiarly his own. James Fergusson, the son of an Ayrshire doctor, joined the family firm in Calcutta in the late 1820s. The firm was on the brink of financial disaster and Fergusson, promptly and wisely, left it to start an indigo business in Bengal. Indigo, a dye made from the leaves of a type of pulse, was, along with opium, the boom crop of the early nineteenth century. Fergusson rapidly made a fortune. Equally rapidly, he developed an interest in architecture, embarked on a series of architectural rambles, and within ten years retired to England.

Bishop Heber, touring India in the 1820s, had formed no good opinion of planters in general and indigo planters in particular. They were 'largely confined to Bengal and I have no wish that their numbers should increase'. Their behaviour was a frequent source of scandal, as much for their notoriously oppressive handling of Indians as for their loose living. Many were Scots, most drank and a good few perpetuated the eighteenth-century custom of keeping native mistresses. They were an embarrassment to the British administration, and their contribution to the study of India's past was negligible.

James Fergusson may well have been an outstanding exception, but the planting fraternity was certainly an unlikely spawning ground for an art historian. He seems to have had no contact with Prinsep and the Calcutta orientalists. Highly self-disciplined, brilliantly self-taught, and latterly somewhat self-opinionated, he approached the confusion of India's monuments like a high-powered executive determined to instil method and logic into the operation of some ailing conglomerate. Schliemann, the explorer of Troy and himself a classic example of the self-made man, dedicated his great work on Tiryns to Fergusson as 'the historian of architecture, eminent alike for his knowledge of art and the original genius that he has applied to the solution of some of its most difficult problems'.

Such a vast subject as the classification of India's architecture was, anyway, beyond Cunningham: he was too busy fending off railway contractors, marching and counter-marching, and forever obsessed with the Buddhist legacy. 'The old campaigner' was, moreover, far too disorganized, a victim of his years, of the depth of his scholarship and of his too close affection for the wide open plains of the north. What the subject needed was a trouble-shooter, a man who could seize on essentials, was not afraid to generalize, not ashamed to improvise; and in Fergusson it got just that. No individual could hope to visit every monument in India, so Fergusson took a short cut. He embraced the latest technology and collected photographs. On his own travels he had used the 'camera lucida' as an aid to making a quick sketch; as soon as photography proper had caught on in India – in the late 1850s – he started accumulating prints. While Cunningham sat at his camp table in a cloud of mosquitoes defending his weatherworn notebooks from the rapacious Indian crows, Fergusson sifted his crisp photographs in a London town house within easy reach of libraries and museums. His forum was not the now persecuted Asiatic Society in Calcutta (recently renamed, and thereby demoted, as the Asiatic Society of Bengal) but the Royal Asiatic Society, its increasingly prestigious London equivalent.

Through much travel and study, Fergusson was soon an equally esteemed authority on the architecture of Europe, Egypt and the

Middle East. It lent much weight and respectability to his Indian studies, and enabled him to place India's monuments in a world perspective. Cunningham had lived and worked too long in north India and Burma; he scarcely acknowledged the existence of architecture in areas, such as the south, where Buddhism had never established itself. But no one could accuse Fergusson of parochialism. Furthermore, he was not bound by any ties of loyalty to the government of India. Cunningham could be scathing enough about individual acts of vandalism: a District Collector who was in the habit of removing local antiquities to his personal collection came in for a vicious broadside when he made off with a pillar of the Gupta period.

> Mr Broadley has omitted to mention two facts which, I believe, may be ascribed partly to his ignorance and partly to his modesty. To the first I should attribute his having fixed the pillar on its brick pedestal *upside down*, in spite of the two Gupta inscriptions. . . . To the second I would ascribe his neglecting to mention that in his anxiety to leave evidence of his own rule in Bihar, he had the whole of the uninscribed surface of the pillar covered with a rudely cut inscription, in which his name figures twice. . . . How fortunate it is that Mr Broadley did not remain long enough to leave more 'evidence of his rule' in other parts of India.

But as an officer and employee of the government of India, Cunningham had to moderate his tone when protesting against official indifference and vandalism. Not so Fergusson. He berated Anglo-Indian officialdom, and especially the military, whenever opportunity offered. He even took the Archaeological Survey to task. Cunningham's obsession with inscriptions often blinded him to more obvious indications of date, his drawings were frequently inaccurate, his reports disorganized and his architectural theories ill-formed.

Needless to say, Cunningham replied in kind. 'My friend, Mr Fergusson,' he called him but there was little love lost between the two Scots. Fergusson's first works were on the rock-cut temples and on the sculptures of Sanchi and Amaravati. Cunningham soon had the measure of his scholarship; the man could not read a single Indian script so no wonder he had got the dates of all these monuments wrong. Dating by architectural styles was all very well, but it could only work when much more was known about them. Meanwhile it was safer to stick to Prinsep's method based on the scripts.

The controversy thus sown would soon have ample grounds on which to flourish. In 1855 Fergusson published *The Illustrated Handbook of Architecture in all Ages and Countries*. A sequel followed in 1862, and both works were revised in 1867 as *A History of Architecture in All Countries from the Earliest Times until the Present Day*. This immediately became a standard work and the second edition, published in 1876, included a whole volume on *The History of Indian and Eastern Architecture* with 700 pages and 400 illustrations, most of them devoted to India itself. Fergusson was nothing if not thorough. He had a note of every known building, including 900 cave temples, and his photographs now covered '3000 Indian buildings, with which constant use has made me as familiar as with any other object that is perpetually before my eyes'. Many sites, especially in Mysore, owe their fame to Fergusson's discrimination; though not one was his discovery. Although well aware that many buildings might yet remain to be discovered, the idea of archaeological exploration did not appeal to him.

His job was simply to analyse and classify; and the *History of Indian and Eastern Architecture* represents the first and by far the most important attempt to present a comprehensive survey of this truly monumental subject. Starting with the Ashoka pillars, Fergusson displayed the whole dazzling panorama of Indian building through 2000 years. He did so with much erudition and ingenuity, yet managed to keep the subject well within the grasp of the general reader.

> My endeavour from the first has been to present a distinct view of the general principles which have governed the historical development of Indian architecture ... [and] I shall have realized a long cherished dream if I have succeeded in popularizing the subject by rendering its principles generally intelligible, and thus ... assisted in establishing Indian architecture on a stable basis so that it may take its true position among the other great styles which have ennobled the arts of mankind.

Popularizing the subject meant making aesthetic rankings: the tomb of Sher Shah at Sassaram was an outstanding example of 'a royal tomb of the second class' (whatever that meant). Likewise Indian architecture as a whole was not on a par with that of Greece or Rome. One of the principles to which he constantly returned was that 'for an exuberance of fancy, a lavishness of labour and an elaboration of detail' it was unrivalled. It was also still a living art. Ernest Havell would find much to criticize in Fergusson's pontifications but he could only approve when Fergusson compared 'the perfect buildings which the ignorant, uneducated natives of India are now producing' with 'the failures the best educated and most talented architects in Europe are constantly perpetrating'.

But perhaps his most curious observation was that 'there is no country where the outlines of ethnology as applied to art can be so easily perceived'. Indeed, according to Fergusson, ethnology held the key to the understanding of the subject. His classifications would obviously depend to some extent on dates, locations and religious associations, but basically Fergusson proposed that the variations in Indian styles of building had something to do with the variety of racial groups that constituted the Indian people. Hence there was Dravidian architecture, Indo-Aryan architecture, Pathan architecture, Moghul architecture and Rajput architecture. All these terms had to be racial— neither regional nor chronological. Even two further classifications, Buddhist and Jain architecture, were not to be regarded simply as religious definitions. For Fergusson contended that Buddhism and Jainism had been adopted by a particular race or group of races, the Dasyus or aboriginal inhabitants. Indeed, it was one of the 'principles of the scientific study of Indian architecture' that these Dasyus, together with the Dravidian races of south India and latecomers like the Pathans and the Moghuls, had between them been responsible for all India's monuments.

On the other hand, the Aryan people, who with their wealth of Sanskrit literature were usually credited with being the cultural and religious trail-blazers of Indian civilization, had made no contribution at all. (The term Indo-Aryan as applied to one of his classifications was simply for convenience; he would have preferred 'Dasyu' but admitted that to most people that would be meaningless.) The oldest Aryan writings, the Vedas, contained no mention of temples, and it had long been something of a mystery that the oldest and holiest cities of north India, Benares and Allahabad, had not a single building more than 500 years old. Cunningham, of course, believed that these places had once boasted temples aplenty, but that they had all been destroyed by the iconoclastic Mohammedans. This was certainly true of Delhi where an inscription recorded that the Qutb mosque had been constructed out of the ruins of twenty-seven temples. But it was odd that in Benares, of all places, there was nothing to testify to an ancient building tradition. Fergusson preferred to assume that this meant that there had never been one. He was inclined to be less harsh on the Mohammedans: Europeans had been equally destructive, and the Hindus, by their neglect and indifference, probably more so than either. But all these factors together could hardly account for there being not a single inscribed stone or mutilated statue of pre-Islamic provenance in the whole of Benares.

Given, then, the Aryan people's lack of interest in any durable kind of architecture, it was not surprising that the great centres of Hindu building were not in the Gangetic plain (where the Aryans had originally settled) but around its perimeter and in peninsular India. Allowing for a few maverick aberrations, and excluding the caves, Fergusson divided his photographs of temples into three main groups – Dravidian, Chalukyan and Indo-Aryan. In describing each of these he selected a simple prototype and traced its stylistic development towards what he regarded as the noblest or best known example of the style.

The Dravidian temples of the extreme south posed the most difficult problem, because they were neither integral buildings nor had much in the way of history. Most had been built within the last 400 years, some within living memory. They were the largest and most imposing temples in India. Yet, 'the fact is that, in nine cases out of ten, Dravidian temples are a fortuitous aggregation of parts, arranged without plan, as accident dictated at the time of their erection'. They were not single buildings, but sprawling congeries in which the main shrine was lost amidst a warren of passages, pillared halls, courtyards, bazaars and bathing pools. Cities within cities, their distinctive architectural feature was not in the temple itself but in the walls that surrounded it and, above all, in the gigantic *gopurams* or gateways.

If the *gopurams* of Madurai, Tanjore, Kanchipuram – Fergusson knew of more than thirty examples – had been a few centuries older they would have ranked with the pyramids as architectural curiosities. Towering hundreds of feet above the flat coastal plains, like the sacrificial towers of some Rider Haggard kingdom, they had attracted the attention of all the early travellers and surveyors, and had been much painted by artists like the Daniells. But Fergusson was one of the first to suggest that, across a gap of perhaps 800 years, they were a development of a style first seen in the *raths* or boulder temples of Mahabalipuram. The rectangular pyramidal shape, the multi-storeyed construction, now adorned with tier upon tier of sculpture, and the barrel-shaped roof, were all anticipated in the little Ganesa *rath* and the larger Arjuna.

Where such structures stood in the architectural hierarchy Fergusson was not sure. The French in the eighteenth century had used the temple walls as fortifications and, later, British surveyors had found the *gopurams* convenient eminences on which to mount their theodolites. But whether their original purpose amounted to any more than a labour-intensive endowment programme seemed doubtful. Fergusson considered that the people of south India, the Dravidians, were devoid of noble feelings: 'their intellectual status is, and always has been, mediocre'.

> All that millions of hands working through centuries could do, has been done, but with hardly any higher motive than to employ labour and to conquer difficulties, so as to astonish ... and astonished we are; but without some higher motive, true architecture cannot exist. ... Much of the ornamentation, it is true, is very elegant, and evidences of power and labour do impress the human imagination, often even in defiance of our better judgement, and nowhere is this more apparent than in these Dravidian temples. It is in vain, however, that we look among them for any manifestation of those lofty aims and noble results which constitute the greatness of true architectural art, and which generally characterize the best works of the true styles of the Western World.

Similar criticisms applied to what Fergusson dubbed the Chalukyan style, although in this case the ornamentation was used to far greater architectural effect. The three classic examples of the style were at Belur, Somnathpur and Halebid. All these places were tucked away in a remote tract of the native state of Mysore, which explained why the style was little known compared with the others. Fergusson did not discover this style, of course, but he deserves much credit for bringing these magnificent buildings to public attention.

As opposed to the rectangular ground plan of both Dravidian and Indo-Aryan temples, the Chalukyan was invariably star-shaped. But a still more distinctive feature of the style was its layered horizontality. Deep cornices line the several façades with strong bands of light and shade; innumerable friezes, steps and ledges continue this effect down to ground level; the whole structure is stretched upon a dead flat expanse of stone terrace, itself lined with more friezes and cornices.

The effect is further emphasized by the fact that the Halebid and Belur temples have flat roofs. Fergusson thought that they should have had low pyramidal towers, like those at Somnathpur, but that for some reason the temples had never been finished.

Maybe, but there was nothing unfinished about the ornamentation. If the ancient Buddhists were inclined to treat sandstone like wood, the Chalukyans (Fergusson considered them a race rather than just a dynasty) treated their distinctive black schist, or potstone, like lace.

> The amount of labour, indeed, which each face of this porch [at Belur] displays is such as, I believe, never was bestowed on any surface of equal extent in any building in the world; and though the design is not of the highest order of art, it is elegant and appropriate, and never offends against good taste.

From the brackets hidden beneath the great roof cornices to the toe-level elephant frieze, and including the elaborately fretted windows, every surface was alive with carving 'of marvellous elaboration and detail'. Every deity in the Hindu pantheon is supposed to be represented at Belur – and most of them many times over. There must be more than 500 elephants in the bottom frieze alone.

Moving to the double temple at Halebid, Fergusson's dismissive attitude began to crumble. Here the elephant frieze was 710 feet in length and 'containing not less than 2000 elephants, most of them with riders and trappings sculptured as only an oriental can represent the wisest of brutes'. Above this was a frieze of lions, then a scroll 'of infinite beauty and variety of design', then a frieze of horsemen, another scroll, and a colossal relief, 700 feet long, of scenes from the *Ramayana*. Above this were beasts and birds, another frieze, an elaborate cornice, windows of pierced slabs of stone, and panels of sculpture. On one side, in place of the windows, there was a frieze of Hindu deities, each five feet six inches high and extending to 400 feet. It included at least fourteen Siva and Parvati groups and considerably more Vishnus.

> Some of these are carved with a minute elaboration of detail which can only be reproduced by photography, and may probably be considered as one of the most marvellous exhibitions of human labour to be found even in the patient East. It must not, however, be considered that it is only for patient industry that this building is remarkable. ... The variety of

outline, and the arrangement and subordination of the various facets in which it is disposed, must be considered as a masterpiece of design in its class. The artistic combination of horizontal with vertical lines, and the play of outline and of light and shade, far surpass anything in Gothic art. The effects are just what the medieval architects were often aiming at, but which they have never attained so perfectly as was done at Halebid.

Fergusson contrasted the Halebid temple with the Parthenon. The one was the absolute antithesis of the other, and all the world's architecture fell somewhere between these two poles. The Parthenon was a product of the intellect, calculated with mathematical precision to such a degree of exactness and complexity that it passed into artistic perfection. Halebid was the exact opposite.

All the pillars of the Parthenon are identical, while no two facets of the Indian temple are the same; every convolution of every scroll is different. No two canopies in the whole building are alike, and every part exhibits a joyous exuberance of fancy scorning every mechanical restraint. All that is wild in human faith and warm in human feeling is found portrayed on these walls, but of pure intellect there is little.

There was more intellect in the soaring outline of the third temple style, what Fergusson called Indo-Aryan although now more commonly known as the Northern or Nagara style. The distinctive feature of this style was the *sikhara*, the curvilinear tower or spire, and there lay Fergusson's biggest problem. 'I have looked longer, and perhaps thought more on this problem than on any other of its class connected with Indian architecture.' But he had found no certain solution. Its forms varied from an almost straight-sided pyramid in some of the earliest examples, to a shape like a bishop's mitre, to the soaring Gothic pinnacles of Khajuraho, to something more like a full-blown pine-apple at Bhuvaneswar. The curvilinear tower was as much the glory of Hindu architecture as the dome was of Mohammedan buildings. Yet where had the idea come from? Fergusson explored several possibilities in vain. He was convinced, though, that it was a purely Indian invention. Indeed, it could only be handled effectively by Indian craftsmen, because only they could bestow on its blank faces the ingenuity in ornamentation needed to break them up and lighten the effect.

Khajuraho's temples were a good example, but Fergusson had never been there and was loth to place too much confidence in Cunningham's descriptions. Instead, he concentrated on the other major temple complexes of north India, at Puri and Bhuvaneswar in Orissa.

> The outline of this temple [the Great Temple or Linga Raja at Bhuvaneswar] is not, at first sight, pleasing to the European eye; but when once the eye is accustomed to it, it has a singularly solemn and pleasing effect. ... Taking it all in all it is perhaps the finest example of a purely Hindu temple in India.

The Khajuraho temples' tapering profiles are certainly more acceptable to tastes tutored on the Gothic arch and the spire: at a considerable distance the Khandariya Mahadeo could almost pass muster as a village church. The Orissa temples, though, are very different. Their porches have tiered pyramidal roofs with upturned cornices suggestive of a Chinese pagoda. And the *sikharas* of the Linga Raja and Rajrani are so elaborately vaned and ribbed that to the unprepared traveller they look as if they belong in an electricity generating station. Fergusson had spent most of his Indian career in Bengal and knew Orissa well. He had verified that every single stone in the Linga Raja's tower had a pattern carved upon it, and that the sculptures were 'of a very high order and great beauty of design'. In short, his eye had become accustomed to it and it therefore outraged his sense of 'true architecture' far less than, say, the *gopurams* of a Dravidian temple.

This, however, was not quite the same thing as taking Indian architecture at its Indian value. For Fergusson, as for Macaulay, Hinduism was still 'the most monstrous superstition the world has ever known'. He made no attempt to master the symbolism and iconography of Hindu temples, and took his stand simply on what he regarded as the universal values of architecture. This dispassionate outlook eased the business of classification and his three temple styles (Dravidian, Chalukyan and Indo-Aryan), though much subdivided, are still accepted today. But one can understand how irritating such pontifications must have been to Alexander Cunningham, whose scholarly bent precluded all aesthetic judgements. Havell, too, rightly insisted that Fergusson's 'true styles of architecture', 'true principles' and 'universal values' were nothing of the sort. They were just a rationalization of his European outlook.

Of the many specific points on which Cunningham and Havell took issue with Fergusson, none proved more contentious than the origin of the arch in India. Moving on from Hindu architecture to Mohammedan – or, as he preferred, 'Saracenic' – Fergusson stated categorically that 'the Hindus up to this time (about AD 1100) had never built arches'. He qualified this by explaining that he was talking about the 'true' arch – one constructed by using wedge-shaped stones, or voussoirs, to achieve the bend, and with a key-stone at the apex. The ancient Hindus had, of course, built small trabeate arches which used brackets and cantilevers to span the gap; but the true, voussoir arch was a purely Mohammedan invention.

Cunningham was at first inclined to accept this. When, in the walls of the great temple at Boddh Gaya, he found some voussoir arches and vaults (now built over) he agreed with Fergusson that this proved that the main structure of the building could not be older than the fourteenth century. But Cunningham later found several other examples of the true arch in buildings that had apparently existed at the time of Hsuan Tsang in the seventh century. By 1870 he realized that Fergusson must have got it wrong again, and in 1892 the old General, now well into his eighties, published a volume re-examining the history of Boddh Gaya.

> Formerly it was the settled belief of all European enquirers that the ancient Hindus were ignorant of the arch. This belief no doubt arose from the total absence of arches in any of the Hindu temples. Thirty years ago I shared this belief with Mr Fergusson ... but during my late employment with the Archaeological Survey of India several buildings of undoubted antiquity were discovered in which both vaults and arches formed part of the original construction.

Cunningham listed three or four examples and showed that the Boddh Gaya temple, though rebuilt more often and more extensively than any other building in India, dated from the fifth century. He was still unsure whether the arches were part of the original building, but they were certainly earlier than the Mohammedan conquest.

Havell agreed and took the argument still further. Concentrating on the pointed arch, which was the hallmark of Islamic buildings, he claimed that not only had the ancient peoples of India known all about it, but the West, and Islam, had originally got the idea from India. A horseshoe arch with a point to it was a characteristic feature on the façades of Buddhist cave temples and a simple pointed arch was found on the image niches that ringed some of the Gandhara *stupas*. When Buddhism, under the Kushans, spread west into Afghanistan, the arch went with it and thus came to the notice of the Arabs. Havell pointed to the façade of St Mark's in Venice, which has a very Buddhist-looking arch, as an example of this East-West trend. But his ideas were highly conjectural. His concern was to stem the tide, to redress the balance; people like Fergusson put far too much in Indian culture down to outside influences. Havell wanted to show that India probably gave as much as she got.

A site which spawned as much controversy and heart-searching as Boddh Gaya was the well known Qutb mosque and minar outside Delhi. In the early nineteenth century the Qutb Minar was considered one of the wonders of the East, second only to the Taj Mahal. It looked even higher than its 250 feet because of the exaggerated tapering and with its elaborate fluting and magnificent symmetry, it seemed the noblest possible monument to the victory of Islam in India. Today our tastes have been somewhat warped by familiarity with industrial shapes. The Qutb Minar has an unfortunate hint of the factory chimney and the brick kiln; a wisp of white smoke trailing from its summit would not seem out of place. But to Fergusson and his generation no praise was too extravagant for it.

> It is not too much to assert that the Qutb Minar is the most beautiful example of its class known to exist anywhere. The rival that will occur at once to most people is the Campanile at Florence, built by Giotto. That is, it is true, thirty feet taller, but it is crushed by the mass of the cathedral alongside; and beautiful as it is, it wants that poetry of design and exquisite finish of detail which marks every moulding of the Minar; ... when viewed from the court of the mosque its form is perfect, and, under any aspect, is preferable to the prosaic squareness of the outline of the Italian example.

Universal as was the praise, it was not at all clear who had built it or whether it could be attributed to Islam. Fergusson placed it firmly in his first category of Saracenic buildings. 'Early Pathan' he called it, although the dynasty that included Qutb-ud-din was Turkish and, as Havell observed, the Pathans were not, and never had been, notable builders. But semantics apart, Fergusson saw it as a classic example of how the lofty ideals of a conquering race, which was already imbued with strong architectural instincts, could exploit the consummate skills of the Indian craftsman and produce something way beyond the latter's limited imagination. In other words, Indians provided the skills and the decoration but foreigners the ideals and the design.

Cunningham, though, was not so sure. As well as numerous inscriptions there was also a wealth of literary evidence for the Qutb. One work put the beginning of the Minar in the reign of the last Hindu ruler of Delhi. Others suggested that the building and rebuilding – the Minar was very susceptible to earthquakes – had gone on over a period of 150 years, and that the top two sections were not added until the fourteenth century. In Volume One of the Archaeological Survey's reports he finally dismissed the idea that the original plan was pre-Mohammedan – only to find his assistant readopting the idea in Volume Four. A hasty retraction was extorted from the unfortunate Mr Beglar, but it showed that the origins of the building were still not a foregone conclusion.

What bothered Beglar and Cunningham was that, for a group of buildings supposedly celebrating the triumph of Islam, there was so little about them that could be called Islamic. The mosque consisted of a courtyard and colonnade, in which the columns were all purloined from Hindu or Jain temples, and in which the most conspicuous object was the famous iron pillar, dating from the Gupta period and celebrating the success of an ancient Hindu dynasty. Even the magnificent arches, though massive even by Islamic standards, were built according to the traditional trabeate design of India. On these, and on the Minar, the ornamentation was typically, and superbly, Indian, while the star-shaped ground plan of the Minar was strongly reminiscent of that of a Jain temple. Indeed, the very idea of victory columns was an Indian one and dated back to the Ashoka columns. There was just not enough in the way of innovation to support Fergusson's hypothesis of a blast of new and nobler ideals somehow releasing Indian architecture from its obsession with ornament and relaunching it onto a higher plane. Apart from the introduction of Koranic graphics in place of animal friezes, the absence of all figure sculpture, and the adoption of massive archways, the buildings were purely Indian.

A hundred years, and three miles, separate the Delhi of Qutb-ud-din (1206–10) from that of Tughluk Shah (1325–51), another of the early Sultans. But in architectural terms they are poles apart. The fortified city of Tughlakabad, and the tomb of its founder, have the cold and uncompromising air of a stern and alien autocracy. The city walls are more than six feet thick, with loopholes and battlements, and are built from some of the most massive stones ever used for constructional purposes. A similar wall surrounds Tughluk's tomb, which has sloping sides emphasizing its indestructibility. All is plain, rough-hewn, solid, making it in Fergusson's view 'the model of a warrior's tomb hardly to be matched anywhere'. Fergusson called this style Late Pathan and thought it marked the final emancipation of Islamic ideals from their initial flirtation with Hindu skills and tastes.

> The Mohammedans had worked themselves entirely free from Hindu influence.... All the arches are true arches; all the details invented for the place where they are found ... and from this time forward Mohammedan architecture in India was a new and complete style in itself, and developed according to the natural and inevitable sequences of true styles in all parts of the world.

These sequences are often expressed in biological terms, as a budding, a flowering and a decay. The Late Pathan was the Saracenic style in the bud, the early Moghul period until the death of Shah Jehan its classical flowering, and the late Moghul period from Aurangzeb onwards its rococo decadence. In this 'natural sequence' the only exception according to Fergusson was the reign of Akbar (1556–1605). He alone of all the Moghuls showed a spirit of tolerance towards the non-Islamic peoples and a willingness to adopt their artistic ideas. Hence the many Hindu features in his palaces at Fatehpur Sikri and Agra, the reappearance of the trabeate arch, fantastically carved brackets, ornate pillars and the peculiar snake-like struts so beloved of the Jains. These buildings were truly Indian, but Akbar was the exception. 'The spirit of tolerance died with him,' wrote Fergusson. 'There is no trace of Hinduism in the works of Jehangir or Shah Jehan.'

Unlike Fergusson, Cunningham was not greatly interested in Islamic architecture. He had reservations about Fergusson's various styles, but he never propounded any grand theory about the relationship between Hindu and Mohammedan styles. Not so, though, Ernest Havell. Whereas Fergusson saw the story of Islamic architecture as one of emancipation from Hindu influences, Havell insisted that, on the contrary, it was one of rapid capitulation to the superior indigenous art of India. Akbar was not the exception but the classic example. His wholesale adoption of Hindu styles and his patronage of Indian craftsmen marked the end of a brief experiment with non-

Indian forms (Tughluk's tomb for example), and the beginning of one of the greatest periods for purely Indian building.

Taking the bull firmly by the horns, Havell turned to the classic age of Moghul architecture, the reign of Shah Jehan (1628–58), and in particular to none other than the Taj Mahal. The great dome of subtle contour, the soaring minarets, the formal Persian garden, the chaste inlay work and tracery, the clustered cupolas – nothing, surely, could be more typically Mohammedan. But Havell was a determined polemicist and a uniquely qualified scholar. His first point was that whatever its inspiration, 'there is one thing which has struck every writer about the Taj Mahal and that is its dissimilarity to any other monument in any other part of the world'. Outside India there was nothing that approached it and, within India, its supposed precursor, Humayun's tomb in Delhi, or the other two white marble tombs, those of Itimad-ud-Daula in Agra and Salim Chishti at Fatehpur Sikri, were so inferior as to be unworthy of comparison.

Fergusson would have agreed with this, though not with Havell's conclusion – that what made the Taj unique was its sculptural quality. Because for this there was no precedent in the strictly non-representational art of Islam. If the inspiration for the building was to be sought in sculpture rather than architecture, then it must be sought in Indian sculpture. The purity of line and subtlety of contour which characterized it were precisely the qualities that distinguished the Mathura Buddhas or the Khajuraho *apsaras*. Fergusson deplored the hint of effeminacy in Shah Jehan's buildings; but to many this represents the great appeal of the Taj. As the tomb of Shah Jehan's beloved Mumtaz Mahal, it is the apotheosis of Indian womanhood, a radiant architectural embodiment of all that is feminine, India's Venus de Milo perhaps. And only an Indian artist with his purely conceptual approach could have created a building that was so blatantly seductive.

It was a measure of the Taj's uniqueness that some even suggested that its designer might have been one of the Europeans employed by Shah Jehan. This idea was, of course, anathema to Havell. It was just another example of foreigners trying to find a non-Indian inspiration for anything in Indian culture that took their fancy. Examining the literary evidence in some detail, he concluded that even the inlay work – cornelian and agate stones embedded in the white marble in the most delicate of floral designs – was not, as was generally thought, of Italian origin. It was true that the *pietro duro* work of Florence was much in fashion at the time, but mosaic inlays had been used in India for centuries: James Tod had mentioned a Jain temple of the fifteenth century with something similar. Besides, the records showed that the inlay artists employed on the Taj were all Hindus.

The gardens, too, which add so much to the staging of the Taj, were the work of a Hindu, from Kashmir. But on this point Havell was prepared to give ground. There was no Indian tradition of formal gardens, divided and subdivided with geometrical precision by neat paths and water courses. From the pools of dense shade to the gay parterres and the gurgling fountains, this was an oasis legacy, the expression of a hard, warrior people's longing for luxury and physical indulgence, a place in which to forget the austerities of the Central Asian deserts and dally with Omar Khayyam and a long glass of sherbet.

Undoubtedly the siting of the Taj Mahal has a lot to do with its unique appeal. The shady gardens and reflecting water-courses, the flanking buildings in sober red sandstone, the dark frame of the great gateway and the backdrop of the Jumna river – all combine to make the sudden sailing into sight of the white marble mirage a dramatic experience. But it was the building itself that Havell was most interested in. He had studied the *silpa-sastras* – the traditional manuals of the Hindu builder – and believed that even the bulbous dome conformed more closely to Indian ideals than those of Samarkand. There was even a sculptural representation of such a dome in one of the Ajanta cave temples. Moreover, the internal roofing arrangement of four domes grouped round the fifth, central, dome conformed exactly to the *panch-ratna*, the 'five jewel' system so common to Indian buildings of all sorts.

All this was not enough in itself to shake traditional views, but Havell was not finished. In the nineteenth century, as now, people were inclined to concentrate too much on the buildings of Delhi and nearby Agra. For most, the Pathan and Moghul styles were the sum total of Islamic architecture, because they were the ones represented in Delhi and Agra. Fergusson, of course, knew better, and devoted considerable attention to the Islamic buildings of Gujerat, Bijapur, Gaur and elsewhere. But he made no attempt to fit these into his 'natural sequence' of Saracenic architecture; they were simply provincial styles, of considerable merit but no lasting significance. Havell, though, examined them much more closely and became convinced that, away from the political turmoil of north-west India, the architectural continuity before and after the Mohammedan conquest was unbroken; and that it was from these provincial centres that the ideals and craftsmen used by Shah Jehan had been drawn. In Gujerat some of the mosques of the first Mohammedan dynasty are indistinguishable from temples; also in Gujerat, white marble had been used extensively by both Hindu and Jain. On the other side of India, at Gaur in Bengal, the Mohammedans inherited the brick building tradition of the Hindu capital that had occupied the same site. Here there were exceptionally versatile masons, familiar with the voussoir arch. The extent to which they were subsequently employed throughout the Moghul empire can be judged by the ubiquity of curved Bengali roofs – even in the Red Fort at Agra. At Bijapur the Mohammedans also inherited a local building tradition, for nearby lay the great Hindu capital of Vijayanagar. European accounts of Vijayanagar before its destruction only hint at its architectural wonders, but certainly the dome and the pointed arch were in general use. It was no coincidence that the great building period in Mohammedan Bijapur began immediately after the fall of Vijayanagar. Encouraged to concentrate on the dome, the erstwhile Hindu architects produced first the Bijapur Jama Masjid and then the giant Gol Gumbaz with one of the largest domes in the world. According to Havell, it was on the skills of these master dome builders that Shah Jehan drew for the Taj Mahal.

In all this there was much speculation. It was fifty years since Fergusson had first put pen to paper, yet new material was still being 'religiously docketed and labelled according to his scheme'. In showing that he could have been wrong about the inspiration behind Moghul architecture, Havell sought to question the whole basis of his work. 'The history of architecture is not, as Fergusson thought, the classification of buildings into archaeological water-tight compartments according to arbitrary ideas of style, but a history of national life and thought.' Its object should be the identification 'of the distinctive qualities which constitute its Indianness, or its value in the synthesis of Indian life'.

This was certainly asking too much of a nineteenth-century art historian. But it was true enough that any scheme of classification must have its faults; and the greatest casualty of Fergusson's was the secular architecture of India. His classifications related primarily to religious buildings, to temples, tombs and mosques. Palaces, forts and public works were tacked onto his various classifications with little regard for their style. Hence the Rajput palaces, arguably the most

'If our poets had sung them, our painters pictured them, our heroes lived in them, they would be on every man's lips in Europe.' Thus, with good reason, wrote E. B. Havell of the much neglected forts and palaces of the Rajputs. In his drawing of Amber (*above*) Bishop Heber strove to convey the impression of 'an enchanted castle'. Gwalior (*below*), 'the Gibraltar of India', furnished the inspiration for the Moghul forts of Agra and Delhi. (Watercolour by Francis Swain Ward, c. 1790.)

To the Islamic architecture of Delhi, the British responded with good intentions marred by questionable taste and occasional spite. The Qutb mosque (*above*) was ably landscaped but its famous *minar* was crowned with a 'silly' pavilion that 'looked like a parachute'. In Old Delhi, Shah Jehan's Jama Masjid was carefully repaired in the 1820s but very nearly blown up by way of reprisal after the 1857 Mutiny.

The tomb of Humayun in Delhi (*above*) anticipates the Taj Mahal in Agra (*below*). In the late eighteenth century, travellers found the Taj well-endowed and much revered; but Humayun's tomb stood neglected and anonymous amidst a wilderness of ruins. The preferential status of the Taj, 'the gateway through which all dreams must pass', was proudly maintained by the British, although not without reservations about whether such a masterpiece could really be Indian.

opposite: Acquired by the Victoria and Albert Museum in 1910, the Sanchi torso owed its celebrity to its supposedly classical modelling. As an example of 'Indo-Grecian art of the 1st century AD' it was one of the few Indian sculptures to win aesthetic approval. Yet, it has now been shown to date from the tenth century AD, a period once dismissed as artistically decadent.

No event contributed more to the European acceptance of Indian art than the discovery of the caves of Ajanta (*right*). Containing the finest gallery of wall paintings (*below*) to survive from any ancient civilization, they were quickly acknowledged as 'the greatest artistic wonder of Asia'. Sadly, attempts to preserve them have done more harm than good. (*right:* drawing by Jas. Burgess of a scene depicting 'The Temptation' in Ajanta Cave XXVI.)

General Sir Alexander Cunningham spent much of his career and all of his long retirement tramping across India in search of its Buddhist past.

Colonel James Tod, historian and champion of the Rajputs, who also brought to notice the Jain temples of Mount Abu and amassed a collection of coins from which the history of western India was largely reconstructed. 'In a Rajput I always recognize a friend.' (Rajput miniature from Udaipur.)

Colonel Colin Mackenzie employed Indian scholars to search out historical materials. The Mackenzie collection of manuscripts, inscriptions and coins is still the best archive for reconstructing the history of peninsular India. (Portrait by Thomas Hickey.)

left: B. H. Hodgson, for fifty years the doyen of British Indian scholars, and 'the highest living authority on the native races of India', spent most of his life in the Himalayas living like an Indian sage.

right: Sir George Everest, most cantankerous of Surveyors-General, who completed the south-north triangulation of the subcontinent, also extended his measurements along the Himalayas enabling the first accurate triangulation of their peaks. The highest was named after him.

E. B. Havell, the principal of the Calcutta School of Art, rejected received ideas about the Indian artist and championed the notion that his art was based on conceptual rather than representational ideals. (Portrait by one of his pupils.)

Sir William Jones was 'the father of Oriental studies'. His discoveries in philology, history and literature provided the first evidence that India boasted a classical civilization to rival those of Greece and Rome.

Lord Curzon, Viceroy of India 1898 – 1905, was the first to acknowledge that India's architectural heritage constituted 'the greatest galaxy of monuments in the world', and that its maintenance and restoration should be an imperial responsibility.

To the discovery of India's past was added a proto-historical dimension with the twentieth century excavation of an urban civilization dating from 2500 – 1500 BC. The 'Harappan' or 'Indus Valley' culture, although widespread and highly sophisticated (witness the statuette of a 'dancing girl', *left*), is likely to remain somewhat enigmatic until the pictographic script (as found on steatite seals, *below*) can be read.

impressive and certainly the most romantic group of buildings in India, were sandwiched incongruously between the latest and least distinguished Indo-Aryan temples and a preamble on the earliest Saracenic buildings. Subsequent works, following Fergusson's scheme, often relegate them to an appendix. For, as Havell rightly observed, there could be no argument that in secular architecture the styles of Hindu and Mohammedan, of Rajput and Moghul, were one and the same. Moreover, the origins of this style were wholly Indian. Witness the great fifteenth-century Man Singh palace in the Gwalior fort. 'One of the finest specimens of Hindu architecture that I have seen ... the noblest specimen of Hindu domestic architecture in northern India,' noted Cunningham. Babur, the first of the Moghuls, evidently agreed. His official diary shows that he admired and coveted this building above all others in India. In due course it became the inspiration for all the palaces of the sixteenth and seventeenth centuries, for the Moghul forts of Delhi and Agra as well as for the Rajput forts of Orchha, Amber and Jodhpur.

> If our poets had sung them [wrote Havell of the Rajput palaces], our painters pictured them, our heroes and famous men had lived in them, their romantic beauty would be on every man's lips in Europe. Libraries of architectural treatises would have been written on them.

Bishop Heber had been equally impressed when he toured the palace of Amber a century earlier.

> I have seen many royal palaces containing larger and more stately rooms – many the architecture of which was in purer taste, and some which have covered a greater extent of ground – but for varied and picturesque effect, for richness of carving, for wild beauty of situation, for the number and romantic singularity of the apartments, and the strangeness of finding such a building in such a place, I am unable to compare anything with Amber. ... The idea of an enchanted castle occurred, I believe, to all of us, and I could not help thinking what magnificent use Ariosto or Sir Walter Scott would have made of such a building.

Even Fergusson was not blind to the romantic appeal of the Rajput palaces. He praised their settings and lack of affectation. But there was no room for them in his scheme of things.

There are some twenty or thirty royal residences in central India, all of which have points of interest and beauty; some for their extent, others for their locality, but every one of which would require a volume to describe in detail.

He contented himself with a description of only the more obvious examples – Gwalior, Amber, Udaipur and Dig – and could only mention the two great palaces of Orchha and Datia. Havell went into more detail, noting the way these buildings seemed to grow organically out of the rocks on which they stood 'without self-conscious striving after effect'. Thus, above all, their romantic appeal; but there is also a grandeur and an elegance of detail beside which the Moghul palaces pale into mere prettiness. Here was Hindu architecture both more virile and more noble than its Islamic equivalent.

Sir Edwin Lutyens, the architect of New Delhi, thought the palace of Datia one of the most architecturally interesting buildings in India. It is also one of the most impressive. Conceived as a single unit, unlike the Moghul palaces, it towers above the little town of Datia like the work of an extinct race of giants. Each side is about 100 yards long and rises from the bare rock so subtly that it is hard to tell where nature's work ends and man's begins. The impression is of immense strength, and only the skyline of flattened domes and cupolas gives any hint of the treasures within. There, the first two storeys are dark and cool, hot weather retreats; then suddenly one emerges into the light and a fairyland of pillared walkways, verandahs and pavilions. Paintings and mosaics adorn the walls, and the verandahs are screened with several hundred feet of the most intricately fretted stone windows.

Datia was built by Rajah Bir Singh Deo in the seventeenth century. The palaces of Orchha were also his work, and here there are more painted halls and dappled pavilions as well as some of the finest carved brackets. But in this case the setting is one of ruination – miles of crumbling stables, overgrown gardens and forgotten temples. Somehow it seems more in keeping with these now forlorn masterpieces. Several thousand people a day visit the Moghul palaces of Delhi and Agra; scarcely a single soul disturbs the rats and the bats at Datia and Orchha. Havell's rhapsodies and Lutyens' admiration have changed nothing. It says much for the formative and lasting character of James Fergusson's work that they have yet to find their true place in the scheme of India's monuments.

CHAPTER TEN

A Subject of Frequent Remark

Sixty miles west of Datia and Gwalior, the long hill fortress of Narwar rises in shaggy scarps above scrubland. A neat white village nestles against its flank, from whence a broad path, paved with slabs of red sandstone, winds up the hill. The steps are shallow enough for cavalry to clatter up and down, and the cusped gateway at the top is big enough to admit an elephant. Today, only one leaf of the great studded door remains, leaning out precariously from a single hinge. The stately flight of steps beyond is spattered with cow dung, and vegetation sprouts from every crack in the stonework. To left and right on the level summit a scene of bewildering devastation unfolds. Trees grow through the masonry of nameless halls, their roots lifting the stone floors. A row of pillars leans sideways, like dominoes frozen in fall. In the prickly undergrowth a hole, no bigger than a rabbit's, reveals vaulted chambers black with bats. And in a sun-filled pavilion projecting out from the cliff-top, where the last of the mirror-work mosaic is flaking from the stucco, herdsmen bivouac amongst their flocks, the smoke of their fire blackening the painted ceiling, fragments of mirror-work crunching underfoot.

Narwar was a Rajput palace in the sixteenth century, and became one of the six great strongholds of the Moghuls in the seventeenth. It reverted to the Rajputs in the eighteenth, and was still in use at the end of the century. But by the time Cunningham visited it in 1864, it was deserted, with the vegetation already in control. Today, its interest lies in the fact that nothing much has ever been done to preserve it: it remains much as it was 100 years ago. Real ruins, those that have escaped the attentions of the archaeologist and the conservationist, have a special appeal. The past seems to cling more closely to them. At

Narwar nature, and not tourism, has taken over. Lizards scuttle across the white marble of the royal bathrooms, and a vulture poses, wings draped, on the highest cupola. Here, away from the manicured lawns and the two rupees admission charge, one senses the romantic beauty of sheer desolation and the very real excitement of archaeological discovery.

In the nineteenth century the neglected state of sites like Narwar was the rule rather than the exception. Thomas Twining, the young man who was privileged to dine with Sir William and Lady Jones in Calcutta, visited Agra and Delhi in the 1790s.

> As we advanced [into Delhi] the ruins became more thickly scattered around us, and at length covered the country on every side as far as the eye could see. Houses, palaces, tombs, in different stages of delapidation, composed the striking scene. The desert we had passed was cheerful compared with the view of desolation now before us. After traversing ruined streets without a single inhabitant for a mile, I saw a large mausoleum at a short distance on our right. I made my way over the ruins towards it with a few of my soldiers, leaving the rest of my people on the road. Dismounting and ascending some steps, I came upon a large square terrace flanked with minarets, and having in the centre a beautiful mausoleum surmounted by an elegant dome of white marble. I had seen nothing so beautiful except the Taje Mehal. It was in vain to look about for someone to gratify my curiosity. The once most populous and splendid city of the East now afforded no human being to inform me what king or prince had received this costly sepulchre. . . . But the name of 'Humayun' in Persian letters of black marble, which chance or respect had preserved untouched, made it probable that this was the tomb of this excellent monarch.

It was indeed the tomb of Humayun, son of Babur and second of the Great Moghuls. But so little cherished was this masterpiece of Moghul architecture, then only 300 years old, that even its identity had become a matter of conjecture.

Within a decade of Twining's visit the British were established in Delhi. This in itself was no guarantee of a more enlightened policy towards ancient monuments. But the Islamic monuments of Agra and

Delhi were safe enough from the terrible depredations of the railway contractors. Their varying fortunes in the nineteenth century had far more to do with swings in official policy.

At first the British Resident and his staff in Delhi were much in awe of their surroundings. The ruins of all those old Delhis – Indraprastha, the Qutb, Tughlakabad, Ferozabad – were poignant reminders of the transitory nature of dominion. Even in Shahjehanabad (the Old Delhi of today) the signs of decay were already there. A Moghul emperor still lived in the Red Fort, the court ritual was still minutely observed. But the reality of power and the sources of wealth had passed away. The imperial treasury was being milked by several hundred dependent relatives and favourites; the palace itself was becoming a shanty town for all these scroungers. In 1825 Bishop Heber found the Diwan-i-Am, the colonnaded audience hall, choked with lumber, and the imperial throne so deep in pigeon droppings that its mosaics were scarcely visible. Pipal trees were sprouting from the walls of the little Pearl Mosque and in the Diwan-i-Khas, or private audience chamber, half the precious stones in the floral inlays had been prised from their white marble setting. 'All was desolate, dirty and forlorn', and in the formal gardens 'the bath and fountain were dry, the inlaid pavement hid with lumber and gardener's sweepings, and the walls stained with the dung of birds and bats'.

The Bishop's next port of call was Agra. As he approached the city he passed by the massive tomb of Akbar at Sikandra, 'the most splendid building in its way that I have seen in India'. Unlike the other Moghul tombs, Akbar's has no central dome and consists of five diminishing storeys bristling with little domed *chattris*. Fergusson, pursuing his theory that Akbar alone adopted Indian architectural styles, would suggest that it derived from the lay-out of a Buddhist monastery. Its other distinguishing feature is a colossal gateway with towering minarets at each of its four corners. According to Twining the top sections of all these minarets had snapped off 'having been struck and thrown down by lightning'; but by the time of Heber's visit money had been granted for repairs and an officer of Engineers was already on site.

The 1820s saw the first spurt of energy in this direction, and in Delhi, too, efforts were being made to restore some of the more important buildings. As Garrison Engineer between 1822 and 1830, Major Robert Smith was the man chiefly responsible. He was an artist of repute and a great admirer of Moghul architecture. One of his first

assignments was to repair the Jama Masjid, the great mosque built by
Shah Jehan. Its skyline is one of the most dramatic in India and it was
the massive dome that, according to a contemporary, most needed
Smith's services.

> The dome had several trees growing out of the joinings in the
> stones, and parts of the back wall had fallen down, and had
> been taken away by some heathen Hindoo to make himself a
> tenement; this part was also repaired. Major Smith is particu-
> larly well qualified for the charge of restoring such magnifi-
> cent relics of art, as much by his exquisite judgement and taste
> in the style of the works, as his acknowledged professional
> talents, which place him amongst the foremost of his com-
> peers.

No doubt emboldened by this success, Smith moved on to the Qutb
Minar. But here, inexplicably, that 'exquisite taste and judgement'
seemed to desert him. In 1803 the building had been seriously damaged
by an earthquake: some of the balustrades were shaken loose, the
main doorway collapsed and, worst of all, the crowning cupola fell
off. Smith's job, as well as clearing and landscaping the whole site,
was to make good this damage. A sketch that had appeared in an early
number of the Asiatic Society's Journal purported to show the original
cupola; Smith rejected this as too much like 'a large stone harp'.
Instead, he produced his own design – an octagonal stone pavilion,
above the dome of which there was to be a smaller wooden cupola
and on top of this a short flagstaff.

The work had barely started when Bishop Heber visited the site and
delivered his oft quoted dictum 'These Pathans built like giants and
finished their work like jewellers.' (He was wrong of course: the
builders of the Qutb were not Pathans; the giants were Turks and the
jewellers Indians.) But by 1829 Smith's work was finished and was
immediately greeted by a storm of protest. 'A silly ornament like a
parachute, which adds nothing to the beauty of the structure,' thought
one observer. According to another, the pavilion made the whole thing
look top heavy and the wooden cupola was like 'an umbrella of
Chinese form'. The Governor-General was more upset about the
flagstaff, 'an innovation which whether viewed as a matter of taste, or
with reference to the feelings of the Moghul court or population of
Delhi, has little to recommend it'.

Smith hit back. The emperor liked the flagstaff, especially since his own flag was flown from it. As for the pavilion, there was no telling precisely what the original had looked like. Moreover, the whole tower was a hotch-potch of inconsistencies, having been built by three different sovereigns and already extensively repaired. His design for the pavilion and cupola was wholly authentic – very similar to the decorative arrangements found on the roof of the nearby tomb of Safdar Jang.

This explanation can have convinced no one. The tomb of Safdar Jang is generally cited as a good example of what happened to the Moghul style when it went to seed. Ornate, florid even, and of a particularly sickening colour of sandstone ('too much the colour of potted meat', thought Bishop Heber), it was an odd model on which to base the restoration of one of the earliest and most admired examples of Islamic architecture.

Perhaps to spare Smith's feelings, no official action was taken; but the wooden cupola was not to last long. 'The lightning struck it off, as if indignant at the profanation.' It was not restored, and in the 1840s, with Smith gone to England, the stone pavilion was quietly moved to the gardens, as a summer-house.

Alexander Cunningham first visited the site in 1839, after the wooden cupola had fallen but while the stone pavilion yet remained. 'The balustrades of the balconies and the plain slight building on the top of the pillar do not harmonize with the massive and richly ornamented Pathan architecture,' he noted in his diary. He thought Smith's repairs were admirably executed, but the restorations were lamentable. It was not only the crowning pavilion that was wrong. Smith had also added balustrades where they were missing and had redesigned the fallen entrance. He should simply have repaired the original entrance but, in his own words, he had 'improved it with new mouldings, frieze and repair of the inscription tablet'. The result, about which Fergusson and Cunningham were for once in complete agreement, could best be described as 'in the true style of Strawberry Hill Gothic'. The flimsy balustrades were 'an even greater eyesore, as they form a permanent part in every view of the building'. Cunningham recommended that they be replaced with something more in the massive style of the Tughlakabad battlements. Smith's balustrades might then be 'sold with advantage in Delhi as they belong to the flimsy style of garden-house architecture of the present day'.

Much more successful was Smith's landscaping of the whole site. The Qutb, like so many of India's monuments, was being ransacked by curio hunters and taken over by squatters. Clapboard hovels and hessian lean-tos buttressed the walls of the great mosque; occasional visitors filed off specimens of the iron pillar and made off with the broken capitals. By clearing the whole site, laying out lawns, and providing for gardeners and caretakers, Smith anticipated the work of the twentieth-century Archaeological Department.

His success can be measured by the decision of the Resident, Sir Thomas Metcalfe, to establish his country residence beside the gardens. For the purpose, Metcalfe conceived the macabre idea of adapting an old Mohammedan tomb, leaving the ground floor with its sepulchre untouched, but converting the next floor and verandah into living apartments, and the grand hall beneath the inevitable dome into a dining room. From this bizarre mansion his daughter would escape into the Qutb itself.

> The grounds on which the pillar and ruins stood had been laid out ... as a beautiful garden and the place was kept scrupulously clean and in excellent repair. ... Many a time have I, with Colonel Richard Lawrence, taken a basket of oranges to the top of the Qutb pillar to indulge in a feast in that seclusion, but we were careful to bring down all the peel etc. as nothing disorderly was allowed within the precincts of those beautiful ruins and buildings.

Robert Smith's other works included some repairs to Shah Jehan's Red Fort. Besides the imperial apartments and the halls of audience, so vividly described by Heber, the fort included a small garrison of troops nominally under the command of the emperor, but recruited and commanded by a British officer. For their protection, and because the place was still considered to be of strategic value, Smith was ordered to repair the walls and to clear the ground in front of them, a task which he apparently carried out with an admirable mixture of military zeal and architectural sensitivity. Otherwise little was done to what Fergusson called 'the most magnificent palace in the East, perhaps in the world'. With the emperor and his entourage still in residence, it was not directly a British responsibility. In the 1830s the first great blast of British vandalism, fired by Macaulay's rhetoric and fanned by financial retrenchment, left the palace untouched. The emperor was refused the pension he thought necessary for the maintenance of the buildings but there was no attempt, as at Agra, to sell off their assets.

The second wave of anti-Indian vandalism came with the Mutiny of

1857. This time neither Delhi, the scene of British carnage and Indian resistance, nor the emperor, considered one of the leading conspirators, was spared. The ransacking of the city when it finally fell, the looting of the imperial palaces, and the desecration of the mosques, form one of the blackest chapters in the history of Anglo-Indian relations. A proposal to raze the whole of Old Delhi was eventually rejected, but within the Red Fort only 'isolated buildings of architectural or historical interest' were preserved. About half the entire complex, including the extensive zenana quarters and the beautiful colonnaded gardens, were simply blown up and replanned as barracks.

> The excuse for this deliberate act of vandalism [wrote Fergusson] was, of course, the military one, that it was necessary to place the garrison of Delhi in security in the event of any sudden emergency. Had it been correct it would have been a valid one, but this is not the case. ... The truth of the matter appears to be this; the engineers perceived that by gutting the place they could provide at no trouble or expense a wall round their barrack-yard, and one which no drunken soldier could scale without detection, and for this, or some such wretched motive of economy, the palace was sacrificed! The only modern act to be compared with this is the destruction of the summer palace at Peking. That, however, was an act of red-handed war, and may have been a political necessity. This was a deliberate act of unnecessary vandalism – most discreditable to all concerned in it.

Even the few architectural gems which were officially reprieved were not exempted from the attentions of looters and prize-agents. The white marble Diwan-i-Khas had already been deprived of the Peacock Throne by the Persian, Nadir Shah, in 1839, of its silver ceiling by the Marathas in 1760, and of much of its jewelled inlay by thieves, according to Heber. Now the kiosks of the four corners of the roof were stripped of their copper-gilt plating by a prize-agent who claimed that they were movable property. The marble paving in front of the building, and the colonnade that surrounded it, went the same way.

In the Diwan-i-Am, the inlaid panels behind the imperial throne were unique. They were of black marble and, since the central panel portrayed Orpheus and a group of animals, almost certainly the work of a European. Fierce must have been the competition to secure such gems. Captain (later Sir) John Jones was evidently first off the mark and, having prised the precious panels off the wall, had what Fergusson sarcastically called 'the happy idea' of setting his loot in marble surrounds as table tops. Two of these he brought back to England and then sold to the government for a not inconsiderable £500; they went on display at the Victoria and Albert Museum.

Meanwhile the Diwan-i-Am itself was turned into a military hospital. As further proof that the fort was now to be regarded solely as a military installation, the ground outside the walls was cleared to a distance of 500 yards. No doubt this action was prompted by memories of the siege of Lucknow; with a field of fire extending to 500 yards, a besieged garrison should be safe from snipers and sappers. How many buildings were thus demolished it is impossible to say; but the compensation paid out amounted to a staggering £90,000. At least one mosque disappeared; but then mosques were in a separate category. The more sacred a building, the more eligible it was for reprisal. Various ideas were entertained about the most suitable fate for the Jama Masjid. Some thought it should be blown up, others that it should be sold or converted into a barracks. A more ingenious idea was to turn it into a hall of remembrance for the victims of the Mutiny; the paving stones of the great courtyard were to be inscribed with the names of all the Mutiny martyrs (British only, of course). But luckily no decision was reached. Five years later passions had died down sufficiently for it to be quietly returned to the Mohammedans of Delhi.

Other mosques had to wait considerably longer. The Fatehpuri Masjid remained in the hands of the unbelievers till the 1870s and the Zinat-ul-Masjid, after a chequered career as a private house and a military bakery, was eventually returned to its congregation by Lord Curzon in 1903. Curzon also managed to restore the gardens of the Red Fort and to get back the black marble table tops from the V & A. With the help of drawings prepared by Major H. H. Cole in the 1880s, and using the services of a specially commissioned Italian mosaicist, the panels were restored to their original position in the Diwan-i-Am in 1909. Cole would have been delighted, for it was he, above all others, who first brought the deplorable state of the palace buildings to official attention. The ceiling of the Diwan-i-Khas was as much a scandal as the missing marbles of the Diwan-i-Am. In honour of a visit by the Prince of Wales it had been 'repainted in black, red and gold instead of the original pattern and the central rose converted into a sort of starved starfish, the effect being extremely harsh and glaring'.

Cole restored the original reds, blues and greens on a gold background and did away with the starfish.

Although designated Curator of Ancient Monuments, Cole, like Cunningham, was not directly responsible for conservation. His job, which lasted only four years, was simply to report on what needed doing and to encourage the local Public Works Departments to get on with it. Their co-operation could not always be counted on, and it is notable that his two major successes were at places where no such department existed. One was Sanchi, the other Gwalior.

Two hundred miles south of Delhi, and commanding the traditional route to the western sea-ports and the Deccan, Gwalior is all that a great natural fortress should be. It towers 300 feet above the plains with castellated walls that march along the contours and merge into the sheer rock faces. Palaces teeter on the brink of the abyss and massive gateways command the only points of access. For as long as history, this has been a place of immense strategic importance, and it was probably fought over more than any other hill on the subcontinent: since the thirteenth century it has changed hands more than twenty times and by the British alone it was stormed three times. Scattered about on the flat summit are Hindu temples, Jain caves, mosques and palaces, testimony to a long and unbroken record of civilization. If ever there was a site that deserved preservation and invited research, this surely was it.

Yet when Cole arrived there in 1881, the place was still neither celebrated nor cared for. Only Cunningham had really examined it. In 1844, long before he started the Archaeological Survey, he undertook, at his own expense, some repairs to the larger of the two beautiful Sas-Bahu temples.

> I found the sanctum empty and desecrated, and the floor of the ante-chamber dug out to a depth of fifteen feet in search of treasure. This hole I filled up; and I afterwards propped up all the cracked beams, repaired the broken plinth, and added a flight of steps to the entrance, so that the temple is now accessible and secure, and likely to last for several centuries.

This probably saved the structure of the building, although it remained for Cole to rediscover its sculptures beneath the smothering of plaster administered by some zealous Mohammedan.

Gwalior was both beautified and desecrated by the Mohammedans. Jehangir and Shah Jehan added palaces to those of the previous

Rajput owners, but their ancestor, Babur, was the man responsible for disfiguring the Jain statues. Admittedly, the full frontal nudity and colossal dimensions of these rock-hewn figures positively invited the attention of iconoclasts. On the other hand, they proved fully a match for the most zealous hammer and chisel: Babur had to rest content with removing more than a hundred sets of genitalia plus a mixed bag of noses, toes and ears.

No doubt the pounding of cannon during successive sieges also took its toll of the fort's antiquities. But it was the brief period during which British troops occupied the place that inspired Fergusson to deliver one of his most damning attacks.

> We have ruthlessly set to work to destroy whatever interferes with our convenience, and during the few years we have occupied the fort, have probably done more to disfigure its beauties and obliterate its memories, than was caused by the Mohammedans during the centuries they possessed or occupied it. Better things were at one time hoped for, but the fact seems to be, the ruling powers have no real heart in the matter, and subordinates are allowed to do as they please, and if they can save money, or themselves trouble, there is nothing in India that can escape the effect of their unsympathetic ignorance.

Gwalior's misfortune was the same as Delhi's: it was taken over by the mutineers in 1857 and its guns were turned upon the British. Its fate, too, was the same – the billeting of a garrison in its palaces and the establishment of a large barracks at the foot of the fortress.

For his information, Fergusson relied heavily on the French traveller, Louis Rousselet, who visited the fort in the 1860s.

> The English [wrote Rousselet] are busily employed reducing the need for archaeology and obliterating this precious source of Indian history. Already all the buildings to the left of the east gate have been reduced to rubble and the same fate is reserved for the rest ... even for the Jain sculptures. When I returned in December 1867, the trees had been cut down, the statues shattered by workmen's picks, and the ravine filled with rubble for a new road being built by the English – rubble in which lay the palaces of the Tomars and the Chandelas [Rajput clans], the idols of the Buddhists and the Jains.

Rousselet was indulging in gallic overstatement, but Cole's sober report of 1880 was no more reassuring. A concrete parade ground now stretched over the rubble to the left of the main gate. The buildings on the right had been spared, but the first, the glorious Man Singh palace, was being used for the commissariat stores. Its two little courtyards, perhaps the most elegant of their kind, had been whitewashed and split up by hideous partitioning. Next door, in the Karan palace, the domed Bara-dari, so much admired by Babur, was being used as the mess. 'I regret to report,' wrote Cole, 'that travellers have removed stone carvings, pieces of coloured tile work, and other fragmentary relics, whilst a few years ago whole columns were taken to adorn gardens in Morar [the barracks], and stones found their way to places even beyond.'

Fortunately Cole's visit coincided with the first pangs of remorse. The British Resident was anxious to make amends and Major Keith of the Royal Scots had been sent to restore what he could, working under Cole's direction. With a grant of £100 from regimental funds, he had just rescued the Teli-ka-Mandir, a ninth-century temple of particular interest in that it failed to conform to any of Fergusson's classifications. One thing about it, though, was certain: it was not meant to be a coffee shop. Major Keith found alternative premises for the regimental elevenses, and set about clearing the place up.

At Cole's suggestion, the temple's precincts were turned into a rough and ready museum where all the statuary and carvings that still littered the fort could be collected together and protected. The most touching relic there is the gateway, a curious monument in that it was painstakingly constructed by Keith from the carved fragments of buildings which fellow comrades-in-arms had destroyed only twenty years before. His penance also included clearing the Man Singh palace of the partitioning, carefully scrubbing off all the whitewash, and ensuring that no more of the beautiful tiling on the outer walls was removed. Six years later the British garrison was withdrawn from Gwalior, and the fort once again became the responsibility of the local maharajah.

The tragedy of both Delhi and Gwalior was that their forts also contained their palaces; the British found it difficult, or simply inconvenient, to distinguish between the two. The same was true of Allahabad. Not only was the Ashoka pillar knocked down to make way for fortifications, but the fort's most precious structure – the Pavilion of the Forty Pillars – was also demolished, 'its materials being wanted to repair the fortifications'. Another pillared building, also from Akbar's reign and known as the Zenana Hall, was spared – only to be turned into an arsenal. The intervals between the pillars were bricked up and, in Fergusson's day, 'whatever could not be conveniently cut away is carefully covered up with plaster and whitewashed, and hid by stands of arms and deal fittings'.

And it was the same story at the Agra fort. There the magnificent Diwan-i-Am became the arsenal and 'was reduced to as near a similarity as possible to those in our dockyards'. The Akbari Mahal became the prison, and the Salimgarh kiosk a canteen. At least one of the white marble pavilions facing the river – perhaps that from which the imprisoned Shah Jehan had gazed forlornly downriver to his Taj Mahal – was commandeered as an officer's quarters. With the marble and its delicate floral inlays liberally coated with whitewash, it was considered a house of elegant simplicity.

Sir John Strachey, Governor of the North-West Provinces in the 1870s, changed much of this. A plaque, discreetly sited in Shah Jehan's palace and dated 1880, was set up by Lord Lytton to commemorate his conservation work. It specifically mentions only the Taj Mahal, although Fergusson reports that his work was concentrated on the fort. Here the worst abuses were rectified, and the first tentative steps at restoration made.

Across the Jumna and somewhat upstream, lies the tomb of Itimad-ud-Daula, another gem of white marble and mosaics. In it Major Cole, who was more used to dealing with Indian squatters than Europeans, found a party of British officers comfortably ensconced. True to type, they too had covered the walls – and especially the magnificent paintings – with regulation whitewash. Cole got them expelled, removed their various partitions and doors, and prepared the most elaborate diagrams to show how the paintings should be restored.

Whether the Taj Mahal was also the victim of such tasteless and irreverent treatment is by no means as clear as one would expect. Lord Curzon, in bestowing upon India's best known building the full weight of viceregal patronage, painted the most lurid picture of past transgressions. English picnickers had been known to 'while away the afternoon by chipping out fragments of agate and cornelian from the cenotaphs of the emperor and his queen'. Drinking parties were given in the gardens and balls on the marble terrace; the *jawab* to the east of the tomb (matching the mosque to the left) was rented out to honeymooners, and the minarets were much in demand for suicides. One can imagine the empty champagne bottles bobbing about in the fountains, an orchestra thumping away in the recessed *liwan*, and a lovelorn subaltern enjoying a cheroot on the tomb of Shah Jehan.

No doubt there was some truth in all this. The gardens were certainly used for picnics and functions; that, after all, was what they were built for. Similarly the *jawab* was intended as accommodation for visitors. It was here that young Thomas Twining had stayed in the 1790s.

> In the evening I walked about the noble terrace and luxuriant gardens of my charming residence, of which I seemed to be the master, for the *derwan* and his men, who had accompanied me from the outer gate, having returned to their post, I saw nobody belonging to the place except a few gardeners among the orange trees. I also rambled about every part of the Taje itself, enjoying a feast that seemed too great for me alone. ... Nothing in architecture can well exceed the beauty of this structure viewed from my pavilion at the corner of the grand terrace.

The deep respect shown by Twining may be regarded as more representative than the acts of vandalism mentioned by Curzon. Moreover, this respect was more than matched by official concern for the fabric of the building. Even in the eighteenth century there were evidently arrangements for its maintenance. William Hodges mentioned that the revenue of certain lands was set aside for the purpose; and another artist, Thomas Daniell, found the building 'in very good repair' in 1788, although the following year the cullice was struck down by lightning and the dome also received 'material injury'.

As well as the earthquake which damaged the Qutb Minar, 1803 saw the capture of Agra by the British. The Taj must have suffered too, and it is probable that the loosening of some of the marble sheets on the dome resulted from this convulsion. By 1810 the situation was serious enough for the Governor-General, Lord Amherst, to call for a report on 'the nature and extent of the repairs which the Taj may require with a view to its being preserved in that perfect state which the reputation of the British government and a regard for the feelings of the population demand'. The committee responsible was in being for fourteen years, and presumably made good the earthquake damage. Certainly Bishop Heber found both building and gardens 'kept in excellent order by government' in the 1820s. According to Emma Roberts, who visited Agra five years later, the bishop had been too ill to appreciate all its beauties; she thought Agra the loveliest city in India and contrasted the considerable government expenditure on the Taj Mahal with the neglect of the city's other monuments.

In 1838 Mrs Postans reported that the Taj 'is a gem of too great value for the British government to lose, and a sum is set aside for the purposes of its repair and preservation'. A similar verdict was reached by the American, Bayard Taylor, in the 1850s: 'the building is perfect in every part. Any delapidations it may have suffered are so well restored that all trace of them has disappeared.' And, perhaps most convincing of all, that severest of critics, James Fergusson, could find no fault with the official attitude to this '*chef d'oeuvre* of Shah Jehan's reign'.

> The Taje Mahal ... has been fortunate in attracting the attention of the English, who have paid sedulous attention to it for sometime past, and keep it now, with its gardens, in a perfect state of substantial repair.

It is thus curious to find, in a recent work on the Taj, the assertion that it was woefully neglected in the nineteenth century, indeed all but dismantled. This startling accusation evidently stems from the notorious efforts of Lord Bentinck, Governor-General in the early 1830s and the patron of Macaulay, to balance the books of the Honourable East India Company. It is true that the marble floor of the bathroom in Shah Jehan's palace in the Agra fort was dug up and auctioned. The bath itself had been removed by one of Bentinck's predecessors, who intended it as a present for George IV. Bentinck thus vandalized an apartment that was already imperfect. Moreover, when the auction proved a dismal failure, the idea of further sales was promptly dropped. But, even if it had been a success, it seems highly improbable that Bentinck would have turned his attentions to the Taj Mahal. And there is certainly no evidence that wrecking crews were already poised to commence operations. Insensitive and arrogant as they undoubtedly often were, the *sahibs* recognized that what Kipling called 'the ivory gate through which all dreams pass' was in a class apart. They admired it unreservedly; indeed, loved it.

This could be said of no other building in India and by the 1890s, in spite of Fergusson's fulminations, in spite of the valiant efforts of Cole and those of a few enlightened Governors like Strachey, India's architectural heritage was a source of shame and embarrassment. 'The means, or rather want of means, taken for the preservation of India's monuments must be a subject of frequent remark,' warned the 1894 edition of Murray's *Handbook for Travellers in India*. All too often the sporadic attempts at conservation, forced on the government by outside pressures, had been left to local Public Works Departments, whose efforts had frequently proved 'seriously injurious to the monuments'. Cunningham's Archaeological Survey had been too academic, Cole's Curatorship too short-lived and ill-funded; it was time to think again.

In 1899, Lord Curzon, the newly-arrived Viceroy, made a speech to the Asiatic Society in Calcutta in which he reviewed the government's archaeological record in terms that must have gladdened the heart of every orientalist.

> There have been periods of supineness as well as activity. There have been moments when it has been argued that the state had exhausted its duty, or that it possessed no duty at all. There have been persons who thought that, when all the chief monuments were indexed and classified, one might sit with folded arms and allow them slowly and gracefully to crumble into ruin. There have been others who argued that railways and irrigation did not leave a modest half lakh of rupees [£3750] per annum for the requisite establishment to supervise the most glorious galaxy of monuments in the world.

Before the year was out Curzon had submitted to London proposals for the reorganization of the almost defunct Archaeological Survey as an Archaeological Department under a Director-General. The responsibility for the exploration, study and conservation of India's monuments was now to be an imperial one as opposed to a provincial one; and the sum of at least £7500 was to be made available from central funds to supplement the contributions of the provincial authorities. The scheme was approved in 1901, and in 1902 John Hubert Marshall, a Cambridge graduate who had been taking part in the Minoan excavations in Crete, arrived as the new Director-General. He was just twenty-six years old and he was to hold the post for twenty-six years.

A law for the protection of ancient monuments had to be drafted, the staff of the new department, including an increasing number of Indian scholars, recruited and trained, and the excavation of selected sites pursued and publicized. But the main preoccupation of both Curzon and Marshall was to provide for a thorough, systematic and continuous scheme of conservation. An idea of the scope of the task can best be gained from what was actually achieved during the first five years.

In the south, the main problem was the vegetation. Numerous sites, including the vast spread of Vijayanagar, were cleared and opened up with paths and approach roads. The temples here, as well as the Kailasanatha at Kanchipuram, were restored, although most of the Dravidian shrines were still in use and maintained by their own Brahmins. In western India, Curzon won the support of the Jains for the careful conservation of the Mount Abu temples, and in Bijapur, Ahmedabad and Burhanpur, structural repairs were made to many of the principal Mohammedan buildings. On the other side of the country, the first serious attempt was made to rescue the site of Gaur from complete obliteration by the jungle; in Bhuvaneswar, those temples not still in use were repaired and protected. At Konarak, the Black Pagoda was treated to preserve it from the ill effects of sea salt. In the process of removing the rubble and sand from its base the famous sculpted wheels and horses were unexpectedly uncovered. They confirmed that the temple must have been planned as a sun chariot. The wheels are some of the most intricately carved objects in the whole of India, and it was the massive strength of the horses that convinced Havell that the Indian sculptor could handle martial themes just as effectively as he could religious ones.

In central India the ruins of the Mohammedan cities of Dhar and Mandu were opened up and partly restored. With the co-operation of the local rajah, Khajuraho's temples were also overhauled and the jungle cut back. But central India was still largely in the hands of native rulers. The Archaeological Department could advise and prompt them, but the initiative and expense must be theirs. A now-famous site like Gwalior was well maintained; others, like Narwar, received only scant attention.

Diverse as was the Department's work, it was the Moghul buildings of north-west India by which its performance was inevitably judged. These therefore received minute attention. In Lahore, much patron-ized by Jehangir, the wall built round the Pearl Mosque when it was used as a treasury was demolished, Jehangir's tomb overhauled, and several other monuments freed of recent tasteless additions. In Delhi, besides the renovation of the 'Pathan' tombs of Tughluk and the Lodi kings, the Red Fort was reinstated as a monument rather than a barracks. Recent military buildings were torn down, the rubble of the

Mutiny reprisals was cleared away, and the famous Diwan-i-Am marbles were in the process of being restored.

Outside Agra, the minarets of Akbar's tomb at Sikandra, broken since before Twining's visit, were at last rebuilt; within the city, the work of Strachey and Cole was continued. In the fort, more military structures were removed to reveal the full glory of the Diwan-i-Am's colonnade, the river front of the so-called Jehangir's Palace (it was built by Akbar according to Cunningham) was completely rebuilt, and the paintings and mosaics of Itimad-ud-Daula's tomb were restored.

And then there was the Taj Mahal. 'If I had never done anything else in India, I have written my name here, and the letters are a living joy', declared Lord Curzon. He personally took the deepest interest in its conservation and he presented the building with the magnificent lamp, made in Cairo, which now hangs beneath the central dome. But it is notable that Marshall found little on the tomb itself that required attention. He refaced and restored the *jawab* where Twining had stayed, and rebuilt sections of the garden walls; but his main achievement was in completely overhauling the red sandstone buildings round the forecourt outside the main gate and along the approaches to it. Then there were the gardens. Curzon himself had a passion for Moghul gardens, and at the Taj, as in the forts of Agra and Delhi, at Humayun's tomb and at Akbar's tomb, detailed consideration was given to their planting and maintenance. Trees that had outgrown their beauty were felled and others planted, the beds were filled with flowers and the lawns carefully trimmed; the pools and water-courses were repaired, the fountains made to play. It was no longer the wild orange grove of Twining's day; a degree of formality was restored and the gardens made to complement the architecture rather than defy it.

Horticulture and landscaping were subjects particularly dear to the English heart. The opening of vistas, the massing of foliage, and the banking of colour were things they understood perhaps even better than the Moghuls. Here was an area in which British taste and expertise could do more than just restore old glories. While the precise geometry of the original was carefully observed, and its formal lay-out restored, a more daring use of foliage and colour was introduced with a more varied and exciting scheme of planting. The Taj Mahal today is a more overwhelming experience than ever. In no small measure this is due, not just to the blending of Indian and Islamic ideals, but also to the incorporation of a peculiarly British feeling for the relationship between art and nature.

CHAPTER ELEVEN
Hiding Behind the Elgin Marbles

In February 1824, at the time when Robert Smith was drawing up his design for the Qutb Minar and Bishop Heber embarking on that mammoth tour of his diocese, a young lieutenant in the 16th Lancers was enjoying some well earned leave in western India. Instead of the flesh-pots of Bombay, Lieutenant James Alexander had opted for a spot of rough shooting in Berar, on what was then the frontier between British territory and that of the Nizam of Hyderabad. Like most frontier regions it was a wild and little visited area. The hilly country, broken up with deep ravines, provided perfect cover for tigers, then as numerous as foxes.

Should he escape the tigers, Alexander was warned that 'the stony-hearted Bhils' would surely get him. An aboriginal tribe every bit as wild as the tigers, the Bhils with their bows and spears had made the few roads perilous ever since the days of Ashoka. Alexander was taking no chances: he made a point of camping in the villages, and it was at a little place called 'Adjunta' that he first heard of ancient caves. In such a wilderness, any evidence of civilization or antiquity was enough to stimulate the curiosity. Next day, at dawn, Alexander was in the saddle and, with the help of a guide, heading for the hilly country above the Tapti river.

After travelling some distance along a stony road and passing several cairns, near which were many bushes covered with rags, pointing out the spot where unfortunate travellers had been destroyed by tigers, we suddenly found ourselves at the top of the precipitous *ghat* or pass. The scene which now opened upon us was magnificent in the extreme. The vale of Candesh was stretched beneath our feet, extending far into the blue distance, and enclosed by wooded mountains. Jungles, small lakes and streams scattered in every direction diversified the face of the valley. . . . Directing our steps towards an opening in the deeply serrated hills we arrived at the *debouche* of the glen, . . . when a low whistling was heard above us to the left, and was quickly repeated from the opposite cliffs. This proved to be the Bhils intimating to one another that strangers were approaching. The guide evinced strong symptoms of fear; but on being remonstrated with, and encouraged with the hope of a handsome present, he proceeded onwards. Some of the Bhils showed themselves, peeping out from behind the rocks. They were a most savage looking race, perfectly black, low in stature and nearly naked. ... Our firearms prevented them from approaching us and we proceeded unmolested.

The glen up which our road lay almost to its termination, where the caves are situated, was remarkable for its picturesque beauty. It continued winding amidst the hills, which rose from the banks of the stream with considerable acclivity, and having their sides clothed with scattered jungle. The hills now began to close in their wild and romantic features upon us and it was with no common interest, and with my expectations intensely excited, that I viewed the low-browed entrance to the first cave.

In all there were some twenty-nine caves strung out along the sheer rock face. Many had elaborately sculpted and pillared entrances like the well-known excavations at Elephanta. But as he rummaged through them, Alexander was at first disappointed. The sculptures could not compare with Ellora: there were fewer figures and they were altogether less elaborate. On the other hand there were paintings – acres of frescoes covering the walls and ceilings – and these exceeded his wildest expectations.

In most of the caves, to compensate for the want of profuse entaille and sculptures, are paintings in fresco, much more interesting, as exhibiting the dresses, habits of life, pursuits, general appearance and even features of the natives of India perhaps 2000 or 2500 years ago, well preserved and highly coloured, and exhibiting in glowing tints, of which light red is the most common, the crisp-haired sect of the Buddhists.

Alexander noted a number of 'spirited delineations' of battles and processions, and admired the portrayal of horses and elephants. But it is doubtful whether, in the poor light and with only a few hours to spare, he was able to take in much more. Sensibly he refrained from aesthetic or technical judgements; there was, after all, nothing with which he could compare his extraordinary discovery. He was also rather preoccupied.

> The fetid smell arising from numerous bats, which flew about our faces as we entered, rendered a continuance inside, for any length of time, very disagreeable. I saw only one cave with two storeys or tiers of excavated rock. In it the steps from the lower apartment to the upper had been destroyed by the Bhils. With our pistols cocked we ascended by the branch of a tree to the upper range of chambers; and found, in the middle of one of the floors, the remains of a recent fire, with large footmarks around it. In the corner was the entire skeleton of a man. On the floor of many of the lower caves I observed the prints of the feet of tigers, jackals, bears, monkeys, peacocks etc.; these were impressed upon the dust, formed by the plaster of the fresco paintings which had fallen from the ceilings.

Nothing more forcibly conveys the plight of India's heritage than this image of primitive tribesmen and wild beasts sheltering amidst the painted splendours of Ajanta. Here was one of the world's great treasure troves of art – the finest gallery of pictures to survive from any ancient civilization. One can only gasp at the idea of peacocks pecking at the dazzling colours, tigers padding softly through the pillared halls, and naked aborigines staring uncomprehendingly at these most aristocratic portrayals of courtly splendour and voluptuous luxury. Forgotten for over 1000 years, their preservation was as miraculous as their rediscovery was fortuitous.

Although Alexander's was the first account of Ajanta, it seems that the existence of the caves had been reported some five years earlier. Then as now, mention of cave paintings was not in itself enough to cause a stampede. Even after his report had been published, few went out of their way to visit Ajanta; and those that did were invariably taken by surprise. Instead of primitive daubings they found a truly classical art; instead of prehistoric hunting scenes, the most convincing and comprehensive depiction of civilized life in the ancient world.

Typical of the unsuspecting traveller's reaction is a wonderfully spontaneous report that Prinsep published in full in the Asiatic Society's Journal in 1836. It consisted of the notes made by a Mr Ralph, interspersed with the verbal comments of his friend, Captain Gresley, as they toured the caves. Actually written on the spot, the report has all the immediacy of a tape recording.

Ralph: These caves are daily becoming more difficult of access. You pass along narrow goat paths with a chasm of fifty or eighty feet below, the footing not nine inches broad, with scarce anything to cling to. ... One cave is inaccessible and several are approached at the risk of life.

Gresley: What a wonderful people these must have been! Remark the head-dresses. Now is this a wig or curly hair? These are chiefly domestic scenes – seraglio scenes; here are females and males everywhere, then processions and portraits of princes which are always larger than the rest. The subjects are closely intermixed; a medallion is twelve or fifteen inches in height; below and above, closely touching, are other subjects. I have seen nothing monstrous. No, certainly there is nothing monstrous except where we see some figure evidently designed for ornament, as in the compartments of the ceiling. The ceiling – aye, everything but the floor and larger statues, everything has been painted. It is done while the plaster is wet – it is fresco painting. I have seen the operation while going about in Rome.

Now, Ralph, look here; can you see this figure? No. Bring the torch nearer. Can you see it better now? Hardly. Let us light some dry grass. Bring grass now; place it here. Now watch while the light is strongest; you may see the whole figure. This is a prince or some chief. It is a portrait. Observe how well fore-shortened that limb is – yes, I can see it now; but throw water on it – now the colours are more vivid. Here is a lovely face – a madonna face. What eyes! She looks towards the man. Observe, these are all Hindu faces – nothing foreign. ... I wish I could make out this story; there certainly is a story. Here is a fair man of full age, dressed in a robe and a cap like some monk or abbot. Here is next to him a half naked Brahmin, copper coloured with shaven crown and single lock on his head. Here is a man presenting him with a scroll on which something is written. He is in a crowded court – he has come to an audience. What can all this be?

Ralph: This zodiac as they call it is very elaborate. ... I think this the best example in the whole series, and evidently done by the same painters who worked in what we call par excellence 'the painted caves'. These medallions in the roof are very handsome. I think they resemble compartments in a Turkey carpet, or what we see in a kaleidoscope – wreaths and coloured radiated patterns. Here are five women with their feet all towards the centre of the circle – their heads alone perfect. Are they angels? There are no winged and two-headed figures anywhere. The zodiac is incomplete. I think about a third of it is missing, and the lower part of the circle can never have been complete for it must have been over this door of the cell.

Gresley: Perhaps they covered the top of the doorway with something in order to complete the circle.

Ralph: You admire it so much you are willing to suppose it must have been complete.

Gresley: What a lovely female! Yes, the last one we discover seems always the sweetest. Here is another heavenly face. This man is her lover – a handsome fellow. You have his profile looking to the left. How eager – how full of ardent desire. The woman has just turned her face towards him, and looks with timid satisfaction and self-approving coquetry. It is excellent. But here is another beauty – she is entreating; her head is turned towards someone above. Is she supplicating or in prayer? Shame to the villains who have destroyed these paintings.

These must have been convents and these paintings to attract the multitude at festivals and to bring pilgrims from afar ...

Ralph: The fewer theories you form, the fewer blunders and dreams you will make.

Gresley: We must form theories – we cannot remain awake and not do so.

Ralph's pet theory was that the Ajanta cave temples, like those of Elephanta, Kanheri and Ellora, were the work of ancient Egyptian conquerors. Whether those Egyptians were supposed to have brought Buddhism with them or to have adopted it on arrival he did not say. But both men were sure that the caves and the paintings were Buddhist. A Dr James Bird, who joined them on site, disagreed. He thought they were Jain and he had brought a learned *pandit* along to read the inscriptions and thus prove his point. He was also preparing an account of the place for the Royal Asiatic Society and intended taking away some of the paintings by prising them from the walls.

Ralph was full of scorn. The inscriptions were in a variation of the still undeciphered Ashoka script; they duly baffled the *pandit*. Moreover there was nothing to suggest that the caves were Jain. And as for removing the paintings, it was quite impossible – except as dust. Nevertheless Dr Bird tried; and 'not withstanding protestations about defacing monuments, this visitor contrived to peel off four painted figures from the zodiac or shield'.

Subsequent visitors followed this sad precedent; at one time there was even a resident caretaker who, for a small consideration, presented all-comers with a souvenir fragment. James Fergusson, who visited Ajanta about 1839, was duly scandalized, and launched the first of many attempts to save the frescoes. To him we owe the now accepted designation of the caves – 'I numbered them like houses in a street' – and the first clear statement of their origin – Buddhist and dating from about 200 BC to AD 650. The paintings were mostly from the Gupta period (fifth, sixth and seventh centuries AD) but some as early as the first century BC. Historically they were as important for the understanding of ancient India as the Bharhut and Sanchi reliefs. But they were infinitely more vulnerable and fragile. If anything was to be saved they must quickly be copied and brought to the attention of art historians.

On Fergusson's recommendation, Major Robert Gill arrived at Ajanta in 1844 and commenced a painstaking record of all the paintings. Twenty-seven years later he was still engaged on the job. In the story of British attempts to record India's past Gill's dedication is unrivalled; sadly, though, it was futile. His oil paintings of the Ajanta murals went on display at the Crystal Palace, London, along with the first Gandhara sculptures to reach England. In December 1866 all were destroyed by fire; the canvases had not even been photographed.

With quite staggering resilience, Gill returned to Ajanta to begin his life's work again; but he died, on site, a year later.

His place was taken, in 1872, by John Griffiths of the Bombay School of Art, and the work of copying continued for a further thirteen years. Again the results were sent to London. They went on display in the Victoria and Albert Museum and again they were destroyed by fire. But this time photographs had been taken. In 1897, nearly fifty years after their discovery, the Ajanta paintings were at last published and the art world could begin to form some opinion of them.

Whether a speedier appreciation of their aesthetic worth would have done much to ensure their preservation is highly doubtful. It is clear that they were already tragically mutilated in the 1820s, liable to crumble at the slightest touch. No doubt they continued to deteriorate; though they might have been better protected from vandals, there was no known method of restoring them. Indeed, any attempt at preservation was liable to be positively damaging. With the idea of resisting the monsoon damp, as well as to bring out their colours, Gill had administered a thick coat of varnish. This tended to blur the original brushwork; and when applied to subjects already encrusted with dirt and smoke, produced just a dingy splodge. In 1871 Clements Markham thought he was writing their obituary: Gill's varnish had 'injured them irremediably and they are now rapidly fading away'.

Although Griffith's work proved that this was not yet the case, another complication surfaced when John Marshall proposed an attempt at their restoration. Ajanta was just inside Hyderabad territory. In the native states, even Curzon's new Archaeological Department had to move with caution, and it was in fact Hyderabad's own Archaeological Department, founded in 1914, which eventually took the frescoes in hand. Thirty miles of road were built up to the gorge and, enticed by the Nizam's liberality, two Italian specialists, Professor Cecconi and Count Orsini, worked at Ajanta from 1920 to 1922. Analyses were made of the pigments and painting process which, incidentally, revealed that they were not, properly speaking, frescoes. (The plaster was not painted while wet, but moistened during the painting.) After many experiments the old varnish, dirt and smoke were removed with alcohol, turpentine and ammonia. Beeswax in turpentine was then used as a fixative, and cement and shellac mixtures used to secure the old plaster. The results were a revelation: a volume of photographs of the restored paintings prompted the *Bur-*

lington Magazine to declare them 'perhaps the greatest artistic wonder of Asia'. Suddenly, if belatedly, Ajanta art had achieved world recognition. In 1923 the great ballerina Pavlova performed an 'Ajanta Ballet' at London's Covent Garden, with choreography based on the gestures and poses of the cave paintings. It was a fitting tribute, because a training in music and dance had been a prerequisite for the original artists. To coincide with the ballet, the *Illustrated London News* published some photographs of the paintings with a long introduction by Sir John Marshall. The Ajanta frescoes were, he declared, 'one of the Wonders of the East'.

> Few things are more impressive than one of these halls at Ajanta seen towards the close of a winter's afternoon. All day long it has lain in shadow, but about four o'clock the sun comes round the shoulder of the hill opposite, and slowly the figures emerge from the gloom, one by one taking definition of form and feature and kindling colour after colour under the touch of the warm and glowing sunlight. Unlike the frescoes in the Sistine chapel, the Ajanta paintings are not the work of a single artist, nor are they homogeneous in design. They have been executed by many hands and at different times – the gifts of donors who gave according to their means. ... Yet in spite of their diversity of size and their varying age and excellence, there is remarkable unity in their general effect; for all the artists of Ajanta followed the same traditional methods in their drawing, and observed the same restraint and reticence in their colouring and tones. ... In these paintings there was no affectation, no striving after meretricious effects. Centuries of experience had taught the artists that in line and silhouette lay the true secret of mural painting, and they brought their drawing to a pitch of excellence that has seldom been equalled.

But the sudden popularity of Ajanta art was not simply the result of new restoration techniques and of publicity. Something much more fundamental had happened: during the first decade of the twentieth century, Indian art as a whole had at last achieved recognition. The role of the outspoken art master, Ernest Havell, in the aesthetic evaluation of Indian sculpture has already been mentioned; and it was Havell who also inspired and initiated the appreciation of Indian painting.

But first he had virtually to resurrect the subject. Back in the eighteenth and early nineteenth centuries, Indian painting meant miniatures, brightly coloured, highly stylized and delicately executed illustrations of court life, birds and animals, hunting scenes and flowers. It was particularly associated with the Moghul emperors and was clearly an off-shoot of the Persian miniature school. Many of the artists had been Persians attracted to India by Moghul patronage and, though the techniques had since been adopted by Indians, the inspiration was still Persian and Islamic. By the time the British arrived in upper India, Moghul patronage was in decline and with it Moghul art. The newcomers, schooled on Gainsborough and Constable, could see no great virtue in what appeared to be an obsession with detail and miniaturization. Thomas Twining much admired Moghul architecture, but found little to praise in Moghul painting.

> The merit of their drawing is almost confined to a very accurate imitation of flowers and birds. I never saw a tolerable landscape or portrait of their execution. They are very unsuccessful in the art of shading and seem to have very little knowledge of the rules of perspective.

A contemporary of Twining's, George Forster, also mentioned their ignorance of 'the rules of proportion and perspective': 'they are just imitators and correct workmen ... they possess merely the glimmerings of genius'. But if this laborious attention to detail and considerable imitative skill could hardly be rated as fine art, it had its uses: in the early 1800s many Indian artists were employed by British patrons to produce souvenir portfolios of buildings, animals, domestic servants and so forth.

Not surprisingly, scholars like Cunningham and Fergusson totally ignored what appeared to them to be purely an applied art. Introduced by one set of outsiders, and now adapted to the requirements of another, it was of little antiquarian interest; Indian painting belonged with enamel work and batik in the arts and crafts section. Even the discovery of the Ajanta murals and similar cave paintings at Bagh (Madhya Pradesh) did not prompt a drastic rethinking. For one thing there appeared to be no possible connection between a Buddhist school of mural painting which died out in western India in the seventh century and an Islamic school of miniature painting which appeared in north India in the sixteenth century. The chasm between the two appeared unbridgeable, and Ajanta could only be explained as some freakish anomaly. To critics who ignored or disputed that its paintings spanned some 700 years, the obvious explanation was that Ajanta was the work of foreigners. The refinement of technique, the impeccable draughtsmanship and the exquisite modelling could only be the product of centuries of artistic development. Since there was no evidence of any such tradition in India, one must look abroad.

> Whoever seriously undertakes the critical study of the paintings of Ajanta and Bagh [wrote Vincent Smith in 1889] will find, I have no doubt, that the artists drew their inspiration from the West, and I think that he will also find that their style is a local development of the cosmopolitan art of the contemporary Roman empire.

If there was Indo-Greek and Indo-Roman sculpture in Gandhara, why not Indo-Roman painting at Ajanta? One of the paintings apparently showed the reception by an Indian sovereign of envoys from Persia. This 'proves, or goes a long way towards proving, that the Ajanta school of pictorial art was derived directly from Persia and ultimately from Greece'.

It was the same old story; and as usual it stimulated Ernest Havell to a vigorous protest. He showed that there was plenty of literary evidence for the existence of an ancient Indian school of painting and argued, most plausibly, that in a country with a climate like India's it was not surprising that so few actual examples survived. Smith's suggestion, that the painting of a Persian envoy demonstrated that Persian influence was paramount, was clearly rubbish. And though north Indian Buddhism was undoubtedly somewhat cosmopolitan, the title of the Ajanta paintings to be considered Indian was 'as valid as that of the schools of Athens to be called Greek, those of Italy to be called Italian and perhaps stronger than that of the schools of Oxford to be considered English'.

Never one to be discouraged by a dearth of evidence, Havell sidestepped the medieval chasm in Indian painting by claiming, ingeniously and correctly, that when Buddhism spread to Central Asia and thence to China, it took the ideals and techniques of Ajanta with it. Less plausibly, he maintained that the Mongols borrowed these traditions of Indian art from the Chinese; the Moghuls, or Mongols, in India were thus repaying their ancestors' debt to Indian culture. In fact, Moghul painting had undergone the same process as Moghul architecture. Initially encumbered with foreign – in this case Persian – ideals, it had been quickly emancipated from the sober formality of the Persians and reanimated by the spirit of Indian art.

Havell considered all Indian miniatures as 'Moghul', and knew of no parallel but distinct Hindu or Rajput school. Indeed, his brand of criticism had little time for schools or styles of any kind. Unlike Fergusson, dissecting India's architecture into 'water-tight compartments', Havell liked to emphasize not the differences but the shared characteristics. Instead of discussing a school of painting or sculpture, he discussed individual works of art. And considering how few were available to him, his selection shows outstanding discernment: most of his examples are still regarded as classics. In the case of painting, whether it was an Ajanta fresco or a Moghul miniature, he concentrated on what was common to both and therefore distinctively Indian – the daring but faultless use of colour, the simple precision of line, the mastery of expressive gesture and pose, the ability to evoke mood and the deep understanding of nature. Of course, Moghul art was more secular and naturalistic than anything in ancient India. But it too, according to Havell, was conceptual in that no subject was drawn from life. Take the famous picture of a turkey cock commissioned by Jehangir. The artist would of course have studied the turkey and frequently referred to it. But the actual painting would have been the subject 'recollected in tranquillity'; hence the result, which says a lot more about a turkey cock, from the precise markings of the feathers to the absurd swagger, than could any accurate painting from life. It is a turkey as one imagines a turkey; but it could never win a poultry club prize.

> Too see with the mind, not merely with the eye; to bring out an essential quality, not just the common appearance of things; to give movement and character in a figure, not only the bone and muscle; to reveal some precious quality or effect in a landscape, not merely physiographical or botanical facts; and, above all, to identify himself with the inner consciousness of the Nature he portrays, and to make manifest the one harmonious law which governs Nature in all her moods – these are the thoughts which he [the oriental artist] keeps uppermost in his mind as soon as he knows how to use his tools with tolerable facility.

Havell's first major work, *Indian Sculpture and Painting*, was published in London in 1908. In spite of the author's harsh words about the ignorance of archaeologists, Sir John Marshall hailed it as 'a splendid protest against the drivelling nonsense on Indian art to which we are usually treated'; 'and so far as one "archaeologist" is concerned it has his very warmest sympathy'. Among those who reviewed it was Roger Fry, the most eminent art critic of his day. Havell, according to Fry, had proved his point. His illustrations alone were a revelation and many of the sculptures 'must appeal deeply to any unbiased and sensitive European'. The business of art could no longer be regarded as that of simply representing things as they appeared to be. 'We can no longer hide behind the Elgin marbles and refuse to look; we have no longer any system of aesthetics which can rule out, a priori, even the most fantastic and unreal artistic forms. They must be judged in themselves and by their own standards.'

Two years later, Havell was invited to address the Royal Society of Arts. The meeting proved a stormy one, but it marks the turning point for Indian art. In the chair was Sir George Birdwood, an authority on Indian crafts and an outspoken exponent of the traditional and dismissive attitude to Indian art. Ranged against him were Walter Crane, the artist, William Rothenstein, and a dramatic looking young man who was to become the greatest of all authorities on Indian art, Ananda Kentish Coomaraswamy. And, of course, there was Havell. If Havell had one serious fault it was his intensely combative approach to the subject. According to *The Times* his teaching career had been characterized by 'vehement and relentless opposition to every trace of European influence [and] constant denunciations of what he deemed utter ignorance on the part of his fellow countrymen of Indian art and civilization'. Seeing everything from the point of view of his Indian students, he had sought to rekindle a pride in their native art by disparaging everything non-Indian – neither the sculptors of ancient Greece nor the painters of the Italian renaissance were spared. But in London such 'irrational exclusiveness' tended only to antagonize his enemies and to embarrass his supporters.

At the Royal Society of Arts, Havell's passionate defence of Indian art brought Birdwood to his feet in a vitriolic outburst. So now India was to be credited with its own brand of 'fine art'. In seventy-eight years Birdwood had not seen a single example to support such a ridiculous theory. India had never prized art for art's sake and the best that it could offer was 'ritualized and generally monstrous representations of gods'. He turned to one of Havell's illustrations, a sculpture of the Buddha in meditation.

My attention is drawn to the photograph, on my left, of an image of the Buddha as an example of Indian 'fine art'. ... Few of us have the faith of the new school of 'Symbolists' in a symbolism that outrages artistic sensibilities and proprieties by virtually regarding art as just a framework for its myths; ... one might as reasonably rave over algebraical symbols as such examples of 'fine art'. This senseless similitude [the Buddha sculpture] in its immemorial fixed pose, is nothing more than an uninspired brazen image, vacuously squinting down its nose to its thumbs, knees and toes. A boiled suet pudding would serve equally well as a symbol of passionless purity and serenity of soul.

Several speakers took exception to the suet pudding, and the controversy spilled over into the letters and editorial columns of *The Times*. As a direct result, the India Society was formed, dedicated to promoting the understanding of – and publishing works on – Indian art. More significant, though, was the reaction of the young Coomaraswamy. His first book, on Sinhalese art, had already been published, but it was from about this time that he espoused the cause of Indian art as a whole. Like Rothenstein, he acknowledged that it was Havell's work that 'marked the beginning of a new order of things'. But it is his own works on Indian art, and especially Indian painting, which have formed the basis for all subsequent criticism.

Coomaraswamy's mother was English and he was educated in England, but he can in no way be identified with the British raj. His father was Sinhalese, his sympathies lay with the rising tide of Indian nationalism, and his career as an art historian was made in the United States. Although the study of Indian art was, even for Coomaraswamy, a process of exploration, he could expound it from within, not just interpret it from without. He was one of India's cultural emissaries rather than one of the West's cultural explorers.

Suffice it, therefore, just to outline his main contributions to the understanding of Indian painting. In the first place, he did for art what Fergusson had done for architecture. A great collector as well as a connoisseur, he identified all the main styles and provided the criteria by which an approximate date and place of origin could be assigned to any work. Jain miniatures, Bengali (Pala) palm leaf paintings and, most important of all, the whole field of Rajput art were virtually his discoveries. But he also insisted on a continuous tradition of Indian painting, and in this respect was far more convincing than Havell. On the ceiling of the Kailasa temple at Ellora, he found traces of frescoes dating back to the eighth century. Though technically reminiscent of the Ajanta murals, their style, and particularly the long sharp noses and exaggerated eyes, clearly anticipated similar modelling in the Jain or Gujerati miniatures. The earliest of these miniatures was painted on palm leaf and dated from the twelfth or thirteenth century. But the tradition of illustrating Jain manuscripts continued right through the medieval period, and the earliest Rajput miniatures (sixteenth century) owed much to the style and lyricism of Jain art. Thus the great hiatus in Indian painting, if not exactly filled, had at least been bridged.

As for Rajput art, it seems quite incredible that as late as Havell's 1908 book, this vast, important and thoroughly delightful school had not so much as been identified. Rajput architecture had, of course, fared little better, and the murals in the palaces of Orchha and Datia, though noticed by Coomaraswamy, are still virtually unknown today. Coomaraswamy's main task was to differentiate Rajput miniatures from the Moghul school. He conceded that there was much interchange between the two contemporary traditions but, whereas Moghul art was essentially secular, academic and factual, Rajput art was always religious, lyrical and poetic. Stylistic distinctions were equally relevant: Moghul tones were softer, the line drawing more precise, and shading more common.

Coomaraswamy also established the two main schools of Rajput painting – first, that of the Rajput states of Rajasthan and Bundelkhand; second, that of the Rajput states of the Himalayan foothills (Pahari). He further broke these down into the individual principalities. Each not only had its own stylistic conventions, but also its favourite themes. Rich in allegory and symbolism, they provided Coomaraswamy with a chance to show the importance of an understanding of Hindu literature, music, dance and iconography to any appreciation of Indian painting.

Perhaps none of this would have cut much ice with Twining and Forster. They would still have bemoaned the absence of perspective and longed for a big watery landscape. But that delightful twosome of Ralph and Captain Gresley would have lent a willing ear to what Coomaraswamy had to say about Ajanta. Their undisguised surprise and admiration had had a lot to do with the fact that the figures in the frescoes seemed to emanate sophistication and classicism. Desirable as was a Mathura *yakshi*, one might have found her conversation limited and her character suspect. Not so, though, the Ajanta beauties; they looked a safe bet in any company. Not only was there 'nothing monstrous', but in fact much grace and delicacy as well as irresistible charms.

Coomaraswamy agreed. 'A more conscious or sophisticated art could scarcely be imagined. Despite its invariably religious subject matter, this is an art of "great courts charming the mind by their noble routine".' It was the very epitome of Gupta art and, like the literature of the period, especially the plays and poems of Kalidasa, it directly mirrored the style and etiquette of India's most classical age.

> The specifically religious element is no longer insistent, no longer antisocial; it is manifested in life, and in an art that reveals life as an intricate ritual fitted to the consummation of every perfect experience. The Boddhisattva is born by divine right as a prince in a world luxuriously refined. The sorrow of transience no longer poisons life itself; life has become an art ...

CHAPTER TWELVE

Some Primitive Vigour

A peculiarity of India's classical past was that its origins invariably defied research. Ajanta art, Mauryan sculpture, even the classics of Sanskrit drama, all seemed to emerge as already mature art forms. They must clearly have had behind them many centuries of development and experiment; but all evidence of these was missing. The dawn, indeed the long morning, of Indian civilization was shrouded in mystery; and the earliest evidence all related to a period close to its high noon.

The incorporation of wooden beams and screens in some of the earliest cave temples suggested that they had been preceded by a long tradition of wooden buildings, all of which had long since rotted away. Stone sculpture, too, was probably a development from more perishable carvings in wood and ivory. An interesting relic of this art, though unfortunately not a pre-classical one, is the little ivory handle of a mirror which was found amongst the ruins of distant Pompeii. The handle is carved into the shape of a highly provocative female figure unmistakably related to the *yakshis* of Bharhut and Sanchi. The eruption of Vesuvius, which fortuitously preserved this one fragment of what was certainly a major craft, occurred in AD 79, a date which incidentally provides a useful cross-reference for the dating of the Buddhist reliefs.

But other aspects of the problem were less easily explained. What, for instance, about the origins of India's religions? The *yakshi* figures are evidence of early Buddhism seeking to accommodate ancient fertility cults associated with tree and snake worship. Hence Fergusson's conviction that Buddhism and Jainism had been more popular with the non-Aryan peoples of north India, the Dasyus or aboriginals.

But who were these aboriginal inhabitants of the subcontinent, and to what extent were they responsible, not only for the iconography of early Buddhist art, but also for its execution?

What, too, of the origins of Hinduism? India's prehistory was generally thought to begin with the arrival, about 1500 BC, of the Aryan peoples. On the strength of their literary traditions, the Aryans were credited with the awakening of Indian civilization. They brought with them to India a strong racial consciousness which, through the developing caste system, provided a society capable of absorbing outsiders without becoming swamped by them. They also brought Sanskrit, their Indo-European language of such immense potential; and they brought Hinduism – or at least a religion to which the origins of Hinduism are usually traced. But Vedic Hinduism (i.e. the religion of the early Aryan invaders as revealed in their *vedas*), was a far cry from medieval Hinduism. Its gods were stern, elemental, all-powerful – lords of fire and thunder, of the sun and the waters and the wind. They were worshipped by sacrifice, invoked by hymns, but never represented by idols or enshrined in temples. The Aryans were an outdoor people – horsemen and graziers; their religion was essentially a wooing of the elements.

But what changed all this? Whence came the softening of this harsh-sounding people, the civilizing of their lifestyle, the lulling of their fear-stricken fantasies? Virtually the whole pantheon of Hindu gods, from the jolly Ganesh to the ghastly Kali – and including Vishnu and Siva – were later additions. So, too, were such fundamental concepts as deities represented in human form, the personal devotion paid to them, and the hallowing of places of worship. Clearly there must have been some other vital ingredient in the development of Hinduism.

Another intriguing subject was the origin of the Indian scripts. Ashoka Brahmi had been successfully identified as the earliest precursor of most north Indian writing. But when found in its earliest form, in the column and rock inscriptions of Ashoka, it was already well developed and fairly standardized. The idea of carving inscriptions on stone seems to have been a Mauryan innovation; but the script itself must have been in use for a long time before that. Some authorities suggested that, like Kharosthi, the script used in ancient Gandhara, Ashoka Brahmi originated in western Asia. Others maintained that it was indigenous to India; and none with more conviction than Alexander Cunningham. For, in the course of his travels as the Archaeological Surveyor, he had located a single and unique piece of evidence.

In the winter of 1872–3, while touring the Punjab, he investigated Harappa, on the Ravi river. It was 'the most extensive of all the old sites along the Ravi', and, according to Charles Masson who discovered it on his way to Afghanistan, it boasted the ruins of a vast brick castle. Cunningham found plenty of bricks, several mounds of them in fact, but no castle. Nor was he altogether surprised. Standing amongst the mounds, he could hear the trains rattling along the new Lahore–Multan line. More than a hundred miles of track had been ballasted with bricks from Harappa.

Cunningham tentatively identified the ruins with a populous city visited by Hsuan Tsang. But he thought the site itself was much older. The pottery had a very archaic character; he described some gigantic stones 'very peculiar in shape' like 'undulating rings of stone'; and he paid particular attention to a colleague's recent find.

> The most curious object discovered at Harappa is a seal belonging to Major Clark, which was found along with two small objects like chess pawns, made of dark brown jasper.... The seal is a smooth black stone without polish. On it is engraved very deeply a bull, without hump, looking to the right with two stars under the neck. Above the bull there is an inscription in six characters which are quite unknown to me. They are certainly not Indian letters; and as the bull which accompanies them is without hump, I conclude that the seal is foreign to India.

Four years later, when writing a book about the inscriptions of Ashoka, Cunningham recalled the odd little seal with its unknown script and wondered whether it was quite as foreign as he had once thought. Could these unknown hieroglyphics (or, more correctly, pictographs) be some archaic form of Ashoka Brahmi? He re-examined the impression he had taken from the seal and decided that they could.

> Taking the characters from the left, the first may be an ancient form of the letter 'l' as it approaches very closely to the shape of the Ashoka character. The third seems to be an old form of 'chh', and the fourth a true archaic 'm', the shape of a fish, *matsya*. The fifth must be another vowel, perhaps 'i' and the sixth may be an old form of 'y'. The whole would thus read 'Lachmiya' [presumably 'Lakshmi', the Hindu goddess of wealth].

Cunningham was thus the first to attempt to decipher what is now known as the Indus Valley script. He had just six characters to go on, and he guessed that they were ancient forms of Ashoka Brahmi. Today we know of several hundred different characters; yet the script, in spite of computer research, remains undeciphered, and the possibility of some connection with Ashoka Brahmi is still wide open. Cunningham's identification of the individual characters is surely wrong and the word is not Lakshmi. Yet, again, he seems to have been on the right track. By intuition, the general had sensed that the little seal held the key to many of the problems surrounding the origins of Indian religion and civilization.

The seal itself eventually found its way into the British Museum, where it was joined by one or two others which came to light during the late nineteenth century. But no further progress was made in probing their significance. It seemed likely that they would forever remain the unclassifiable jetsam of some forgotten people, pieces of an archaeological jigsaw that had been packed in the wrong box.

Certainly Sir John Marshall attached no immediate importance to them. Knowing Cunningham's reports intimately, he must have realized that Harappa was a prime site for research into India's prehistory. But for twelve years after his appointment as Archaeological Director, no one visited the place. The new Department's first priority was conservation; excavation and research had to wait their turn and, if the Department was to justify its existence, could be undertaken only in places where there was a good chance of noteworthy finds. Hence early excavations were concentrated on Taxila, Sarnath, Sanchi and other Buddhist sites where sculptures and readable inscriptions could be guaranteed.

When one of the Department's staff finally visited Harappa in 1914, it was just to survey it. He did indeed recommend that the main mound be excavated, but it was not until 1921 that work started. In that year, more pottery and more seals were discovered, as well as a number of stone implements. But still the significance of these finds was doubtful. They were too few and too trifling to suggest a whole new civilization and, though apparently belonging to some chalcolithic culture (i.e. stone and bronze but no iron), they gave no hint of their true age.

But the breakthrough was imminent. A year before, R. D. Banerji, one of Marshall's Indian recruits, had been travelling in the sandy wastes of Sind 400 miles south of Harappa and near the mouth of the Indus. At a place called Mohenjo-daro, he stopped to investigate a

ruined Buddhist *stupa* and monastery, both built in brick, and he
noticed in their vicinity several other promising-looking mounds. He
thought they represented 'the ruins of a village or township which had
grown up around the *stupa*' and, knowing the Archaeological
Department's interest in Buddhist sites, recommended excavation.

Two years later a trial dig got under way. Banerji quickly discovered
more ruins but, since everything was built of the same small bricks, he
had no reason to assume that they pre-dated the *stupa*. Then some
engraved pieces of copper and some seals were found. One of the seals
depicted what was thought to be a unicorn; and all bore pictographic
letters which Banerji immediately recognized as belonging to the same
class as those on the Harappa seals. The hot weather was just beginning and nowhere in India is hotter than Sind. Banerji himself was
feeling the strain and would in fact have to retire after this arduous
season. But his curiosity was aroused. His small party redoubled their
efforts, and two new mounds were excavated. Below the *stupa* he
identified four different strata. The top one he dated to the second
century AD; the bottom one must therefore be of very considerable
antiquity. Studying the seals and their script, and recalling what he had
learnt from Marshall of the excavations in Crete, Banerji boldly
suggested that there appeared to be similarities with the Minoan
world. He was later proved wrong; but here at last was a hint that they
were dealing with a true civilization, and that it might be one of the
world's oldest, antedating the earliest events in India's reconstructed
history by two or three thousand years.

In 1924, Marshall compared the finds from Mohenjo-daro with
those from Harappa, and recognized that they belonged 'in the same
stage of culture and approximately to the same age, and that they were
totally distinct from anything known to us in India'. The date of these
'somewhat startling remains' was still a complete mystery, but in a
report to the *Illustrated London News* in 1924, Marshall could not
conceal his excitement.

> Not often has it been given to archaeologists, as it was given
> to Schliemann at Tiryns and Mycenae, or to Stein in the
> deserts of Turkestan, to light upon the remains of a long
> forgotten civilization. It looks, however, at this moment, as if
> we are on the threshold of such a discovery in the plains of
> the Indus. Up to the present our knowledge of Indian anti-
> quities has carried us back hardly further than the third

century before Christ. ... Now, however, there has unexpectedly been unearthed, in the south of the Punjab and in Sind,
an entirely new class of objects which have nothing in common with those previously known to us, and which are
unaccompanied by any data that might have helped to establish their age and origin.

His report was illustrated with photographs of clay toys 'to amuse
little prehistoric people of the Indus Valley', jewellery and trinkets 'as
worn by prehistoric Indian beauties' and of course the famous seals
with their 'unknown picture writing'.

After a further season of digging trial trenches at Mohenjo-daro,
Marshall was prepared to go further. An aerial survey had been made
of Harappa; another chalcolithic site had been found in Baluchistan;
and there was a report of a further find in Rajasthan.

From these and other researches it has now become evident
that this Indus civilization must have developed and
flourished in western India for untold centuries and that it
extended over an immense area.

Instead of Minoan Crete, Marshall suspected parallels with the
Sumerian culture of Mesopotamia which was now coming to light. It
seemed possible that these two chalcolithic cultures were contemporary; and when an Indus Valley seal was found in Iraq amongst debris
of the third millennium BC, an approximate date could at last be
inferred. For a time Marshall called his new discovery 'the Indo-
Sumerian civilization', though he adopted this 'merely as indicating
the close cultural connection between the prehistoric civilization of the
Indus and that of Sumer, not as implying that the peoples of these two
regions were of the same stock or spoke the same language'. In fact, he
was already certain that the Indus culture was quite distinct from any
other and, to avoid confusion, soon preferred to call it simply the
Indus Valley civilization.

Of the two principal sites, Harappa appeared the larger, but it was
far from being the better preserved. Mohenjo-daro, on the other hand,
was comparatively undisturbed: silt brought down by the Indus river
had smothered the ruins deep enough to hide them from railway
contractors, but not so deep as to make excavation prohibitive. Here,
then, Marshall would concentrate his resources. Eight hundred
labourers, a team of technical assistants, and six officers of the
Department, including Marshall himself, descended on Mohenjo-

daro for the 1925–6 season. A road to the site was hastily constructed; offices, workrooms and living quarters mushroomed; a museum was laid out. Mohenjo-daro was to be the Indus Valley's showpiece – India's Knossos.

Needless to say, Marshall was now sure of his ground. The finds themselves had not been sensational, and he warned that nothing like the royal tombs of Egypt could be expected. All the indications were that they were dealing with a less flamboyant, more practical people. He was already impressed by their drainage system, a subject beloved by archaeologists and a not inappropriate indicator of the prevailing life style. The houses, which were unexpectedly roomy, had each its own well and bathroom, from where a waste pipe connected with covered conduits which ran the length of every street and alley. They were built of finely chiselled brick 'laid with a precision that could hardly be improved upon'. This implied a 'social condition of the people much in advance of what was then prevailing in Mesopotamia and Egypt'.

He was also now aware that the Indus Valley civilization was far more extensive than those of Sumeria and Egypt. Besides covering the whole of what is now Pakistan, a westwards extension along the Arabian Sea to Iran seemed possible. This suspicion was soon confirmed, but more impressive are recent discoveries of its eastward extent. Indus Valley sites have now been found round the Arabian Sea coast almost to Bombay, beyond the deserts of Rajasthan to near Delhi, along the banks of the Jumna, and north to the edge of the Himalayas near Chandigarh.

During the years 1926–31, Mohenjo-daro was systematically excavated. Harappa followed later, and many other Indus Valley sites have since been explored. The subject, though, is far from exhausted and new discoveries could yet overturn current interpretations of what has proved to be the most enigmatic of civilizations. In recent years, speculation seems to have overtaken the flood of finds: Sir Mortimer Wheeler has complained of the available evidence being 'flogged to death'. For every ingenious suggestion from the archaeologists, the historian could raise a dozen objections and the layman as many counter-suggestions.

So little is known for certain. The great bath at Mohenjo-daro may not be a bath at all, the dock at the port of Lothal not be a dock – Lothal itself not a port. The citadels may not be citadels, the vast granaries not granaries. No building has been positively identified as a temple, the distinction between 'toys' and 'cult objects' is far from clear, and the purpose of the seals, which seem to tell us so much about the Indus Valley religion, is still not certain.

Nevertheless, there are certain fundamental characteristics of the Indus Valley civilization which are even more intriguing. The first thing that strikes every visitor to Mohenjo-daro or Harappa is the extraordinary regularity of their street plans. The streets are all straight, and they all cross one another at right angles. In other words, these are planned cities and represent not only the earliest known examples of town planning but, until recent times, virtually the only ones known in India. This regularity of lay-out applies to all the Indus Valley sites, giving the whole civilization an archaeologically disappointing, but not insignificant, uniformity. The seals show no local peculiarities, and in houses 1000 miles apart the bricks used are identical, even in size. No other ancient civilization, and very few modern ones, has followed such a consistent building pattern.

Another peculiarity was the apparent inflexibility and conservatism of the Indus Valley people. For perhaps 1000 years, there is virtually no evidence of change. The script does not develop, tools remain the same, and architecture is as regimented as ever. At Mohenjo-daro, the silt brought down by the Indus floods meant frequent rebuilding. But the opportunity this offered was never taken: houses were built with exactly the same ground plan as those they replaced.

This apparent conservatism has led archaeologists to infer either that the Indus Valley people were very unimaginative, or that they were at the mercy of firm government or orthodox religion. Often all three explanations are advanced, creating the image of a dour and down-trodden people, prosperous in their way, but devoid of noble aspirations and obsessed with domestic comfort, order and cleanliness. Not a single building shows any decorative effects; the outside walls are blank and windowless, giving the cities a grim and soul-less aspect. It is hard to imagine a people and a civilization less Indian.

To some extent this is also borne out by the artefacts that have been recovered. Indus Valley pottery is well made but remarkably plain. There are many rather clumsily-made terracotta figures and simple but primitive jewellery. In a totally different class, though, are a handful of figurines and some of the engravings on the seals. Here one suddenly comes face to face with a degree of artistic skill and awareness which belies every other generalization about the Indus Valley people. It is as if these were the work of a totally different culture; but though controversy has raged around the origin of some of them, there can be no argument, for instance, about the seals. And not only do these few examples exhibit a tantalizingly advanced art, but they also clearly anticipate important features of the later religious and artistic life of India.

Working his way along 'Ninth Lane' in the southern sector of Mohenjo-daro, one of Marshall's colleagues reached House LV. Compared to the 'comfortable little House LIV' next door, LV was in ruins. But one room had a particularly well-paved floor.

> At one end of this paving is a little fireplace, by the side of which was lying one of the most interesting antiquities unearthed during the season. It is a bronze statuette of a naked, slender-limbed dancing girl cast in the round. It is four and a quarter inches high and in good preservation save for the feet, which are broken off. The figure is characterized by negroid facial features and executed with some primitive vigour.

Whether this lissom little figure in fact represents a dancing girl, and whether her features mean that she belonged to some subordinate negroid or aboriginal race, is pure conjecture. But there is no gainsaying the far from primitive modelling and the highly effective exaggeration of her long gangling limbs. Head held high, hand on hip and left leg forward, she could pass for a spindly mannequin or a nubile disco-dancer. The small pointed breasts and slender hips suggest a very modern ideal of feminine beauty — the antithesis of the full-blown figure usually associated with Indian art. Yet her nakedness but for bangles and necklace, and the careful modelling of the lower abdomen, anticipate similar conventions in later Indian sculpture. Perhaps, too, there is a hint of the south Indian bronzes in the exaggerated pose and the attenuated limbs.

Marshall was particularly impressed by her back view, with smoothly rounded buttocks and hips. But this was not to be compared with two even more surprising statuettes, this time from Harappa.

> When I first saw them I found it difficult to believe that they were prehistoric; they seemed so completely to upset all established ideas about early art. Modelling such as this was unknown in the ancient world up to the Hellenistic age of Greece, and I thought, therefore, that some mistake must surely have been made; that these figures had found their way

into levels some 3000 years older than those to which they properly belonged.

Had there been just one of these small stone torsos, or had both been found in the same place, this explanation might have stood, but in fact they were found some distance apart. It was inconceivable that each could independently have worked its way six to ten feet deep into the dense rubble. Moreover, there were peculiarities about the two figures themselves which meant that they could not readily be assigned to any known school of sculpture. One torso was of grey stone and the other of a more reddish stone, neither of which was used in any other school of sculpture. Nor was the technique of attaching head and limbs separately in socket holes used by either Indian or classical sculptors.

> Indeed, what we have to realize ... is that it is almost as difficult to try and account for them on the assumption that they belong to the historic, as it is on the assumption that they belong to the prehistoric age. ... [Gandhara sculptures] give us the form, not the substance, of Greek art. Superficially they call to mind the Hellenic prototypes of which they are to some extent transcripts. But they miss altogether that characteristic genius of the Greek which delighted in anatomical truth and took infinite pains to express it convincingly. Now, in these statuettes, it is just this anatomical truth which is so startling; that makes us wonder whether, in this all-important matter, Greek artistry could possibly have been anticipated by the sculptors of a far-off age on the banks of the Indus.

Havell would have been delighted by this suggestion. He had always maintained that the Indian artist could handle anatomy as well as anyone, but had progressed beyond simple naturalism. Marshall, too, was no mean judge of Indian art; Vincent Smith had placed him alongside Havell and Coomaraswamy as a pioneer in its appreciation. Though the red figure was 'work of which a Greek of the fourth century BC might well have been proud', the execution was typically Indian as was 'the set of the figure with its rather pronounced abdomen'. The grey figure, evidently of a male dancer, was more liberally endowed with socket holes. One was clearly designed to sport an erect phallus, and those on the neck must have been for three heads. Here then was what might well have been an early representation of the famous Siva Nataraja, the dancing Siva of so many later sculptures and bronzes.

No doubt Marshall was emboldened to make this suggestion by the earlier discovery of a very curious seal. This shows a figure sitting in the posture of a yogi. The figure has enormous horns and a long, lugubrious face which, on close inspection, appears to be three faces. He also appears to be exposing an erect phallus, although this could be a pendant from his belt buckle. Around him are shown various animals, and beneath his low stool, two deer. To Marshall he was 'at once recognizable as a prototype of the historic Siva'. The cross-legged posture, like the inflated abdomen of one of the Harappa torsos, showed that the Indus Valley people were already familiar with yoga; and Siva was, par excellence, the Mahayogi. He was also traditionally three-faced and still very much associated with the lingam, of which, incidentally, the Indus Valley sites had yielded several unmistakable examples. Finally, he was also Lord of the Beasts; hence the animals. The image of deer under the throne would be precisely the convention adopted by early Buddhist sculptors to evoke the Buddha preaching his first sermon in the deer-park at Sarnath.

In all, some 12,000 steatite seals have been discovered. Although their script still defies solution, they constitute much the most comprehensive source material for the religion of the Indus Valley people. Horned female figures, big of bust and broad of hip, cavorting amongst the trees, almost certainly represent the earliest forms of the *yakshi*; evidently the fertility cult associated with trees was already prevalent. But the commonest subject of all is animals – elephants, tigers, rhinoceroses, buffaloes and, above all, bulls. There are also numerous mythical beasts, some part man, part beast – like the later *Varaha* versions of Vishnu boar-headed – others made up of various animal parts. It seems clear that some at least must have been cult objects and that the Indian habit of deifying animals was already well established. In the frequent use of the bull, further evidence is seen of Siva worship, the Nandi bull being Siva's 'vehicle'.

Even more remarkable is the execution of these animal seals. Most are about an inch square. Allowing space for the script, this means that many of the designs are no more than half an inch by three-quarters. They are cut intaglio, using the simplest bit and chisel. And, as yet one more constraint, the artist has had to bear in mind that for the seal to stamp clearly he must further reduce his conception to the very barest essentials. Yet the results are often startlingly effective. The famous humped bull with its enormous ruff-like dewlap is a masterpiece by any standards. It occupies the narrow zone of genius where the purely representational and the conceptual overlap; it has the universal appeal of, say, the Sanchi torso. Anatomically, it appears perfect; but the artist has also managed to suggest the bull's great bulk and strength and, by stylizing the dewlap and twisting the horns through ninety degrees, to produce a composition which is also a delight to the eye. The same skills may be seen in the prancing tiger, the armour-plated rhino and the backward-glancing deer. Marshall, for one, was convinced that the artists who could produce these little gems of design could also have created the more contentious Harappa torsos.

But who were these Indus Valley people, and what became of them? On this highly debatable question Marshall was extremely cautious. He argued, convincingly, that they could not possibly be Aryans and that Mohenjo-daro and Harappa predated the first Aryan invasions (1500 BC) by at least 1000 years. But he would not commit himself on whether they might have been Dravidians. From pockets of the Dravidian language that still survived in Baluchistan, it was assumed that the Dravidian peoples of south India (today the Tamil, Malayali, Telugu and Kannada speakers) had once extended over most of the subcontinent. The most obvious theory, therefore, was that the Indus Valley civilization was a Dravidian achievement and that it was overthrown, when already in decline, by the invading Aryans. This is the line taken by Sir Mortimer Wheeler, though it is by no means generally accepted. A change of climate, a cataclysmic flood, a weakening of the central authority, any of these things could have caused, or contributed to its collapse. But whoever the Indus Valley people were, the discoveries of Marshall and his colleagues served to focus attention on the non-Aryan element in Indian culture.

CHAPTER THIRTEEN
New Observations and Discoveries

When Sir William Jones founded the Asiatic Society back in 1784, he envisaged a far wider field of enquiry than is nowadays associated with indology. 'You will investigate whatever is rare in the stupendous fabric of nature; will correct the geography of Asia by new observations and discoveries; will trace the annals and even traditions of those nations who from time to time have peopled or desolated it.' In fact such things as literature, architecture and painting came right at the end of his list. The physical and natural sciences had a vital role to play in the discovery of India, and to many this was what it was all about. The revelations of every bug and butterfly collector, of every meteorologist and seismologist, are beyond the scope of this book; such specialized studies contributed more to the advancement of their individual sciences than to the understanding of India. But in a very different class are those broader fields of survey indicated by Jones – geography, ethnology, botany and zoology. The government itself recognized this, devoting considerable sums of money to them and, in the case of India's geography, promoting one of the most ambitious undertakings of the nineteenth century.

Jones's insistence on scientific enquiries was not simply a reflection of his own extraordinary range of interests. In those days there was no such thing as the 'two cultures'. Men of learning took a lively interest in both the sciences and the arts. The journals of the Asiatic Society carry no fewer, and perhaps more, contributions on birds, plants and tribes than on buildings and inscriptions. When Jones died, his fellow members desired to immortalize his memory: instead of erecting a monument or founding a scholarship, they named a tree after him, the *Asoca jonesia*. No doubt the great man would have been deeply touched by this apt and modest memorial.

Right from the start, the discovery of India had been more than a cultural and historical exercise. Thomas Coryat, the eccentric Elizabethan traveller, had told the emperor Jehangir that he had four reasons for visiting India. First – very diplomatic – was to see the Great Moghul; second, to see an elephant; third, to see the Ganges ('captain of all the rivers in the world'); fourth, to get a passport for Samarkand. John Marshall – not the twentieth-century archaeologist but his seventeenth-century namesake – 'the first Englishman who really studied Indian antiquities' – was equally intrigued by natural phenomena. His observations on Ashoka pillars and Hindu mathematics are punctuated by enquiries about the sex life of elephants, 'mairmaids' (only found in Mozambique, where the natives 'do often ly with them when they catch them'), and the salinity of sea water (according to the Hindus, 'one of Adam's sonnes drank up all the water and then pissed it out again, which made it salt').

To many of the early scholars, including Jones, the height of the Himalayas was as intriguing an enigma as the antiquity of Sanskrit. Cunningham was a notable ethnologist; Fergusson's first work was not on architecture but on the geography of the Ganges delta; and Prinsep's not on inscriptions, but on the topography of the Benares area. The important role played by surveyors and engineers in the discovery of India's antiquities has already been noted: Khajuraho was discovered by Franklin, and the painted caves of Bagh by Frederick Dangerfield, another surveyor. But these were essentially chance discoveries; by the time the mapmakers reached central India, the degree of professionalism demanded of them usually precluded other interests.

This was far from being the case in the early days of the Survey of India. In the south, where the mapmaking started, surveyors were encouraged to extend their enquiries well beyond the purely geographical; most of south India's antiquities were first made known in their reports. In 1799, Tippu Sultan of Mysore had been finally defeated by the forces of the East India Company and its allies under Arthur Wellesley, later Duke of Wellington. The whole of peninsular India lay exposed to the British, and the new century dawned with a flurry of surveying aimed at exploring the upland interior and at establishing cartographical contact between the east and west coasts.

This surveying took three distinct forms. There were route surveys, which could provide an interim picture of the country and its main arteries, as well as constituting a preliminary reconnaissance for the other surveys. A topographical survey filled in all the detail essential to a map. A trigonometrical survey aimed at establishing a framework of precisely determined positions and at laying down the geographical proportions of the peninsula.

Dr Francis Buchanan was despatched from Madras on a series of route survey journeys north and west across Mysore and Kerala in 1800. This was the same Buchanan who later carried out a similar survey in Bengal and Bihar, and who at Boddh Gaya reached some important conclusions about the origins of Buddhism. A Scot by birth and a surgeon by training, he was typical of that class of pioneers whose accomplishments were so varied that he is almost impossible to classify. His researches into Buddhism and Indian antiquities are more than matched by his work as an agriculturalist, a botanist and a zoologist; he later founded India's first zoo, and his last post was as Superintendent of the Calcutta Botanical Gardens.

The extent of his interest is reflected in the objectives of his survey in Mysore. These are minutely detailed in the title of the book that resulted: *A Journey from Madras through the Countries of Mysore, Canara and Malabar, performed under the orders of The Most Noble the Marquess of Wellesley, Governor General of India, for the Express Purpose of Investigating the State of Agriculture, Arts and Commerce, the Religion, Manners and Customs; the History, Natural and Civil, and Antiquities in the Domains of the Rajah of Mysore and in the Country acquired by the Honourable East India Company, in the late and former Wars, from Tippoo Sultan.* With such a title there was no need for an introduction. Day by day, Buchanan recorded his observations. With an eye for new crops that might benefit British India, he paid particular attention to agriculture. He despatched vast quantities of seed to Calcutta and when seed was not available, he carefully drew the plant in question. By May 1801, with the rains just breaking, he was exploring the tobacco growing areas west of Mysore city when he stumbled upon the first of the famous Chalukyan temples. He was not impressed: the building was 'utterly destitute of either grandeur or elegance', and as for the sculpture, 'I have not yet had the good fortune to meet with a Hindu image that was tolerable'. Next day he reached Halebid. In size, at least, the main temple 'exceeded any Hindu building I have seen elsewhere' and he much admired the highly polished pillars. But the famous sculpted friezes still did not please him.

> Its walls contain a very ample delineation of Hindu mythology; which in the representation of human or animal forms is as destitute of elegance as usual; but some of the foliages possess great neatness.

On the basis of an inscription, he dated the temple to 1280, and he correctly identified Halebid as the capital of the thirteenth-century Hoysala Ballala dynasty.

Next came Belur. The temple was again too ornate for his taste; but his day was made by a chance meeting with some cochineal farmers. Here was an unusual branch of husbandry, and one that intrigued Buchanan greatly. The farmers, or rather drovers, were herding their livestock along the cactus hedges. As the scarlet insects devoured one plant, a small colony was set to work on the next. In a good year the farmers expected to harvest close on half a ton of dead and dried insects. With indigo rivalling opium as India's most lucrative cash crop, Buchanan could see a rosy future for cochineal.

As the rains grew heavier and the going harder, he reached Sravana Belgola three days later. This was the most important Jain shrine in southern India. Already Buchanan, who had just returned from Burma, was far more drawn to Buddhism and its sister religion, Jainism, than to Hinduism. In particular he looked forward to seeing 'the colossal image of Gomata Raja'. This statue, which towers above the lake and Jain temples, is reputedly one of the highest free-standing sculptures in the world. Ironically, though, Buchanan, the first visitor to Sravana Belgola, failed to see it.

> This [the statue] I was not able to visit, owing to an inflammation that attacked my eyes the day before, and rendered the light almost intolerable. I sent my painter and interpreter to inspect the hill.

They reported the statue as seventy feet high, and the painter did a sketch which, as the Duke of Wellington would observe, bore not the slightest resemblance to the original. Next day Buchanan was worse. He was quite blind, and had to be carried to the nearest military base for treatment. It was three months before he could take to the field again and complete his survey. His report, in three volumes, was published in 1807 and remained the most reliable and exhaustive description of Mysore throughout the nineteenth century. It was reprinted in 1870 and is still a classic.

Fergusson declared the colossal statue of the Jain saint 'among the most remarkable works of native art in the south of India ... Nothing grander or more imposing exists anywhere out of Egypt and, even there, no known statue surpasses it in height.' He thought it must have been carved out of an existing rock pinnacle rather than erected on site. Coomaraswamy would agree, giving its date as AD 983. The site, though, appears very much older, and legend has it that both Chandragupta Maurya and Ashoka visited it.

According to Fergusson, the first visitor actually to see the statue was Wellesley. But Buchanan seems to make Wellesley's visit later than that of Colin Mackenzie, the man in charge of the Mysore Survey and the future Surveyor-General of India. Mackenzie was certainly the first to measure it (fifty-seven feet, not seventy), and there is a famous portrait of him, by Thomas Hickey, in which the Sravana Belgola statue, alongside a 'pole and basket' survey marker, is shown in the background.

Mackenzie, like Buchanan, was a Scot of wide interests and exceptional ability. The son of the first postmaster at Stornoway in the Outer Hebrides, he served the first ten years of his career as the local customs officer. But he was also a brilliant mathematician and, while collaborating on a life of John Napier (the inventor of logarithms), he became fascinated by the mathematical discoveries of the ancient Hindus. With that extraordinary resolve which 200 years ago seems to have been quite taken for granted, he left forever the windswept scapes of Lewis and, with no certainty of either a passage or employment, set off for India in search of the Hindu system of logarithms. It was 1783 and Mackenzie was twenty-eight, somewhat late to be starting an Indian career.

In Madras he was gazetted as an Ensign of Infantry but he soon transferred to the Engineers and made his first survey in 1784. Opportunities for distinction as both a siege engineer and surveyor then came thick and fast. He served during the Third Mysore War (1790–92), was present at the siege of Pondicherry in 1793, and served with the Nizam of Hyderabad's troops in 1795 and at the siege of Colombo in 1796. There followed more surveying in Hyderabad territory, during which he prepared a detailed study of the famous diamond mines. He also reported on a remarkable temple that he had discovered at 'Perwuttum' on the Kistna river.

In 1798, the Fourth and last Mysore War saw his prompt recall from survey duty. As chief engineer with the Nizam's forces, he fought alongside Arthur Wellesley. He was the only man with Wellesley during the famous episode when the future Duke became separated from his men during a night advance. This incident was widely regarded as a blemish on Wellesley's prospects. Revealingly, a contemporary rejected any such heresy on the grounds that 'any imputation of deficiency of courage [on Wellesley's part] must equally have applied to Colonel Mackenzie whose bravery and sangfroid in action are proverbial'. Wellesley himself regarded Mackenzie as indispensable. 'I shall say nothing of Mackenzie's merits as a surveyor; his works are a strong proof of them. He was under my command during the campaign and I never saw a more zealous, a more diligent, or a more useful officer.' Mackenzie played a vital role in the final siege of Tipu's capital, and immediately after the war was appointed to take charge of the survey of Mysore.

The Mysore Survey was India's first large-scale topographical survey. It covered some 40,000 square miles and took nine years to complete. The methods devised by Mackenzie, and the organization and training of his staff, became standard procedures for the extension of the survey to the whole of India. Its success proved that such an ambitious scheme was well within the realms of possibility. Starting on the northernmost frontiers of the state, Mackenzie and his staff covered the whole country with a network of carefully determined positions; from these, individual survey parties carried out minor triangulations and then toured the ground, fitting in roads, rivers and all the other human and physical features that go to making up a map. For months on end, these small detachments would disappear into the mountains and jungles. 'Fever and ague' might prostrate the whole team, and the rains would pen them within their tents for weeks on end. But the work went on; the reports and survey sheets accumulated. Mackenzie himself was in the field for up to two years at a time; but, as completion drew near, he increasingly immersed himself in the preparation of the final maps, plus a memoir, in seven folio volumes, on the conduct and results of the survey.

This memoir – and indeed, the whole Mysore Survey – was remarkable for the information collected on non-geographical subjects. Unlike Buchanan, Mackenzie was no naturalist; and the botanist attached to the Survey failed to stay the course. But in the report on the 'Perwuttum Pagoda' Mackenzie had already shown a deep and sympathetic interest in Indian antiquities and history. Three years later, he discovered the remains of the Amaravati *stupa*, the most important Buddhist monument in south India. And at about the same time, he secured the services of a Brahmin, Kavali Venkata Boriah, through whose learning Mackenzie believed that 'a new avenue to Hindu knowledge was opened'. Throughout the period of the Mysore Survey, Mackenzie not only directed the operations of his survey parties, but, through Boriah, also a network of antiquarian scouts. Scouring the country in search of inscriptions, historical records, coins and architectural curiosities – for all of which Mackenzie paid from his own pocket – their activities covered the whole of peninsular India. Later they were extended to Java, where Mackenzie was employed from 1811–13, and to Bihar and Bengal, when he became Surveyor-General in 1815.

The Mackenzie collection was far and away the largest and most important hoard of historical materials amassed during the nineteenth century. It included 1568 manuscripts in various scripts and languages, 8076 inscriptions, 6218 coins, 3000 engraved copper plates recording land tenures, and 2630 drawings of sculptures and monuments. What this means in terms of shelf space can best be gauged from the 8000 volumes in the Madras Library – only a fraction of the total, much of which found its way to Calcutta and London.

No man, even with a university of Brahmins at his elbow, could hope to translate and digest all this material; it would be 1828 before the bulk of it had even been catalogued. But for once the government was far from blind to its importance. Even Lord Bentinck, no great respector of Indian antiquities, was filled with admiration.

His [Mackenzie's] ardour, perseverance and contempt of all climate and danger in pursuit of this object have been quite extraordinary. No man that ever was in India has had the same opportunity, has incurred the same expense, or devoted the same time to these investigations. If it is possible ... to clear away the impenetrable darkness with which this Indian system, its origin and its progress, has been involved, the efforts of Colonel Mackenzie promise the finest hopes of success.

In old age, Mackenzie became something of an institution, like Cunningham fifty years later. Bemused by his dedication, the government continued to endorse his researches. No one could fault his management of the Indian surveys or criticize his eminence as one of India's outstanding geographers. Yet increasingly he immersed himself in his antiquarian studies. In an historical sketch of south India's history during the sixteenth and seventeenth centuries, he made a rare attempt to interpret some of his materials. He had also written, in 1797, a notable account of the Jains, on the basis of which he is sometimes credited with the discovery of this important faith. But basically his object was to collect and preserve. He firmly believed that all the materials for a history of pre-Islamic India still existed. But they were scattered about, forgotten and unread. They must quickly be discovered and recorded before the inscriptions were erased by time and the manuscripts destroyed out of ignorance. During the 1820s, James Tod in western India and Brian Hodgson in Nepal would subscribe to exactly the same belief and religiously follow Mackenzie's example. Stimulated by the sums paid to Mackenzie for his collection – his executors received £15,000 from the East India Company for the bulk of it – travellers throughout India and beyond took a new interest in antiquities; the spate of coin collecting and inscription copying in the 1830s, which resulted in the reconstruction of India's classical past, can be attributed as much to Mackenzie's example as to Prinsep's exhortations.

The year 1800, which saw Buchanan embarking on his route survey and Mackenzie launching the first major topographical survey, saw yet a third party of surveyors heading out of Madras for the rolling uplands of Mysore. In charge was William Lambton, a Yorkshireman of uncertain, probably humble, origins who had delayed his Indian debut even longer than Mackenzie. He had now been just two years in India and, though holding only the rank of lieutenant, was already in his mid-forties. Somehow the military establishment had forgotten about William Lambton. As a barrack-master he had whiled away the previous thirteen years in the backwaters of eastern Canada. While Mackenzie had been studying logarithms in Stornoway, Lambton had been teaching himself geodesy and astronomy in New Brunswick. And there, no doubt, he would have stayed. But there came a scrutiny of the regimental records and then a summons. By now his regiment had moved to India, was commanded by Wellesley, and about to see stirring action in Mysore. Lambton was needed.

He went first to Calcutta and announced his presence by delivering a paper to the Asiatic Society on *The Theory of Walls* ('wherein some particulars are investigated which have not been considered by writers on fortifications'); this was closely followed by another on *The Effect of Machines When in Motion*. Wellesley, understandably, was not sure what to make of either the man or his achievements. But during the Mysore War he became impressed by both and, when Lambton confided in him the great scheme that was forming in his mind, Wellesley became one of his most ardent supporters. The scheme in question was for a trigonometrical survey stretching right across the Indian peninsula and capable of being continued 'to an almost unlimited extent in every other direction'.

> It is scarcely necessary to say [wrote Lambton] what the advantage will be of ascertaining the great geographical features upon correct mathematical principles; for then, after surveys of different districts have been made in the usual mode, they can be combined in one general map.

In other words a trigonometrical survey would provide an extremely accurate framework within which topographical and route surveys, like those of Mackenzie and Buchanan, could be fitted. The principle had already been established in Britain by General Roy's Ordnance Survey, which no doubt gave Lambton the idea. While the topographical surveyor must carefully sketch and measure every inch of the ground, the trigonometrical surveyor leaps across the countryside from one eminence to the next. Extreme accuracy was of the essence: the stations he established would become the pole stars of all future topographical surveys. Though comparatively few surveyors would be needed, the instruments required were complex and cumbersome. Factors such as the curvature of the earth had to be taken into account, and it was one of Lambton's great ambitions to establish precisely what this amounted to in a latitude such as India's. The scheme therefore had both practical and scientific implications, both of which recommended themselves to Mackenzie as the Madras Surveyor-General.

But in the enthusiastic support that Lambton received from Wellesley and the Governor-General, there must also have lurked a political consideration. The trigonometrical survey was of no immediate military or strategic relevance, was not essential for the purposes of revenue assessment and was unlikely to lead to the discovery of useful plants, interesting buildings, etc. Unlike all the other surveyors, Lambton would not be sidetracked onto matters other than his triangles.

But what the trigonometrical survey did do was embrace the whole of India. In its adoption lay the seed of an idea that would soon translate itself into the reality of an all-Indian empire; and in its completion would lie the important acknowledgement of India's physical integrity. Just as Ashoka had staked out his empire with pillars and stone-cut inscriptions, so the British would stake out their own claim with trig stations and the maps that resulted.

Between 1800 and 1802, Lambton carried out what amounted to a practice exercise around Bangalore. Trigonometrical surveys started with measuring, along the ground, a base line using a specially wrought chain, levelled and stretched to give absolute accuracy. The chain, along with all the other instruments used by Lambton, had been bought secondhand from a Dr Dinwiddie in Calcutta. They would have been in Peking but for a lucky coincidence: the Chinese had not regarded chains, and what looked like other instruments of torture, as suitable presents for His Celestial Majesty. Dinwiddie was therefore escorting them back to England via India, and only too happy to be relieved of his charge.

Outside Bangalore, a suitably level piece of ground was selected and operations began. The chain, of blistered steel, was 100 feet long. To ensure that it was taut, level and not subject to extremes of temperature, it was housed in five long wooden coffers, each twenty feet long. These in turn were supported on tripods equipped with elevating screws for levelling; the coffers were also equipped with thermometers, as temperature was an important factor in any expansion of the chain.

The base line in this case was 7.44 miles long, so the chain, coffers and tripods had to be dismantled and re-erected nearly 500 times. This was done by a carefully drilled squad, twenty men to the chain, more to the coffers, acting on the word of command. The whole operation took fifty-seven days. Flooding, possibly contrived by the locals, interfered; but Lambton was confident that 'no error exceeding eight or ten inches' over the whole distance was possible. Then came a series of astronomical observations to establish the latitude at each end of the base line. For this an instrument called a zenith sector was required; the one bought from Dinwiddie was held in two large coffins which it took fourteen men to carry.

Finally, the base line measured and its position determined, triangulation could begin. A suitable hill was selected, a pole was erected on top of it and, using a theodolite, the angle between the base line and a line to the hill was measured at each end of the base line. Knowing, now, the length of the base and the two angles, the length of the other two sides could be worked out and the position of the hill minutely ascertained. One of the lines to it then became the base for the next triangle. And so on. The survey could at last stride off across the country. From time to time it was essential to check for accuracy by measuring another base line and by taking further observations. But, theoretically, so long as the original base was precisely measured, and the necessary allowances made for variations of altitude, the curvature of the earth, and refraction, the deviation should never exceed a few inches.

Although the base lines and triangles measured in 1800–2 were only a practice run, the principles and procedures remained the same throughout what became known as the Great Trigonometrical Survey (GTS). There were difficulties – the lack of suitable hills in the plains, for instance. And there were refinements – flashing lights instead of poles, for one. But Lambton's scheme based on 'correct mathematical principles' did indeed prove capable of being continued 'to an almost unlimited extent'.

In 1802, provided with new instruments from England, including the Great Theodolite weighing exactly half a ton, Lambton started his coast-to-coast series. He measured a base line above the beach in Madras and from this extended triangles up and down the coast to measure a short arc of the meridian which would give him the curvature of the earth in that latitude. Then, in 1803, he headed west, reaching the Malabar coast near Mangalore two years later. His measurements showed the peninsula to be 360 miles wide at this point, forty less than current maps showed.

In 1807, he started south to extend his triangles to Cape Comorin so as 'to form a complete skeleton of the peninsula'. He tried going down the coast, but at Nagore, south of Pondicherry, ran into difficulties.

> The work was here brought to a standstill owing to the height and the thick growth of the palm trees which everywhere obscured the view. The difficult and dangerous method was adopted of building scaffolds on top of the highest pagodas [temples] and of hoisting the heavy apparatus up by machinery constructed for the purpose, but without success; no stations whatever could be found with the necessary visibility and it was with some difficulty that the pagoda at Nagore was laid down.

He decided to move inland and, using more temples, reached Tanjore. Here this 'difficult and dangerous method' resulted in disaster, and the whole GTS was placed in jeopardy. The great tower of the Tanjore temple, 216 feet high, had proved irresistible; but in winching the half-ton theodolite to its summit, the guy rope used to keep it clear of the structure snapped; the theodolite crashed against the tower. Any damage to the temple Lambton does not record; he was far too concerned about his instrument.

> The blow was received on the tangent screw and its clamp. The case, being insufficient to protect it was broken, and the limb, instead of being a beautiful circle, was so distorted as to render it to all appearances worthless.

It looked as if operations would have to be suspended indefinitely. Lambton retired to the nearest ordnance depot and shut himself away in his tent with his beloved theodolite. No one, except a couple of assistants, was allowed to enter.

> He then took the instrument entirely to pieces [writes his successor] and, having cut out of a large flat plank a circle of the exact size that he wanted, he gradually, by means of wedges and screws and pulleys, drew the limb out so as to fit into the circumference; and thus in the course of six weeks he had brought it back nearly to its original form. The radii, which had been bent, were restored to the proper shape and length by beating them with small wooden hammers.

The work could begin again. By 1810 Lambton had finished his triangulation of the southern tip and returned to his original coast-to-coast series to extend it northwards. He was now approaching sixty, and increasingly left the triangulation to his assistants, concentrating his own flagging energies on new base lines and calculations. But, reliable as his assistants were, there was as yet no one who could be considered as his natural successor. 'Someone possessing zeal, constitution and attainments' was desperately needed.

In 1818 the government rose to the occasion by nominating George Everest, a young artillery officer with an outstanding aptitude for mathematics and a good surveying record. At about the same time, the Survey reached Hyderabad territory and was transferred from the Madras government to the Supreme government in Calcutta. It was officially designated as the Great Trigonometrical Survey, and its extension to the whole of India right up to the Himalayas was sanctioned. The future was assured. But Lambton, now a Colonel, was slowing up. 'Men cannot last forever', observed Everest in 1822, 'the Colonel's infirmities have evidently subdued all but his spirit.'

> It is now upwards of twenty years since I commenced it [the
> Survey] on this grand scale [wrote Lambton]. In this long
> period of time I have scarcely experienced a heavy hour; such
> is the case when the human mind is absorbed in pursuits that
> call its powers into action. A man so engaged, his time passes
> on insensibly. ... I shall close my career with heartfelt satisfac-
> tion and look back with increasing delight on the years I have
> spent in India.

But there was to be no time for looking back. Aged seventy, he
embarked on the 400-mile journey across the Deccan from Hyderabad
to a new headquarters at Nagpur. Fifty miles short of his destination
he died in his tent. 'As he ever looked forward to dying, so he died, at
his post', wrote a later Surveyor-General.

Everest was to prove a worthy successor to Lambton in everything
except constitution and temperament. Whilst Lambton was seemingly
impervious to India's climate, Everest succumbed to every fever going
and was never free from 'my old complaint' – probably amoebic
dysentery. His correspondence is filled with detailed bulletins. In 1824
he was paralysed for a time and had to be lifted in and out of his seat at
the zenith sector. In 1835 his hip seized up and he recovered only after
'the application of some hundreds of leeches – fomentations administered night and day – a due abstraction of blood from cupping – and a
course of gruel diet'. Three years later he collapsed again.

> I was attacked in November last near Sironj with a severe
> illness. ... Dreadful rheumatic pains in my bones – fever – loss
> of appetite – indigestion – intestines totally deranged –
> stomach totally powerless – my strength entirely gone – the
> whole system apparently destroyed and forever undermined.
> I recovered gradually ... but found to my indescribable dis-
> may that my memory was in a great measure gone – that my
> mind was affected – that whatever I did or thought of during
> the day preyed on me at night – and worst of all I found
> myself oppressed by a dreadful foreboding of ill – a horror of
> being awake in the dark – an apprehension even whilst I was
> wide awake, of some spectre or monster of fancy coming to
> hold converse with me ... I thought it would certainly end in
> madness.

Apart from five years home leave (1825–30), this state of perpetual
convalescence was not allowed to interfere with the progress of the

Survey; but it certainly contributed towards making George Everest one of the most cantankerous *sahibs* in history. When he took over the GTS most of Lambton's assistants promptly resigned. Those who succeeded them were bullied and browbeaten unmercifully. Everest seemed incapable of sustaining any professional relationship other than as a vendetta. He chastised his native staff, berated local officials, and met every directive from Calcutta with a howl of protest. No man can have been less prone to misgivings about the importance of his work, and woe betide anyone who interfered with its smooth progress. Any dog or cat straying into his camp was promptly shot, and an officer whose horse presumed to neigh outside the Surveyor-General's tent was threatened with a court-martial for insubordination.

But, if not exactly loved, Everest commanded great professional respect. No one could question his dedication. During twenty years as Superintendant of the GTS he carried Lambton's triangulation from Berar through the wilds of central India and across the plains of the Ganges to Dehra Dun in the Himalayas. The line of triangles, stretching from Cape Comorin to the mountains, was the longest arc of the meridian ever measured, and of immense geodetic importance for calculating the curvature of the earth. This great arc was Everest's most important achievement, and it has formed the backbone of maps of India ever since. But he did not neglect the rest of the skeleton – from the great arc, another series of triangles stretched east to Calcutta, and a third was started, east along the base of the Himalayas. These two were connected by further meridional series and a grid was thus thrown over a large part of north India.

All this was possible thanks to more accurate instruments, a much larger staff, increased expenditure and a number of innovations. Everest rejected Lambton's chain for base line measurements in favour of the new compensation bars, which eliminated the stretch caused by expansion. The first time these bars were used was for the Calcutta base line measured in 1832. A sketch of the operation by James Prinsep, ever an enthusiast in such matters, shows the bars mounted in coffers and supported on tripods as in Lambton's day; in the background can be seen one of the towers erected at each end of the line. Towers became an essential part of the survey in the plains of the north. With a heavy smoke and dust haze invariably covering the ground, and with no handy *gopurams* or hills, scaffolding towers of bamboo, seventy feet high, were erected, as well as some masonry towers for the more important trig stations. Even then, a clear view over a distance of fifty miles was seldom possible. Everest therefore introduced the use of heliotropes – mirrors reflecting the sun – for day working, and blue flares for night work. He also pioneered what he called 'ray-tracing' – fixed telescopes trained on the distant flares. The accuracy was now staggering. The difference between the Dehra Dun baseline as measured on the ground and as triangulated from a baseline on the great arc 400 miles away was just 7.2 inches.

Sir Clements Markham would hail Everest's completion of the great arc of the meridian as 'one of the most stupendous works in the whole history of science'. But, in terms of human endeavour as well as scientific achievement, the North-East Himalayan Series of triangles along the base of the Himalayas was scarcely less remarkable. Started by Everest it was completed by his successor, Andrew Waugh, to whom goes the credit for finally determining the height of the Himalayas and discovering the world's highest point. According to Markham, the North-East Himalayan Series entailed 'dangers and difficulties in the execution which were far greater than have been encountered in the majority of Indian campaigns'; it was 'the most desperate of undertakings and the average slaughter was greater than in many battles'. Because the Nepalese refused to co-operate, the survey had to be carried through the dreaded Terai, a belt of jungle and swamp between the plains and the foothills. Between 1845 and 1850 five survey officers worked on this series. Of these, two died of fever, two were compelled to retire, and only Waugh survived. In one season alone, forty native assistants fell victim to the climate, and in another, an entire survey party had 'to be conveyed in a helpless condition from fever to Gorakhpur'.

But somehow the series was completed, and from the principal trig stations it was at last possible to triangulate the precise position and height of the snowy peaks along the northern horizon. For as long as the British had been in India, the height of the Himalayas and their distance from the plains had been matters of avid speculation. From near Patna, John Marshall observed 'very high hills to the north' in 1671. They seemed more distant than 'any object my eyes ever beheld' – perhaps, he thought, as much as 300 miles away. According to travellers he had met, Armenians 'which come from China and have travelled the most countries in the world ... these Botton [i.e. Bhutan, by which he meant Tibet] hills are the highest hills they ever saw or heard of'.

Sir William Jones first saw the Himalayas on his excursion to Benares.

> Just after sunset, on the fifth of October 1784, I had a distinct view from Bhagalpur of the Chumalury peak [possibly Chomolhari in Bhutan], and the adjoining mountains of Tibet. ... From the most accurate calculations I could make, the horizontal distance at which it was distinctly visible must be at least 244 British miles.

Taking account of other recent observations, Jones boldly asserted that 'we saw from Bhagalpur the highest mountains in the world without excepting the Andes'. As so often, he had guessed right – but few in Europe would yet concede the point. Oddly, it was the mountain on the island of Tenerife that was then regarded as the highest, at least in the Old World: 'the peaks of Nepal cannot be supposed to be less elevated than the peak of Tenerife' ventured William Kirkpatrick in 1793. The next visitor to Nepal, none other than the ubiquitous Dr Buchanan, fresh from his route survey in Mysore, declared the mountains to be 'of vast height'; with his companion, Major Crawford, he attempted to measure eight peaks – 'Result: 11,000 to 20,000 feet above stations of observation.'

Another man much intrigued by the subject was Henry Thomas Colebrooke, who succeeded Jones as the leading Sanskrit scholar of the day. In 1807, he measured from the plains the peaks of Nanda Devi and Trisul. After giving the basis of his calculations he agreed wholeheartedly with Jones's verdict.

> Two of these mountains will therefore be more than five miles in perpendicular height above the level of the plain on which I stood. ... I must for the present postpone any further remarks or calculations until I can compare my observations with those of Major Crawford, who observed the same mountains in Nepal, and with the observations which have been made of the Andes in South America and of the peak of Tenerife ... but I trust that I shall then be able to prove that the mountains of Tibet are not only higher than any in the ancient hemisphere but also in the known world.

By 1816, Colebrooke decided that the point was beyond dispute. He had just worked out that Dhaulagiri was 26,862 feet; the Himalayas were considerably higher than the Andes and might be declared 'the loftiest range of Alpine mountains which have yet been noticed'. Surveyors working in the wake of the Gurkha war agreed, declaring that there were at least twenty peaks in Garhwal alone that were higher than Chimborazo, supposedly the highest of the Andes peaks.

But the armchair geographers at home were still far from satisfied. The trouble with all these computations was that they were based on observations made from positions whose distance apart had not been accurately determined. Until the base for the triangles to the distant peaks was either measured on the ground or itself trigonometrically established, the results had to be in doubt. This, of course, was where the work of Lambton, Everest and Waugh came in. With the completion of the suicidal North-East Himalayan Series, a network of unimpeachably accurate base lines extended right along the foot of the mountains. In the late 1840s and early 1850s, Waugh triangulated the heights and positions of seventy-nine peaks. Some had names, the rest were given numbers. The highest of all, measured at 29,002 feet above sea level, was No. XV. On Waugh's recommendation, it was named, after his old boss, Mount Everest.

CHAPTER FOURTEEN

An Idolatrous Affection

Vast as the output of British scholarship was during the raj, one has to cover many yards of library shelving before encountering any work that can be regarded as a classic. In the genre of memoirs and travelogues there are a few notable productions – Bishop Heber's *Travels* for example; but somehow writers on architecture, sculpture, archaeology, geography, and even history, failed to produce much of outstanding merit. For the most part they confided their discoveries to the journals of the Asiatic societies, or incorporated them in official reports. When a separate volume was contemplated, the most influential literary format seems to have been that of the government gazetteer. It was as if the facts and discoveries should speak for themselves; the cake needed no icing.

But exception must be made for two monumental works written by Colonel James Tod. *Annals and Antiquities of Rajasthan* and *Travels in Western India*, in spite of their different sounding titles, are really sister books. Both are part history and part travelogue; the second merely extends the field of enquiry to include Gujerat and thus cover the whole of western India. Together their 1500 pages of tight print occupied Tod for sixteen years. The general reader might find the plethora of unfamiliar names and places discouraging; the India specialist might jibe at Tod's often uncritical approach; but neither could deny that here at last was a real classic, rich in instruction, resounding with conviction and eminently readable, a work that might worthily stand beside Gibbon and Carlyle.

The depth of Tod's scholarship and the breadth of his vision are remarkable in a man whose education was undistinguished and whose career was as active and demanding as any. But still more surprising is his magnificent command of language and the deep sympathy for his subject which inspires it. The long rumbling periods, like distant thunder, somehow evoke the vast skies of the western deserts, the well-turned phrase echoes the simple harmony of a camel and rider silhouette. There is a wealth of classical and medieval metaphor which lends to the exploits described an added degree of conviction. Tod was writing from the heart. The Rajput clans, whose martial traditions constitute the bulk of *Annals and Antiquities*, had won more than just his sympathetic curiosity. 'In a Rajput I always recognize a friend,' he confided; and for Mewar, the most illustrious of the Rajput principalities (capital Chitor and later Udaipur), he felt both filial loyalty and paternal solicitude.

> I look upon Mewar as the land of my adoption and, linked
> with all the associations of my early hopes and their actual
> realization, I feel inclined to exclaim with reference to her and
> her unmanageable children, 'Mewar, with all thy faults, I love
> thee still'.

Tod's close identity with a people who were not even a part of British India coloured his career as well as his books. Born in London, he came to India in 1799, aged seventeen, as a military cadet. Six years later he was assigned to the escort of the British Agent at the court of the Maratha chief, Daulat Rao Scindia of Gwalior. The Marathas were at this time masters of most of Rajasthan whose Rajput princes, spurned by the British and hopelessly divided amongst themselves, were proving an easy prey. In 1806 Tod made his first visit to Udaipur where he witnessed the final degradation of the Maharana of Mewar, scion of the Rajputs. The scene was one of horrifying intrigue. The Maharana, a weak but noble figure, was at the mercy not just of the Marathas but of various other adventurers; and outside his gates his natural allies, the Rajput chiefs of Jodhpur and Jaipur, were warring for the hand of his daughter and a share in the spoils. Swayed this way and that by evil counsellors he eventually consented to the murder of his lovely Kishna Kumari as the only way out of the impasse and the only chance of preserving Rajput independence. But no man could be found to deliver the fatal blow; and, in a scene tailor-made for Italian opera, 'the flower of Rajasthan' herself took up the poisoned cup and thrice drained it before 'she slept a sleep from which she never awoke'. Tod was so moved by all this that he seems to have resolved there and then to espouse the Rajput cause. But as yet there was little he

could do; and, between 1806 and 1817, Mewar was ravaged by the
Marathas as never before. Tod kept in touch with events through a
network of informers covering the whole of western India. He became
the East India Company's leading authority on the region and when,
in 1817, the Rajputs were finally accorded British protection, Tod was
nominated as Political Agent in western Rajasthan. His return to
Udaipur through burnt-out villages and overgrown fields was a
funereal progress.

> All was desolate; even the traces of the footsteps of man were
> effaced. The babool (*mimosa arabica*), and gigantic reed,
> which harboured the boar and the tiger, grew upon the
> highways; and every rising ground displayed a mass of ruin.
> Bhilwara, the commercial entrepot of Rajasthan, which ten
> years before contained 6000 families, showed not a vestige of
> existence. All was silent in the streets – no living thing was
> seen except a solitary dog, that fled in dismay from his lurking
> place in the temple, scared at the unaccustomed sight of man.

On a practical level, Tod's mission was to win the confidence of the
Rajput princes and to restore peace and prosperity which the country
had not known since before the arrival of Islam. A measure of his
success can be gained from the comments of Bishop Heber who passed
safely through the western deserts only eight years later. By then
Bhilwara was again thriving; it had 'a greater appearance of trade,
industry and moderate, but widely diffused, wealth and comfort than I
had seen since leaving Delhi. The streets were full of hackeries laden
with flour and corn, the shops stored with all kinds of woollen, felt,
cotton and hardware goods', etc. Everybody sang Tod's praises, and
Heber was told that the place had almost been renamed 'Tod-ganj' –
'but there is no need for we shall never forget him'. It was the same
story throughout the Rajput states.

> We were continually asked by the *kotwals* (village heads)
> after 'Tod Sahib', whether his health was better since he
> returned to England, and whether there was any chance of
> their seeing him again. On being told it was not likely, they all
> expressed much regret, saying that the country had never
> known quiet till he came amongst them, and that everybody
> whether rich or poor ... loved him. He, in fact, loved the
> people of this country and understood their language and
> manners in a very unusual degree.

Tod's achievement of political and economic reconstruction was one thing; but this espousal of the people's manners and traditions was even more important. He recognized in the Rajputs the ancient warrior race of Hindu India. They were a feudal aristocracy as imbued with traditions of chivalry, and as fond of martial epics, as King Arthur and his knights. Tod pried deep into their history and, like Mackenzie, he found ample material. Not only were there ruins, inscriptions and coins but a wealth of literary and oral evidence, especially the poems of the bard, Chand, 'the Rajput Homer, the Indian Ossian'.

As he explored the ruins of Chitor, Tod would be told tales of its heroic defences and tragic capitulations. In Udaipur, beside the waters of the Peshola Lake, he would sit in the Jagnivas lake palace and hear the epics of old just as had the princes of Udaipur two centuries before.

> Here they listened to the tales of the bard as they slept off their noonday opiate amidst the cool breezes of the lake, wafting delicious odours from myriads of lotus flowers which covered the surface of the waters; and as the fumes of the potion evaporated, they opened their eyes on a landscape to which not even its inspirations could frame an equal; the broad waters of the Peshola with its indented and well-wooded margin receding to the terminating point of sight, at which the temple of Brinpoori opened on the pass of the gigantic Aravalli, the field of the exploits of their fathers.

Through the rocky defiles of many an ambush Tod traced the history of their desperate encounters with Mohammedan and, later, Maratha foes. In the mirrored and marbled halls of Amber and Jodhpur he listened to whispered stories of court intrigues and harem scandals. And in the libraries of Jaipur and Bikaner he tracked down the chronologies and records. If he was inclined to romanticize it was hardly surprising. He was not just studying the past, he was reliving it. Nor was this romantic approach out of place. In their palaces and paintings, as well as in their history and their poetry, the Rajputs evinced a love of pageantry and setting. By rescuing and recording such traditions – and above all, by reverencing them and recognizing them as still vital – Tod restored to the Rajputs a pride of race which more stringent standards of scholarship might simply have destroyed. In short, Tod, single-handed, did for the Rajputs what it would take several generations of scholars to do for the people of India as a whole.

In the preface of *Travels in Western India* he restated his commitment to the Rajput cause but with an important addition.

> Heart and soul did I labour for the one [*Annals and Antiquities*] and with the same idolatrous affection for the subject have I given up every pursuit, every thought to this [*Travels*] in the hope of making the Rajputs known by their works; but I linger awhile in the skirts of Rajasthan and lead my reader into the hardly less interesting region of Saurashtra and to the mounts sacred to the monotheistic Jains.

The Jains were traditionally the administrators, merchants and bankers of western India. Already Tod was deeply indebted to their scholarship. His principal *pandit* was a Jain and he had located whole libraries of Jain texts. ('We can only pity', he wrote in a veiled response to Macaulay's rantings, 'the overweening vanity which has prompted the assertion that the Hindus possess no historical records.') As a reformed sect comparable to, and contemporary with, the Buddhists, the Jains had once been numerous throughout India; but they now survived only in scattered pockets centred on their main places of worship. Such places were often lofty hills, on or around which the Jains sculpted their colossal naked statues and built their trim little temples. Gwalior, Parasnath (Bihar) and Sravana Belgola were typical examples; but the most important were in western India and of these the most celebrated was the isolated mountain of Abu, 5000 feet high, which rears up out of the western desert.

Tod was determined, before leaving Rajasthan, to see this famous shrine. By 1822 he was a very sick man (like Everest, he seems to have suffered from permanent dysentery). But he resolved to turn his journey down to Bombay into a sort of Jain pilgrimage. He visited the mountain of Girnar, bristling with whitewashed temples, and there first discovered the famous Ashoka rock inscription. He also explored the ruins of Anhilwara and discovered a pointed arch which, like Havell nearly a century later, he took as evidence that the Jains and Hindus had anticipated the architects of Islam. But Abu, unvisited by any European, was his greatest goal.

> It was nearly noon as I cleared the pass of Seetla Mata, and as the bluff head of Mount Abu opened upon me, my heart beat with joy as, with the sage of Syracuse, I exclaimed, 'Eureka'.

Too weak to climb 'the Indian Olympus', Tod accepted the offer of a ride in a pilgrim's chair. Thus, swinging from a bamboo pole, he was borne aloft, from the desert scrub through the dense jungles and up the steep scarps to the rolling meadows and woods of the summit plateau. On 14 June 1822 he was deposited, 'in a high fever and unable to articulate', beside the clump of mango trees in which nestles the Dilwara complex of temples.

> Beyond controversy this is the most superb of all the temples of India and there is not an edifice besides the Taj Mahal that can approach it. The pen is incompetent to describe the exuberant beauties of this proud monument of the Jains. ... The whole is of pure white marble, every column, dome and altar varying in form and ornament, the richness and delicacy of execution being indescribable. . . . The most fastidious admirer of chaste design need not apprehend that his taste would be shocked by the accumulation of details, or that the minuteness of ornament would detract from the massive dignity of the whole; on the contrary. ... When we reflect that all this magnificence is found on the summit of an isolated mountain on the verge of the desert, now inhabited by a few simple and half-civilized people [the tribal Bhils again] the association cannot fail to enhance one's impression of wonder.

Like many a subsequent visitor Tod was unable to analyse the beauty of the temples. 'The dazzling rays of a vertical sun, reflected from the marble pavement, drove me for shelter into the piazza.' The domes and pillars, walls and floors are all of white marble; they trap the light, eliminating all shadow, and they glare with the blinding effect of a glacial serac. In the brittle intricacy of the sculpted detail there is, too, a vitreous quality, as hard and as bright as a diamond. But the design and ornament are all too easily forgotten in what is essentially a physical experience. Like Tod, one reels away to the deep shade of a mango tree with eyeballs seared and senses seduced by the impossible smoothness of the marble flagstones.

'Now that my pilgrimage is over, wrote Tod, 'I feel content; it is one of my desiderata accomplished.' He retired to his camp-bed, feverish, but clutching a copy of the *Ramayana*. Next morning he was worse. 'Abu has completely demolished me, the fever raging, my hands and face prodigiously swollen. ... The European traveller should distrust his physical powers on this seductive mount.' After such a gamble with his health, he was understandably tenacious about his discovery. Others, including Heber, published accounts of Abu before his own came out. But 'the discovery was my own; to Abu I first assigned a local habitation and a name; and if I am somewhat jealous of my rights in this matter, it is the sole recompense for the toils I have gone through and no small deterioration of health as well as of purse'. For the man who launched the study of Indian coins, who contributed to the solution of the Ashoka script, who pieced together much of India's medieval history and who, above all, rescued the Rajputs from obscurity and related their history in one of the noblest monuments of British scholarship, the discovery of the Abu temples was indeed a most fitting reward.

What Tod did for the Rajputs, others would do for all the tribes and castes of India. Joseph Cunningham, for instance, the Archaeological Surveyor's brother, wrote the first history of the Sikhs, and Edgar Thurston compiled a massive handbook to all the tribes and castes of south India. The country's quite exceptional human diversity was a perpetual source of wonder and had intrigued even the earliest visitors. John Marshall, he of the 'yogis' and 'mairmaids', was much interested in the tribal peoples of Nepal who descended to the plains during the winter. Having never known shoes, 'nothing will hurt them to tread upon it, for they are at the soles like hoofes'. He noted 'but few hares [sic] in their beards', and credited the women with a most disagreeable habit.

> The women of Nepal are said usually to piss in the streets in the day time before people, which I am apt to believe, being at Hajipur whither came many women from Nepal, I saw one woman (that passed by me as I was walking), who almost as soon as she was past me, sat her down in the middle of the path before me and pissed.

Nepal was to provide one of the classic fields for ethnological research. This was partly due to its geography which had kept its various tribes isolated and distinct; but it also owed much to the presence, there and in Darjeeling, for nearly forty years, of that remarkable scholar, Brian Hodgson. Hodgson's contributions to the discovery of India cover so many different subjects and such a long span of years that one might be excused for thinking he was several different people, members of the same family perhaps, with a long connection with the Himalayas. But no, Hodgson whose collections of

Nepalese and Tibetan texts won him the title of 'founder of the true study of Buddhism', was also Hodgson the naturalist, 'the father of Indian zoology', Hodgson the ethnologist, 'the highest living authority on the native races of India', and Hodgson the promoter of India's vernacular languages and protagonist of Macaulay. 'I doubt whether any Englishman of our century,' wrote his biographer, 'received so many distinctions from so many learned bodies representing both the scholarly and the scientific sides of research'. At the Linnaean Society and the Royal Society, the Ethnological Society and the Zoological Society his name was as much revered as in the purely orientalist societies of India, Britain, Germany, France, Italy and the United States. No man better represented Sir William Jones's vision of the scope of Indian studies and no man better typifies the spirit of the discovery of India.

Born in the year 1800, Brian Houghton Hodgson had no sooner arrived in India than his health collapsed. He was advised to return to England immediately and seek another career; and no doubt he would have done so had it not been for the necessity of supporting his impoverished parents and their several other children. Instead, therefore, he opted for service in the Himalayas, particularly Kathmandu, where alone the climate was considered mild enough for his delicate constitution. And there he stayed for twenty-four years in self-imposed exile. As Assistant Resident and then Resident at the Nepalese court, he rarely had the company of more than two of his fellow countrymen. The frequent hostility and constant feuding of the Nepalese, coupled with the often unsympathetic attitude of the government in Calcutta, made his position as perilous as it was lonely. Yet somehow he survived. He fought off the loneliness not only by immersing himself in his studies but also by the now much frowned on expedient of 'forming a domestic connection' with a young Mohammedan lady. They had two children to whom Hodgson became devoted.

In 1833 he wrote to his sister describing his various activities.

> The antiquities of the land afford me much entertainment; I pore over the pictorial, sculptural and architectural monuments of Buddhism. But the past chiefly interests me as it can be made to illustrate the present — the origin, genius, character and attainments of the people.

His first paper was not on ancient Buddhism but on the modern

Buddhists, and this highly practical approach coloured all his researches. The chronic instability of Nepal he traced to the under-employment of its manpower. Trade was a possible solution and he desperately tried to open new markets and commercial routes. More important, though, was his recognition of the martial traditions of the people; until some outlet for their fighting spirit could be found, peace must always be fragile. Hodgson studied each of the tribes in great detail, contributing a paper on them to the Asiatic Society as early as 1833. And he was the first to recommend that, so far as the Gurkha peoples were concerned, the only solution was recruitment into the Company's forces. The Gurkha regiments of the Indian, and later the British, army are amongst his least expected legacies.

The Gurkhas apart, Hodgson's main interest in ethnology was in India's most primitive peoples, the aboriginal tribes. Before the Aryans, before the Indus Valley people, perhaps even before the Dravidians, there were layers of indigenous peoples whose modern representatives still survived in the jungles of south and central India and in the hidden valleys of the eastern Himalayas. In the Himalayas alone he discovered and studied a host of hitherto unknown peoples. He compiled vocabularies and grammars for their unwritten languages, noted their customs and beliefs, and measured their crania. By circulating questionnaires he extended his enquiries further and further into the subcontinent until they reached Ceylon and the Indus. In twenty-one separate papers submitted to the Asiatic Society he identified all the main regions, from the Nilgiris to the Himalayas, in which aboriginal tribes still survived and he examined their anthropological and linguistic affinities. Much work remained to be done but, as in so many other fields, Hodgson prepared the ground, laid down the direction of future researches and inspired others to pursue them.

Meanwhile he himself came to conform more and more to the ideal of the Himalayan sage. In 1839 he had given up meat and liquor and lived, like a Brahmin, on the strictest vegetarian diet. His success in Nepal owed as much to his reputation as a guru as to his political astuteness. When relieved of his post by the inconsistencies of Lord Ellenborough's policies he simply moved a few hundred miles east, and a few thousand feet higher, to Darjeeling, then an equally isolated spot. And there, in a hill-top house half lost in the clouds, he continued his studies for another thirteen years, withdrawn, and more than ever the 'Hermit of the Himalayas'.

CHAPTER FIFTEEN

The Stupendous Fabric
of Nature

In that same letter of 1833 to his sister, Hodgson described all his various 'amusements' and gave pride of place, not to Buddhist studies or ethnological researches, but to natural history.

> Zoology in the branches of birds and quadrupeds amuses me very much. ... I possess a wild tiger, a wild sheep, a wild goat, four bears, three civets and three score of our beautiful [Himalayan] pheasants. And my drawings now amount to 2000.

That Hodgson, in the mid-nineteenth century, should be credited with fathering Indian zoology might seem strange given that the country's fauna had always been one of its main attractions. Visitors to the Moghul court in the eighteenth century invariably sent home wide-eyed reports of the emperor's 14,000 elephants, of his camels and cheetahs, and of his 'unicornes' or 'rhinocerots' ('which are large beastes as bigge as the fayrest oxen England affords; the skins lie platted, or, as it were, in wrinkles upon their back'). The same writer, Edward Terry, paid particular attention to the elephants. Although no longer regarded as beasts of legend, they were still virtually unknown in Europe; Terry felt obliged to render a description – no easy task – of their anatomy.

> Their trunks are long grisselly snouts hanging downe twixt their teeth, by some called their hands, which they make use of upon all occassions. ... The male's testicles lie about his forehead, the female's teates are betwixt her forelegges.

He was right about the teats, wrong about the testicles. But, then, the whole question of where lay the elephant's generative organs, and of how these strange creatures contrived to mate, was perhaps India's single greatest zoological mystery. John Marshall, with his talent for spotting the curious and controversial, earmarked the subject for particular enquiry.

> Mr Hatton saith, elephants when they gender, the male gets upon the female as a horse doth a mare and putting his yard under the female's belly, hee bends it back againe (it having a joynt in it ⅓ part from the end), which he puts into the female into that part which distinguisheth her sex, which lies under her belly; which was a wonder formerly how they should engender, some affirming it was as woman to man, and others that the female kneeled down etc.

Marshall was on the right track; but the theory of their mating face to face survived well into the nineteenth century and, as late as 1903, a paper on the subject was published by the London Zoological Society.

Like Hodgson, many Englishmen of an earlier generation had formed their own menageries. Jones himself, with his tiger cub, his herds of sheep and goats and his tortoise, had something of the sort. William Carey, another great Sanskritist and the promoter of the Bengali language, kept a small zoo, the Duke of Wellington kept and studied cheetahs, and his brother Lord Wellesley, the Governor-General, founded the first official menagerie at Government House in 1804. Wellesley attached great importance to natural history and urged the East India Company to provide funds for its research. 'Many of the most common quadrupeds and birds of this country are either altogether unknown to the naturalist or have been imperfectly and inaccurately described. The illustration and improvement of that important branch of natural history ... is worthy of the munificence and liberality of the East India Company and must necessarily prove a most acceptable service to the world.' He commissioned a magnificent series of some 3000 drawings of plants, birds and animals, and he installed the indefatigable Dr Francis Buchanan, late of the Mysore Survey, as superintendent of the menagerie. Buchanan did noble work collecting and describing hundreds of species; but, with his going on leave and Wellesley's recall, the initial impetus failed. The East India Company had not been impressed by the Governor-General's scheme and the Government House menagerie degenerated into a fairground.

A further stumbling block to the development of the scientific study of India's fauna was the, for once, far from encouraging attitude of Sir

William Jones. Nothing shows more clearly the great man's influence over the course of indological studies and nothing better exemplifies his extraordinarily humane outlook. In his tenth Anniversary Discourse to the Asiatic Society he stated his position plainly.

> Could the figure, instincts and qualities be ascertained ... without giving pain to the object of our examination, few studies would afford us more solid instruction, or more exquisite delight; but I never could learn by what right nor conceive with what feeling, a naturalist can occasion the misery of an innocent bird, and leave its young, perhaps, to perish in a cold nest, because it has gay plumage; or deprive even a butterfly of its natural enjoyment, because it has the misfortune to be rare or beautiful.

No doubt this deep compassion had much to do with the reverence for life which pervades all Indian religions and cultures and which Jones had imbibed so deeply. Certainly, it was never more nobly expressed; and, given the tragic consequences of ignoring it, one might regret that Indian zoology ever progressed beyond the menagerie stage.

But, to Hodgson's credit, he at least seems not to have confounded science and sport. As in all his other 'amusements' he was entirely self-taught, but he brought to the examination of every species a minute attention to detail and structure. This could only be satisfied by the dissection and analysis of dead specimens. But he was also a great field naturalist, fully conscious of the importance of observing behaviour and habitat, and an outstanding collector. His menagerie included some of the rarest Himalayan goats and pheasants, and he is the only man known to have tamed an Indian jackal. In 1833 he attempted to send some of his collection to the Zoological Society in London. The mortality rate amongst sea-borne zoo specimens in those days was appalling. An Indian gaur (or bison) sent by the Asiatic Society had just perished at sea, and a rhinoceros in the same cargo had first created havoc on deck and then, 'a storm coming on, the captain thought it only prudent to throw him overboard'. Hodgson's specimens fared no better.

> One of the deer leapt overboard, the other knocked itself to death against the bars of its cage. The pheasants and pigeons lived until the vessel got into the colder latitudes, when they died, one after the other.

In all, his zoological studies resulted in 127 articles, most of them published in the Asiatic Society's journals. His first, in 1826, was an account of 'the Chiru, or Unicorn, of the Himalayas' and his last, in 1858, the description of a new species of Himalayan mole. Long-legged thrushes, cat-toed plantigrades, Tibetan badgers, and the fifteen species of Nepalese woodpecker – all were grist to his insatiable researches. His drawings, now in the London Zoological Society, form the most complete folio of Himalayan fauna and his collection of specimens, now in the Natural History Museum, is said to number 10,500. He was the first to describe some thirty-nine new species of mammal and about 150 new birds.

The question of claiming and naming new species was a particularly sore point. Hodgson was a stickler for precise description and careful identification. He hesitated to proclaim any new discovery until he had studied at least two or three specimens. But some of his contemporaries were less scrupulous. 'If any person who chances to lay hold upon a single shrivelled skin may forthwith announce a new animal,' wrote Hodgson in 1836, 'the real student of nature must be content to leave what is called discovery to the mere nomenclator; and the science must continue to groan under an increasing weight of fictitious species.' Three years later he was even more bitter and, in announcing a new species of cuckoo, pointed the finger even at the zoological societies.

> Amongst the numerous new birds forwarded by me to London some years back, when I was young enough to imagine that learned societies existed solely for the disinterested promotion of science, was a very singular form of *cucuculus*. Unceremoniously as many of my other novelties have been appropriated, this one, I believe, still remains undescribed, and I therefore beg to present a description and sketch of it.

Hodgson's successor in the fields of zoology and ornithology was Edward Blyth, curator of the Asiatic Society's Natural History Museum from 1841–63. If Hodgson was the Jones of ornithology, Blyth was its Prinsep. As a struggling pharmacist in the London borough of Tooting he had conceived a passion for studying and dissecting birds. When the pharmacy failed he sailed for Calcutta and the ill-paid, over-worked and underrated post of museum curator. And in this humble position he remained until, after twenty years, his health finally collapsed. He contributed some forty erudite papers to the

Society's journal and catalogued their entire collection. But more important was the stimulus he provided to every would-be naturalist in India. Like Prinsep he was an inveterate correspondent. To sportsmen and animal lovers alike he sent out a call for specimens; and soon, from the four corners of India, stuffed birds and skins, drawings and descriptions, came flooding in. Working round the clock, he acknowledged them, catalogued them, published them – and asked for more. He became a walking encyclopaedia, ridiculed by some but revered by those, including Charles Darwin, who shared his love for pure science.

The catalogue of the Society's collection was incomplete when he was forced to retire. It was taken over by T. C. Jerdon, a doctor in the Madras army. In the 1860s Jerdon published the first standard handbooks to *The Birds of India* and *The Mammals of India*. Twenty years later a further series on *The Fauna of India* was commissioned by the government with the geologist W. T. Blanford, as editor. Jerdon recorded some 242 mammals but by Blanford's time this tally had risen to over 4000. However, the decline in the numbers and distribution of the more distinctive species was already evident. Probably Indian zoology owed as much to the improvement in firearms as to the example of Hodgson or the encouragement of Blyth. As the matchlock gave way to the breech-loader and the breech-loader to the express rifle, sport and science grew in popularity prodigiously. Sadly, in India as elsewhere, no distinction was made between the two, and Jerdon, for instance, could devote much of his entry on *sus indicus* to a lyrical description of pig-sticking.

The accounts of men like Tod, Buchanan and Mackenzie who, in their different roles, marched and counter-marched across the subcontinent in the early years of the nineteenth century, show plainly that tigers were a terrible curse. Buchanan records whole villages and crops deserted because of their depredations. Alexander tells the same story of the area around Ajanta and as late as the 1860s Blanford notes that nearly a thousand people a year were killed by tigers in Bengal alone. Leopards, too, could be just as deadly; one is on record as killing 200 people in two years. And these, of course, were only the man-eaters – perhaps one in a hundred of the total; but all preyed on domestic cattle.

The government had instituted a system of rewards, which could be as much as fifty rupees for a tiger, to encourage native huntsmen; the sporting *sahibs* needed no encouragement. But by Jerdon's time, the 1860s, this had apparently had little effect; 'the tiger's numbers appear to be only slightly diminished'. By the 1880s it was a different story.

Blanford noted that 'within the last twenty or thirty years the number of these destructive animals has been greatly reduced, and they have now become scarce, or have even in some cases disappeared entirely, in parts of the country where they were formerly common'. Blanford evidently did not consider this a matter for concern, rather for congratulation. Twenty years later Lord Curzon, like his predecessors, would religiously observe the rituals of the ceremonial tiger shoot. Although no man understood better than Curzon the need to conserve India's monuments, it is doubtful whether any Anglo-Indian appreciated the need for conserving her wildlife.

The Indian lion, found by Tod in Rajasthan and reported by Heber as far north as the Punjab and by Cunningham as far east as Bharhut, was by Blanford's day 'verging on extinction' and restricted to the Gir forest of Saurashtra where alone it still survives – just. The rhino, which was met by the emperor Babur on the Indus and still found in the Terai in Jerdon's day was, by Blanford's time, reduced to just 473 specimens, all in Assam. Even the killing of elephants was for a time subject to a government reward. The idea that the country's fauna was as important a part of its national heritage as Sanskrit, or that it had inspired as many artistic masterpieces as the Buddha story, seems not to have occurred to either naturalists or orientalists.

A happier tale by far is that of the discovery of India's flora. To a trading concern like the East India Company the natural productions of the country, and the extent to which they could be improved and augmented, were matters of vital concern. It was the spices of the Malabar coast that had attracted the first Europeans and it was opium, indigo, cotton, tea and jute which successively financed the British raj. Botanical studies thus had great practical and commercial value as well as the purely scientific, and they were funded accordingly. Sir William and Lady Jones might adopt botany as 'the loveliest and most copious division in the science of nature' but they also watched with approval the founding of the Calcutta Botanical Gardens in 1786. A similar institution was already in existence in Madras and it was from there that in 1793 William Roxburgh came to Calcutta to take over as superintendent. Roxburgh, 'the Indian Linnaeus', 'the father of Indian botany', was, like Francis Buchanan, a Scot and originally a surgeon in the Company's navy. This was of course no coincidence. The best medical schools were in Scotland and herbalism was still an important part of medicine; botany was in fact included in the medical curriculum. But whereas Buchanan became essentially a roving field-worker, collecting and surveying his way across Burma, Mysore, Nepal and Bihar, Roxburgh was a scientist and horticulturalist, studying, cataloguing, laying out his gardens, and experimenting with new varieties.

During twenty years he transformed the Calcutta garden into the most extensive and scientifically organized in Asia. Like the great banyan tree in its midst, which steadily put out more branches and roots till it covered an area a quarter of a mile in circumference, the gardens grew under Roxburgh's care from a collection of 300 species to one of 3500. For the purposes of study he instituted a herbarium, and trained a number of Indian artists in the production of scientific plant drawings, a field in which the Indian's supposed genius for portraying minute detail could be put to good use. By the time Roxburgh retired in 1814 some 2500 plates had been completed. There were also two books in manuscript, one a catalogue of the garden which included at least 500 species new to science, and the other an unfinished *Flora Indica*.

This last was eventually edited and published by William Carey, the orientalist, and Nathanial Wallich. After a brief period in which Francis Buchanan took charge of the Calcutta garden, Wallich became the new superintendent and held the post for thirty years. He had originally come to India as surgeon at the Danish settlement of Serampore just upriver from Calcutta. But in 1813, when the British at last found a pretext for ousting the Danes, Wallich was taken prisoner and then, in recognition of his botanical knowledge, rehabilitated. Though perhaps less erudite than Roxburgh, he proved an even greater traveller and collector than Buchanan, visiting Nepal, Singapore, Penang and Burma as well as all the more botanically interesting regions of India. His greatest contribution to science, though, was the distribution in Europe of his herbarium, numbering some 8000 different species, together with vast quantities of seeds and plants. Joseph Hooker declared this 'the most valuable contribution of the kind ever made to science'. In one fell swoop Wallich made available to the botanists of Europe the flora of 'the most varied botanical area on the face of the globe'.

There only remained the production of a standard work of reference on the subject. Roxburgh's *Flora Indica* was far from comprehensive and was, anyway, incomplete. Several other works on the flora of particular areas had appeared and it was by using these, as well as drawing on their own collections from north India and the Himalayas, that Thomas Thomson, another Scottish medico-botanist, and Joseph Hooker set about a new *Flora Indica* in the 1850s. Volume One appeared in 1855, Thomson himself covering the cost. It was hoped that the government would see the value of the work and finance the remaining volumes. But, at this rate, the subject was expected to run to some 12,000 pages, or twenty further volumes. The government procrastinated, Thomson was called away to take charge of the Calcutta botanical garden, and the project lapsed. It was not, however, forgotten and in 1870 Hooker revived it on a reduced scale. With official backing and a new staff of collaborators he laboured away at Kew Gardens for a further twenty-seven years until the last of the seven volumes of *Indian Flora* was published.

Hooker, the greatest of all British botanists and the friend and colleague of Darwin, had made botanical forays in India, Nepal and Tibet; but he never served in India and never had reason to identify with the country. In Darjeeling he was privileged to win the affection of Brian Hodgson and even to stay in his house. Hodgson became 'one of my dearest friends on earth' and he named a celebrated rhododendron, as well as one of his children, after him. But it seems doubtful whether Hooker ever really understood the strange passion that fired such a man. The botanist was all youthful enthusiasm and curiosity. Hodgson, now surrounded by cats and shunning all society, seemed impossibly aloof and eccentric, lost amidst his books and his multifarious enquiries. In age there were seventeen years between the two men, but it could have been fifty. Hooker represented all that was modern in terms of science and scholarship, Hodgson recalled the older, wider traditions and the looser disciplines of Jones or Mackenzie.

Meanwhile, following the example of Madras and Calcutta, other botanical gardens had sprung up in different parts of India. At Saharanpur north-east of Delhi, John Forbes Royle, yet another Scottish medico-botanist, made an important collection of flora from Kashmir and the western Himalayas. The Saharanpur garden was located in what had originally been a Moghul garden, and though planned as much for research as for amenity value, it no doubt provided useful experience for the later rescue of more famous Moghul gardens. The lovely sunken parterres between the palaces of Dig in Rajasthan furnish an even better example than the Taj of how the formality of a Moghul garden could be complemented by the horticultural and botanical skills of the British.

Later in the nineteenth century Saharanpur became famous for its collection of fruit trees. Likewise, the Madras gardens concentrated on the growing of tobacco, pepper and cardamom. All the gardens were in fact as much government research stations as pleasure groves, and from them went out the steady stream of seeds and seedlings which gradually changed the pattern of Indian agriculture. In 1835 Hodgson announced from Kathmandu, 'I am felling, and digging, and sowing potatoes and oats – yea, with my own proper hands.' Both crops were recent introductions and it was said that, if the British disappeared from India overnight, the extent of their influence in the country could still be clearly measured by studying the distribution of the potato. Bishop Heber agreed, regarding it as 'perhaps the most valuable present they [the people of Kumaon, in this case] are likely to receive from their new masters'. He was not so much denigrating the benefits of British rule as extolling the virtues of this new addition to the staple diet.

All this was, of course, before the arrival of more celebrated products. At Saharanpur, Royle was already advocating the introduction of a Peruvian tree known as chinchona. The name came from that of a Spanish contessa who had been cured of fever by taking a liquid extracted from its bark. In the 1880s Clements Markham revived Royle's idea and, through the botanical gardens, chinchona was successfully established in India. As quinine, it did as much to reduce deaths from malaria as, later, did DDT.

Another crop with which Hodgson, amongst others, experimented was the tea bush. As early as 1778 Sir Joseph Banks, the great naturalist and promoter of exploration, had recommended tea to the East India Company as a crop that might profitably be introduced into India. He even suggested that, with the seeds or shrubs, some Chinese planters should also be imported. Banks urged Lord Macartney's mission to China – the same that included Dr Dinwiddie and the surveying instruments ultimately acquired by Lambton – specifically to investigate this possibility. Seeds and plants were apparently forwarded to the Calcutta garden, and in 1819 Dr Wallich was able to supply both to an official anxious to experiment with the crop in Assam.

But the real breakthrough came with the discovery, both there and in Nepal, of an indigenous tea plant. In its wild state this was more a tree than a bush and, during the 1820s, Wallich was unable to confirm whether it was in fact tea or whether it was a camellia. The government, in danger of losing its monopoly of the China tea trade and faced with an insatiable demand from the British tea drinker, now moved fast. A committee was set up to investigate the subject, a mission was despatched to China to acquire more seeds and know-how, and Wallich was sent to investigate the Assam trees. He not only confirmed that they were tea but also discovered that they were much more widespread than was thought.

> The result of the researches of the tea-deputation despatched to Assam under Dr Wallich, respecting the tea plant in that country, gives every reason to expect that tea will become in a short time a prime article of export from India. The plant has been found in extensive natural plantations and the localities are such as to encourage the belief that it exists far more extensively than has been actually discovered, and to warrant the conclusion that Assam, and our northern frontier gener-ally, will afford the most ample field for tea-cultivation of every variety.

Three years later, in 1839, the first Indian tea was offered for auction in London. By the end of the century it had completely ousted the China variety and India was the largest grower of tea in the world.

The report quoted above of Dr Wallich's deputation to Assam was published in the Asiatic Society's journal for 1836. A plump leather-bound volume of 840 pages, it covers a breadth of material that may be taken as typical for any year. The first article is from Charles Masson on his haul of coins from Begram in Afghanistan. Then comes a piece from Hodgson quoting Sanskrit texts in support of his reconstruction of Buddhist beliefs. Then follows a report on the great fossil finds being made in the Siwalik hills, including the bones of a creature the size of an elephant but more like a camel and with four horns (it was called the Sivatherium after the god Siva). Colonel Stacy reports his find of that Bacchus relief from Mathura and there is news of a new pillar inscription in the Gupta script. In this single volume Hodgson contributes twelve articles on new birds and mammals, and Prinsep nearly as many on translations of coins and stone inscriptions.

For the Society 1836 was not a good year. The Orientalists were still smarting from their defeat at the hands of Macaulay in the previous year. Sanskrit studies were virtually proscribed and Prinsep, in his preface, felt constrained to offer some encouragement. There was still 'a tide of popular favour, or at least a diminutive wave of it', which reached 'the secluded estuary of oriental research'. If Calcutta was distinctly hostile, London, Paris and Vienna still appreciated their studies. The work would go on. 'We shall ever study to infuse into these pages a pleasing variety of original information on all subjects, of man's performance or nature's productions, within the wide range prescribed to us by our allegiance to the Asiatic Society.' The spirit of Jones lived on.

Sources and Bibliography

In a book of this nature it seemed inappropriate to burden the text with references and notes. The sources quoted at length are, in any case, generally self evident from the context. Likewise, the publications listed below no more represent an exhaustive bibliography of the subject than they do the extent of my own reading. They are simply those which have been found most relevant. In particular I should like to single out the journals of the various Asiatic Societies – especially those of the Asiatic Society of Bengal (Calcutta). They are the fields whence this story has been garnered. (Except where otherwise stated the place of publication is London).

PRIMARY SOURCES

Blanford, W. T., *Fauna of British India – Mammalia*, 1888–91
Brown, P., *Indian Architecture*, Bombay, n.d.
Buchanan, F., *Journey through Mysore etc.*, 1807
Buchanan, F., (ed. M. Martin), *Eastern India*, 1836
Cole, H. H., *Preservation of National Monuments*, vols I–X, Calcutta, 1881–85
Coomaraswamy, A. K., *Indian and Indonesian Art*, 1927
Cumming, J. (ed.), *Revealing India's Past*, 1934
Cunningham, A. C., *Archaeological Surveys of India*, vols I–XXIII, Calcutta, 1981–87
Cunningham, A. C., *The Bhilsa Topes*, 1854
Cunningham, A. C., *Inscriptions of Ashoka*, 1877
Cunningham A. C., *The Stupa of Bharhut*, 1879
Cunningham, A. C., *Maha-Bodhi*, 1892
Daniell, T., *Views of Taj Mahal*, 1789
Fergusson, J., *Rock-cut Temples of Western India* (second ed.), 1864
Fergusson, J., *Tree and Serpent Worship* (second ed.), 1873
Fergusson, J., *A History of Indian and Eastern Architecture* (second ed.), 1897

Fergusson, J. and Burgess, J., *Cave Temples of India*, 1880
Foster, W. (ed.), *Early Travels in India*, 1921
Havell, E. B., Havell Papers in India Office Library and Records
Havell, E. B., *Indian Sculpture and Painting*, 1908
Havell, E. B., *Indian Architecture*, 1913
Havell, E. B., *Ancient and Medieval Architecture of India*, 1915
Hooker, J. D. and Thomson, T., *Flora Indica*, 1855
Hunter, W. W., *Life of B. H. Hodgson*, 1896
Huxley, L., *Life and Letters of Sir J. D. Hooker*, 1918
Jerdon, T. C., *Mammals of India*, Roorkee, 1867
Jones, Sir W., *Letters of Sir William Jones* (ed. G. Cannon), 1970
Keene, H. G., *A Handbook to Delhi*, 1899
Macaulay, T. B., Minute on Education, 2 February 1835
Macaulay, T. B., Speech on the Gates of Somnath, 9 March 1843
Markham, C., *Memoir of the Indian Surveys* (second ed.), 1878
Marshall, J. (ed. S. A. Khan), *John Marshall in India*, 1927
Marshall, J. H., *The Monuments of Sanchi*, 1931
Marshall, J. H., *Mohenjo Daro and the Indus Civilization*, 1931
Marshall, J. H., *Buddhist Art of Gandhara*, 1960
Mitra, R. L., et al, *Centenary Review of the Asiatic Society of Bengal*, Calcutta, 1885
Phillimore, R. H., *Historical Records of the Survey of India*, vols I–V, 1945–65
Prinsep, J. (ed. E. Thomas), *Essays on Indian Antiquities*, 1858
Rapson, E. J. (ed.), *Cambridge History of India*, vol I, 1922
Tod, J., *Annals and Antiquities of Rajasthan*, 1829
Tod, J., *Travels in Western India*, 1839
Wilson, H. H., *Ariana Antiqua*, 1841
Wheeler, M., *My Archaeological Mission to India and Pakistan*, 1976
Wheeler, M., *Civilization of the Indus Valley and Beyond*, 1961

PERIODICALS

Asiatic Researches, vols I–XX, 1788–1839
Journal of the Asiatic Society of Bengal, vols I–X, 1831–41
Journal of the Royal Asiatic Society vols 1–5, 1829–33
Transactions of the Bombay Literary Society, vols 1–11, 1819–20
Archer, M., 'Forgotten Painter of the Picturesque; Henry Salt', *Country Life*, 19 November 1959
Archer, M., 'India and Natural History', *History Today*, November 1959

Archer, M., 'India and Archaeology', *History Today*, April 1962
Archer, M., 'Indian Miniatures', *Art International*, 5 December 1963
Archer, M., 'An Artist Engineer; Col. Robert Smith', *The Connoisseur*, February 1972
Marshall, J. H., 'The Cradle of Indian Art – Ajanta', *Illustrated London News*, 11 September 1923
Marshall, J. H., 'First Light on a Long Forgotten Civilization', *Illustrated London News*, 20 September 1924
Marshall, J. H., 'Unveiling the Prehistoric Civilization of India', *Illustrated London News*, 27 February 1926
Havell, E. B., Obituary in *The Times*, 1 January 1935

TRAVELOGUES AND SOCIAL BACKGROUND

Atkinson, G. F., *Curry and Rice*, 1858
Busteed, H. E., *Echoes of Old Calcutta*, 1908
Eden, Emily, *Up the Country*, 1830
Eden, Emily and Fanny, *Letters from India*, 1872
Fay, Eliza, *Original Letters from India*, 1925
Heber, R., *Journey Through the Upper Provinces of India*, 1828
Hickey, W. (ed. P. Quennell), *Memoirs of William Hickey*, 1960
Hodges, W., *Travels in India, 1780–83*, 1793
Jacquemont, V. V. J., *Letters from India*, 1834
Kincaid, D., *British Social Life in India, 1608–1933* (second ed.), 1973
Murray's *Handbook to the Bengal Presidency*, 1882
Murray's *Handbook to India*, 1894
Murray's *Handbook to India etc*, 1975
Postans, Mrs M., *Western India in 1838*, 1859
Roberts, Emma, *Sketches and Characteristics of Hindostan* (second ed.), 1837
Valentia, G. A., *Voyages and Travels*, 1809

SECONDARY SOURCES

Arberry, A. J., *The British Orientalists*, 1943
Arberry, A. J., *Asiatic Jones*, 1946
Archer, M., *Indian Architecture and the British*, 1968
Archer, M., *Company Drawings in the India Office Library*, 1972
Archer, W. G., *India and Modern Art*, 1959

Basham, A. L., *The Wonder that was India*, 1954
Basham, A. L. (ed.), *A Cultural History of India*, 1975
Blunt, W., *The Ark in the Park*, 1976
Cannon, G., *Oriental Jones*, New York, 1964
Carrington, R., *Elephants*, 1958
Carroll, D., *The Taj Mahal*, New York, 1972
Craven, R., *Concise History of Indian Art*, 1972
Crowe, S., et al, *Gardens of Moghul India*, 1972
Dictionary of Indian Biography (ed. Buckland)
Dictionary of National Biography
Gascoigne, A. B., *The Great Moghuls*, 1971
Griffiths, P., *History of the Indian Tea Industry*, 1967
Hawkes, J., *The First Great Civilizations*, 1973
Keay, J., *When Men and Mountains Meet*, 1977
Keay, J., *The Gilgit Game*, 1979
Kopf, D., *British Orientalism and the Bengali Renaissance*, Los
    Angeles, 1969
Lipsey, R., *Coomaraswamy, His Life and Work*, 1977
Markham, C., *Peruvian Bark*, 1880
Marshall, P. J. (ed.), *The British Discovery of Hinduism etc,* 1970
Mason, P., *The Men Who Ruled India*, 1954
Mason, P., *A Matter of Honour*, 1974
Mukherjee, S. N., *Sir William Jones*, 1968
Narain, V. A., *Jonathan Duncan and Varanasi*, Calcutta, 1959
Philips, C. H., (ed.), *Historians of India, Pakistan and Ceylon*, 1961
Rowland, B., *Art and Architecture of India*, 1967
Sewell, R., *A Forgotten Empire*, 1900
Sharma, R. C., *Mathura Museum of Art*, Mathura, 1967
Singh, Madanjeet, *The Cave Paintings of Ajanta*, 1965
Spear, P., *Twilight of the Moghuls*, 1951
Spear, P., *The Nabobs*, 1963

Index

217

The Great Arc

The Dramatic Tale of How India was Mapped and Everest was Named

John Keay

'A wonderful and fascinating book' LAWRENCE JAMES, *The Times*

'More extraordinary than any fiction'
CHARLOTTE CORY, *Mail on Sunday*

The Great Indian Arc of the Meridian, begun in 1800, was the longest measurement of the earth's surface ever to have been attempted. The 1600-mile survey took nearly fifty years and cost more lives than most contemporary wars. Hailed as 'one of the most stupendous works in the history of science', it was also one of the most perilous. Through hill and jungle, flood and fever, an intrepid band of surveyors carried the Arc from the southern tip of the Indian subcontinent up into the frozen wastes of the Himalayas. William Lambton, an endearing genius, conceived the idea; George Everest, an impossible martinet, completed it. Both found the technical difficulties horrendous. With instruments weighing half a ton, their observations had often to be conducted from flimsy platforms ninety feet above the ground or from mountain peaks enveloped in blizzard. Malaria wiped out whole survey parties; tigers and scorpions took their toll.

Yet the results were commensurate. India as we now know it was defined in the process. The Arc also resulted in the first accurate measurements of the Himalayas, an achievement which was acknowledged by the naming of the world's highest mountain in honour of Everest. More important still, the Arc significantly advanced our knowledge of the exact shape of our planet.

'This wonderful book – surely Keay's most compelling, and one of the most remarkable works of non-fiction to be published this year – is a fitting monument not just to Everest but also to the Great Arc itself' WILLIAM DALRYMPLE, *Sunday Times*

0-00-653123-7

India: A History

John Keay

'In an environment where every fact is infinitely malleable, every interpretation politicised, the need for clear, accessible and unbiased popular history is all the greater. It is hard to imagine anyone succeeding more gracefully in producing a balanced overview than John Keay has done in *India: A History* . . . a book that is as fluent and readable as it is up-to-date and impartial. Hardly a page passes without some fascinating nugget or surprising fact . . . one can only hope that John Keay's *India* will be widely read, and its lessons taken to heart.'

WILLIAM DALRYMPLE, *Guardian*

'[John Keay's] astute commentary on the development of Indian history is a delight . . . one of the best general studies of the subcontinent.'   ANDREW LYCETT, *Sunday Times*

'Certainly the most balanced and the most lucid [one-volume history of the subcontinent] . . . his passion for India shines through and illuminates every page . . . puts Keay in the front rank of Indian historiographers.'   CHARLES ALLEN, *Spectator*

0-00-638784-5